CANADA
NORTH OF SIXTY

CANADA
NORTH OF SIXTY

Editors
Jürgen F. Boden and Elke Boden

Text Authors
Valerie Alia, John U. Bayly, Ethel Blondin, Jonquil Graves/Anne Gunn,
Ann M. Hanson, Jerome Knap, Brian Lewis, Jeff MacInnis, Lynn Maslen,
Beth Mulloy/Louise Profeit-LeBlanc, Dick North, Randal Pokiak,
Erik Watt, Florence Whyard, Renee Wissink

Photographers
Wolfgang R. Weber
and
Mike Beedell, Barbara Brundege/Eugene Fisher, Richard Hartmier,
Douglas C. Heard, Fran Hurcomb, Tessa Macintosh, Kim G. Poole,
Richard A. Popko, Wendy Stephenson, Wayne Towriss,
plus many more

Illustrations
Germaine Arnaktauyok

M&S

Produced by: Jürgen F. Boden
Art director: Hartmut Brückner

Canadian Cataloguing in Publication Data

Main entry under title:

Canada — North of 60

ISBN 0-7710-1581-X

1. Canada, Northern — Description and travel.
2. Canada, Northern — Description and travel — Views.
3. Canada, Northern — Civilization.
4. Natural history — Canada, Northern. I. Boden, Jürgen F.

FC3956.C363 1991   971.9'03   C91-093619-6
F1090.5.C363 1991

Published in Canada in 1991 by
McClelland & Stewart Inc.
The Canadian Publishers
481 University Avenue
Toronto, Ontario
M5G 2E9

Acknowledgements:

- Map on northern Canada courtesy of Canada Centre for Mapping, Energy, Mines and Resources Canada
- Illustrations by Germaine Arnaktauyok courtesy of the Department of Renewable Resources, Government of the Northwest Territories
- Fourteen photographs courtesy of the Department of Culture and Communications, Government of the Northwest Territories
- Four photographs courtesy of Travel Keewatin, Government of the Northwest Territories
- Canadian copy-editing of all text matter by Dr. Richard Tallman

Published simultaneously in Canada by McClelland & Stewart Inc., Toronto, and in the Federal Republic of Germany by Alouette Verlag, Oststeinbek

Printed and bound by Tien Wah Press in Malaysia

Foreword by the Editors

When, in July, 1989, the 1,700-kilometre international canoe race down the Mackenzie River from Fort Providence to Inuvik took place to commemorate the 200th anniversary of Alexander Mackenzie's first journey deep into the wilderness of the western Arctic, it reminded Canadians of a time when European powers fought for predominance in the northern part of the North American continent, when Canada was yet far from becoming a nation. The explorations of Alexander Mackenzie and his Nor'westerners had an impact on the aboriginal people in the Far North that should last forever. For thousands of years the Native peoples had survived in a land that alternated between the harsh and the bountiful, and they had developed values and skills to deal with their environment. The impact of these early explorations in the North was even greater than that of the 1668 voyage of the *Nonsuch*, which led to the establishment of the Hudson's Bay Company and its royal charter.

Change of scenes. A classroom at Maani Ulujuk School, Rankin Inlet, August 23, 1988, shortly after the late May to mid-August summer holiday is over. The daily morning routine for Bill Belsey's twenty-six grade 5 youngsters, from Stacy Anawak to Jolene Ippiak, from Jacky Price to Chris Tiktak: 8:50 — toothbrushing (once a month there is a party if no case of caries has occurred); 9:00 — "O Canada," the national anthem, is sung; 9:05 — announcements, during which each pupil is encouraged to tell the class and the teacher about events and happenings of the previous day or of the weekend, such as: "we went hunting and my father got a caribou" or "my aunt went down to Winnipeg to get her baby"; 9:15 — journals, where pupils are to write down little pieces about everyday things such as the breakdown of their family's television set, the repair of the three- or four-wheeler, or anything else, this exercise also being meant to encourage shy boys and girls to express themselves in writing; 9:45 — beginning of the regular lessons. This elementary school has a large gym with an indoor track and a stage for school theatre productions, a science lab, a computer room, a photographic darkroom, a woodworking shop, home economics facilities, an animal-skin preparation room, and even a dental therapist's office. The school includes pupils from kindergarten to grade 9. There are now comparable schools in many other communities of the Northwest Territories and Yukon. Elementary and high schools as well as colleges in the North still have a large portion of non-Native teachers and lecturers, which is gradually changing.

Empathetic modern education with modern facilities is most likely how the Native youth of Canada's North can find a stable road for themselves out of the enormously difficult conflict between two entirely different cultures that they still face and which their parents and grandparents had and have to cope with. The life of a subsistence hunting and gathering society which, at least for the Inuit, was largely nomadic, has been in conflict with a highly technological Western civilization since the days of Alexander Mackenzie. With a well-founded education and with sufficient knowledge of their natural environment and of living from the land and the sea, the young Native generation might be able to take and use the advantages of both worlds to their and their families' benefit and, thereby, for the welfare of all Canadians.

As editors, we wish to express our deeply felt and sincere gratitude to the people of the North, especially to the authors of the essays and legends, who all have generously contributed their broad knowledge and their feelings of and for the land and its people, and who have allowed us an insight into their world. Our thanks go as well to the many northern photographers and to Wolfgang Weber, the principal photographer, whose contributions are so important to illustrate this immeasurably vast, wild, beautiful country and its people. Other northerners have granted us their support and good advice in facilitating our research and our attempts to comprehend most of the issues of this region of Canada, and they have helped in many other ways as well. To name a few of those to whom we owe thanks: Shirley Adamson of Laberge; Jerry Antoine of Fort Simpson; Brent Boddy of Iqaluit; Sharon Buness, formerly of Iqaluit; Phoebe Cellaire of Fort Simpson; John Cournoyea of Inuvik; Cheryl Grant-Gamble of Yellowknife; Colleen Haight and Darcy Grieshuber of Norman Wells; Al Huestis, formerly of Pond Inlet; Jim and Helen Janson of Fort Good Hope; Bezal and Terry Jesudason of Resolute Bay; Marion LaVigne and Ronne Heming of Yellowknife; Della Lewis of Yellowknife; Father LeMuer of Fort Good Hope; Susan Makpah of Rankin Inlet; Joe Mercredi of Fort Simpson; David Monteith of Iqaluit; Dennis Thrasher of Paulatuk; and Max Ward of Edmonton/Yellowknife.

Not forgotten are also MP Jack Anawak's elaborate lessons for us about many aspects of Inuit life and his great help in obtaining Canadian passports, permissions, and financial support for the Rankin Inlet girls' soccer team, whom we invited in the spring of 1989 to Germany to play in youth tournaments in Hamburg, Bremen, and West Berlin, as well as to show them some of this country's culture.

And last, but certainly not least, thanks go to George Sinfield of Whitehorse, who, along with Paul Vallillie from Yellowknife, must be held somewhat responsible for the publication of this book, because these two suggested the idea to us over fiddleheads, shrimps, and cocktails at a Canadian dinner in Berlin many years ago.

Finally, Wolfgang Weber has asked us to convey his gratitude also to these northern ladies and gentlemen: Phil Bastien, Jim Broadbent, Fred Carmichael and Micky O'Kane, Judith

Currelly, E.J. (Ted) Grant, David and Eva Howe, Alan Kaylo, Abraham Pijamini, Cecil Reilly, John Sheehan, and Andy Williams.

The list of names of people has become long, but as our author John Bayly writes: "And I will wager that fifty years after, when the details of the travel have blurred and the photographs are faded, it will be the people you camped with and whose trails you crossed that you remember best. The people of the North — people constantly on the move in a land where all travel is an adventure."

Table of Contents

Brian Lewis
Canada's Northwest Territories

It wasn't until 1953 when the Royal Canadian Air Force completed its aerial photographic survey of the Arctic that the true dimensions of Canada's Northwest Territories were fully understood. Even today much of this vast wilderness area has not been explored on the ground. The Northwest Territories with its 3.3 million square kilometres covers an area more than twice the size of Alaska, the American northland, and is bigger than the entire subcontinent of India. And yet only about 55,000 people are living here. Air travellers who take the polar route from western Canada to Europe spend roughly one-third of their journey crossing the Northwest Territories. Aklavik, near its western boundary, is further west than Los Angeles; the eastern coast of Baffin Island is on the same longitude as Barbados. The most northerly island, Ellesmere, is only 800 kilometres from the North Pole.

This massive extension of Canada north of 60 degrees consists in its western part of one of the great river systems in the world, the Mackenzie, which winds its way from the headwaters of the Peace and Athabasca rivers in Alberta to the Arctic Ocean. It is the largest river in Canada and second only to the Mississippi in North America. Into this river drain two large lakes, Great Bear Lake and Great Slave Lake, the first slightly larger, the second slightly smaller than Belgium. These lakes form the western boundary of the Arctic mainland or tundra, which extends in an enormous broad horseshoe around Hudson Bay. The Arctic mainland is a vast, glaciated plateau of granite, covered with slow-moving streams and stagnant lakes and pools in summer, and a featureless snowscape in winter. Much of the land exploration in the Northwest Territories is done on the Arctic mainland, since it is part of the Canadian Shield and the explorers are prospectors in search of gold, uranium, base metals, and rare earths.

The eastern part of the Northwest Territories extends furthest north. It consists largely of the Arctic islands, the homeland of most Canadian Inuit. Many of the islands have high mountain peaks, glaciers, and fjords, reminiscent of Norway. Several of these islands are uninhabited but the largest, Baffin Island, is the fifth largest island in the world and its largest community, Iqaluit, is home to 10 per cent of the Canadian Inuit population.

The most distinctive geographical feature of the Northwest Territories is, perhaps, the treeline. As the traveller moves north the white and black spruce, birch, alder, tamarack, and poplar become more sparse and weatherbeaten. On the Canadian Shield, trees survive in small pockets of earth among the rocks, but these are gradually replaced by small jack pine and scrub willow and, eventually, by mosses, lichens, and small Arctic plants and shrubs. Of course, the northern limit for trees does not mark the limit for plant growth. Every year in the short summer season the tundra explodes into a multi-coloured quilt of Arctic plants, the flowers contrasting magnificently with still remaining patches of snow. The treeline is also currently a feature marked by political controversy. The Inuit in the eastern Arctic would like the treeline stretching from the Mackenzie Delta on the Arctic Ocean to the mouth of the Churchill River on Hudson Bay to be the western boundary of their homeland, a new territory they call Nunavut (Our Land). When Canada invited the world to visit Vancouver on Canada's west coast for Expo 1986 the Northwest Territories pavilion drew some of the largest crowds. Inside the simulated iceberg formation of the pavilion, visitors learned about Canada's first peoples, the Inuit (Eskimos) and the Dene (Indians), and their more than 400 years of contact with non-Native people. They also learned about an enormous wilderness called "the Territories," the one-third of Canada that extends north of the provinces to the North Pole.

Although contact with the outside world has brought changes to the North over a long period of time, the face of the North did not change dramatically until the Second World War. Many people throughout the world still think of northern Canada as a land of snow houses, skin tents, log cabins, traplines, canoes, fur-clad hunters, lonely trading posts, and red-coated policemen. Elements of all these still exist and continue to make the North unique and appealing to the visitor.

This is the world the American military first encountered when they built the Canol pipeline, the Alaska Highway, and airstrips along the Mackenzie Valley in 1942 when they feared a Japanese assault on North America through Alaska. Imagine the shock to the trappers of the small village of Fort Smith on the Alberta border when they woke up on June 20, 1942, to find 2,000 black troops camped nearby and thousands of tons of pipeline and earth-moving equipment making the sixteen-mile portage around the nearby rapids on Slave River. There was no access into the Northwest Territories except by water and small bush plane — but that was about to change.

The waterways are no longer the main transportation routes through the wilderness, but there are few roads from the south to replace them. The capital city, Yellowknife, is linked to the south by a road originally built to serve the gold-mining industry. Although it is used for passenger traffic, including a bus line to Edmonton, the capital of Alberta, the northern 400 kilometres of the road are still gravel. The Mackenzie Highway, which forks east to cross the Mackenzie River to

Yellowknife, continues north for another 287 kilometres on the western side of the river to Fort Simpson. This community, once a major fur-trading centre, was the site chosen for Pope John Paul to meet the aboriginal peoples of Canada's North in 1984. South of Fort Simpson the road continues southwest through the Liard Valley into British Columbia. Many visitors to the Fort Simpson area take this route and visit closeby Nahanni Butte, site of a small but spectacular national park. The Nahanni River attracts canoeists from all over the world. Some want to challenge the many rapids; others take the easier routes and, at a more leisurely pace, enjoy the incredible natural beauty of the canyons and sub-arctic meadows.

For many years northern people have dreamed of a road north up the Mackenzie Valley to the Arctic Ocean. It is possible to get within about 100 kilometres of the Arctic Ocean by road but this means taking the Dempster Highway through the Yukon to Inuvik, so very little of the journey is within the Northwest Territories. There is no road link between the eastern and western parts of the Northwest Territories. For all the communities in the Northwest Territories east of Yellowknife the only contact with the capital city or with southern Canada is by air. Even those people who live along the highway system travel a lot by air because distances are so great.

Edmonton, the most accessible southern city for northerners, is 1,450 kilometres south by road from Yellowknife. Food and supplies are trucked along this road throughout the year with short delays in the spring and fall when the ferry cannot cross the Mackenzie River. Until the mid-seventies many of the communities along the river were supplied by barges out of Hay River, which is connected by rail with Alberta. The railway is not as active as it once was because the nickel mine at Pine Point, for which the railroad was built, closed down in 1988. Fewer barges are needed on the river since oil and gas exploration began to decline in the Beaufort Sea over the past ten years.

Most visitors to the Northwest Territories who come by road end up in Yellowknife, a gold-mining town and mineral exploration centre for more than fifty years. Although visitors will see Dene and Inuit in the streets, they will feel at once that this is not the true North. Shopping malls, high-rise apartment buildings, and a modern airport with frequent daily jet service to the south are part of the cultural landscape of Yellowknife. But the old "frontier spirit" has not completely disappeared. In the summer months the colourful "Old Town" of the city on the waterfront of Great Slave Lake springs into life. Water bombers and helicopters come and go during the dry season carrying supplies to the fire-fighting crews in the bush. Float planes dodge past canoeists and sailboats on the lake. Prospectors and mineral exploration parties head out into the wilderness. Tourists seeking a true wilderness adventure head out by canoe along the waterways and over portages toward the Arctic coast or east toward Hudson Bay. Some fly in to fishing lodges in pursuit of lake trout, pike, pickerel, and grayling.

Except for a seventeen-mile road between Arctic Bay and Nanisivik, a lead and zinc mining community on northern Baffin Island, the eastern Arctic has no highways. The main link with southern Canada is by jet service through Montreal. Visitors to Baffin Island land in Iqaluit, the largest Inuit community in Canada. From there they can proceed north to Resolute Bay, a staging point for expeditions to the North Pole and for scientific parties doing research on the Arctic islands. Near Iqaluit is the picture postcard community of Lake Harbour with its Greenlandic-style houses with their high-pitched roofs set against multi-coloured polished rock faces around the snug harbour. Between settlements travel is mostly by De Havilland Twin Otter, a perfect plane for landing on very short runways. The flight to Lake Harbour takes about thirty minutes but in winter the journey can be made by snow machine along an ice road.

North of Iqaluit is Pangnirtung, once an important whaling centre but now the centre for Auyuittuq National Park. The scenery is reminiscent of Norway and the park attracts hikers and naturalists as well as climbers looking for new peaks to conquer. For those interested in Inuit arts and crafts, they will find some in most Inuit communities, but Cape Dorset, west of Iqaluit, is where soapstone carving and printmaking began to attract the attention of the art world in the 1950s. After thirty years there continues to be strong world-wide interest in the annual Cape Dorset print collection.

One of the biggest surprises for visitors to Canada's Northwest Territories is the climate. In the western part, summers can be very hot, temperatures sometimes climbing to 35° Celsius, with inland communities like Fort Liard and Fort Simpson and even coastal places like Coppermine recording the highest temperatures in Canada on any one day. Gardeners in the west can grow a wide variety of fruit and vegetables. Yellowknife has only one less frost-free day than Edmonton. The summer is short but the days are long and the major challenge for the gardeners is not climate but soil, since most of it was scraped away by the glaciers of the ice age. On the other hand, Baker Lake, the only inland Inuit community, suffers the worst extremes of a continental-type climate. It is too far away to enjoy the warming influence of the sea and its bitterly cold days are made even more unpleasant by the high winds that blow from the barren lands. In winter, Baker Lake people wear heavily quilted wind pants even for a short walk to a neighbour or to the store. With the wind chill, temperatures can be more than 55° Celsius below zero.

Origins

Before the first human appeared in the North to make a barely distinguishable impact on the landscape, the land had experienced three billion years of geological change. Around 600 million years ago life forms living in a northern marine environment developed hard shells and their fossil remains tell the story of long successions of sea cover. Around three million years ago the climate began to cool enough for glaciers to be created. They gradually moved southward, reaching thicknesses in some places of 2,000 metres. Glaciers much thicker than this still remain on the Greenland ice cap. These glaciers created the lakes, the gravel ridges, and the gouged, scratched, and polished northern landscape of today.

The question of how and when humans made their appearance in the northland remains an enigma. Petitot, a French Catholic priest who worked in the Mackenzie Valley and along the Arctic coast in the 1860s, is the first to be credited with the suggestion that aboriginal people in North and South America had an Asiatic origin. The theory was that when the glaciers formed the sea level dropped. Over the land bridge created across the Bering Strait in Alaska, man made his first appearance in the New World, at the end of the last ice age — more than 22,000 years ago. At this time Alaska and the most northerly part of Canada had no permanent ice cover. As the glaciers retreated north around 13,000 years ago, the southern migration was no longer impeded by ice and aboriginal people began the settlement of the Americas. This theory is being hotly contested by aboriginal people today. In pursuing their land claims with the government of Canada they do not wish to be considered merely as early settlers of the land. They lay claim to land because they believe it has always been theirs, not because they were the first immigrants.

The Dene

Most anthropologists have not revised the "Asiatic origin" theory of the aboriginal settlement of the Americas. Accordingly, it is assumed the ancestors of the current Indian population in the western Arctic (now called Dene — from Tinne — their word for "people") arrived in North America around 12,000 years ago. The Dene bear a close similarity to Native peoples living along the river valleys in Alberta and British Columbia and to many tribes in the western United States, including the Navaho. They belong to a large group of tribes speaking variations of the same language group called Athapaskan.

Before contact with non-Native settlers and visitors, the Dene lived in harmony with their environment, their lives following a pattern of seasonal migrations in pursuit of game. They were primarily fish and meat eaters, though plants obtained in the short summer season were a source of medicine and a food supplement. The main source of food was the caribou, highly valued in winter not only for meat and fat but for its skin, which was perfect for winter clothing. The mark of a successful hunter was a lodge made from caribou skin; people normally used birch bark. Moose were as well of importance to the Dene: the hides of this solitary animal are very durable and its meat is delicious. In the Mackenzie Delta the hides were used for jackets and footwear more so than anywhere else because moose were available here in larger numbers.

Throughout the year fish was the most reliable food supply: caught by nets under the ice in winter, with spears at the ice edge in spring, and, when the river was full of ice, by using fish-trap baskets made out of willow. Life was a constant struggle for survival, with little time for recreation and creative activity, as there was among the Native people on the British Columbia coast where the climate was gentle and the food abundant.

Drumming, singing, and gambling were the main forms of amusement. The Dene had a unique form of gambling in which teams of men, to the accompaniment of singing and drumming, tried to outguess each other. Sticks were passed from hand to hand under a blanket, then held out in clenched fists and the opposing team was challenged to locate the hidden stick or *idsi,* as it was called. The game is still popular today and each tribe has variations of this "hand game."

The Inuit

Like the Dene, the Inuit did not have a written language until very recent times so information about their history is limited to written observations made by visiting Europeans, oral tradition, and archeological evidence. Like the Dene, they prefer to be known by their own name, Inuit, their word for people. The name "Eskimo" ("eaters of raw meat" in the Indian Chippewa dialect) is considered a pejorative by modern young Canadian Inuit, though "Eskimo" is still in common use throughout the polar world. While the Dene migrated south along the river valleys the Inuit were attached for the most part to the sea coast. The present-day Inuit (and the Inuvialuit of the western Arctic, as they have called themselves for the past twenty years) are descended from the Thule people who hunted whales about a thousand years ago in the Bering Strait off Alaska.

The Inuit developed a complex technology that allowed them to survive in a harsh environment. This included the construction of sea craft out of skins, driftwood, and bone, notably the kayak, the long craft paddled by the single hunter; and the umiak or woman's boat, used for family and cargo transportation. They developed the articulated harpoon to spear sea mammals such as the seal, walrus, and whale. They developed the *avataq,* an inflated bag made from skins to keep their prey afloat. On land they created the incredible igloo or snow house and, for transportation, the sled or *qamutiq (komatiq* in other dialects) pulled by dogs, each one singly attached to it via a central loop by leather ropes cut from the skin of the bearded seal or *udjuk.* They made hunting bows cleverly constructed from whale bone, as well as hand-held fish spears, throwing spears, and knives for varying purposes, including the large snow knife for making snow houses and the woman's knife or *ulu* with the crescent-shaped blade, the most versatile knife of all. Today most travellers in the Arctic wear winter clothing copied from ancient Inuit designs.

Others

Those people who live in the Northwest Territories, some Native but mostly non-Native, who do not have a special relationship with the federal government through treaties are often referred to as "others." Until the 1950s they were a small group confined mostly to the west and associated with the mining industry, though there were non-Native trappers, traders, public servants, and small businessmen even in the smaller communities. In the past twenty years these non-Native "others" have increased dramatically in numbers because of the fast growth of government, which required a wide variety of skilled people. The urban centres, apart from Yellowknife, have no commercial or industrial base. They only exist because they have become area or regional centres for government. In these communities the "others" are in the majority. They are also by far the largest group in the industrial centres of Norman Wells (oil) and Nanisivik (lead and zinc). In the smaller traditional Native communities, non-Native "others" are still employed as school teachers, nurses, technicians, and managers. The Northwest Territories still depends heavily on skilled non-Native people to work in government, business, and industry, though major initiatives are under way to increase the number of Native people working in government.

A generation ago most of the "others" were associated by Native people with a colonial government in Ottawa. To attract them to work in the Northwest Territories the federal government gave its public servants many incentives, including good housing and low rent. To the poor hunter and trapper with little or no education, the "others" were a privileged class. The regional administrators of government seemed like all-powerful colonial governors. They helped to form a social class from whose activities Native people were largely excluded. Levels of education were identified as the major difference between Native people and the "others." The federal government insisted that if Native people were going to run their own government they would need a modern education.

One of the major sources of disagreement between Native people and the "others" has been education. The "others" expected their children to get an education little different from what existed in the provinces. The Native people saw education as one more colonial imposition that would destroy their language and culture and alienate children from their parents.

The majority of non-Native people are not settlers who have committed themselves to living permanently in the Northwest Territories. They have come north to work for a variety of reasons. Some are attracted by large salaries and a chance to save money for further schooling or investment in a house or business in southern Canada. These usually don't stay long when they experience the high cost of living. Some seek valuable work experience. Others come out of a sense of adventure and fascination with the culture of Native peoples. A small number see the North as part of the "Third World" and believe they can be of service to underprivileged people.

This view of the North by non-Native people is changing to some degree as second-generation children realize their roots are northern and decide to return from college or university in the south to work in the North. Unlike in the Yukon, where there are fourth- and fifth-generation non-Native families that can trace their origins to the Klondike gold rush, most non-Native people who come to the Northwest Territories have either stayed for a few years and then left, or they have married into one of the Native tribes.

Flora and Fauna

The image of the North as a barren wilderness covered with ice and snow for most of the year is misleading. There are abundant fur-bearing wildlife, crystal clear waters rich in several species of fish, and plant life which, in the short summer season, shocks the visitor by its profusion and brilliancy of colour. Trees do not reach the dimensions of those in milder climates and there are few species. On the barrenlands dwarf willow, just a few inches high, may be several hundred years old. Unlike Japanese bonsai, they have been twisted into fascinating shapes by snow, ice, and wind, not by the patient hands of the gardener.

An enduring image of the North for most people is the polar bear, a symbol that appears on the unofficial flag of the Northwest Territories and on everyone's distinctive polar bear-shaped vehicle licence plate. But even those who do not live on the Arctic coast are rarely far from bears.

The curious black bear is always close to the local garbage dump. Campers are often awakened by noises in the night as black bears help themselves to last night's leftover supper. Just as formidable and dangerous to man as the polar bear is the grizzly bear. They exist in the mountainous areas west of the Mackenzie River, but another species, the barrenland grizzly bear, lives above the treeline and sometimes rears ten feet above a clump of willows to distract the hunter in search of caribou.

The animal that provides meat for Inuit and Dene is the

caribou. To the tourist the herds of thousands of caribou on the move are awe-inspiring. To the Native hunter they represent millions of dollars worth of food that does not have to be imported from the south. Another source of food is the muskox. This unusual member of the bovine family exists in large numbers on the Arctic islands, especially on Banks Island. Another very large inland herd exists on the Thelon River, which has been part of a game sanctuary since the 1920s.

One of the more interesting areas for naturalists is around the community of Fort Smith on the Alberta border. The town is the administrative centre for Wood Buffalo National Park. This is the largest national park in Canada and was established in 1922 to protect the wood buffalo or bison, indigenous to the area, and to save the smaller plains bison from extinction. In addition to the park's hybrid herd of now less than 3,000 animals — tragically about half of them being infected — there are, further north, two herds of pure wood bison that are disease-free. On the rapids close to the community are colonies of pelicans, and in the swamplands the breeding grounds of the rare and still heavily endangered whooping crane.

Throughout the Northwest Territories below the tree line even the motorist on the long, lonely, gravel highways is likely to see some wildlife. Near Fort Providence on the banks of the Mackenzie there may be a bison or a black bear on the road, or a moose in a nearby swamp. In the wetlands there are muskrat, mink, marten (Canadian sable), and beaver.

In the eastern Arctic there are fewer land mammals. Only the white fox, the wolf, and the polar bear are caught for their fur to generate some cash income to support a hunting economy. Seals, which at one time provided both meat for the family and cash for the pelts, are not the major part of the economy they were twenty years ago. Culturally great importance is still attached to the hunting of walrus and whales, even though the need for vast quantities of meat has declined with the virtual disappearance of dog teams.

Although people visit the Northwest Territories for a wide variety of reasons, few will forget the sight of a northern evening sky alive with an incredible variety of water fowl heading north to their nesting grounds in the spring or to Central and South America in the fall. On the land, in the water, or in the air, in the eastern or western parts of the Northwest Territories, what seems at first a desolate, lifeless part of the world rewards the sensitive, interested observer with a unique insight into life in a cold climate.

Exploration and Settlement

The European discovery of North America is credited to the Vikings; they were also very probably the first European visitors to Canada's North. Greenland is only a good day's sail from Baffin Island and the likely Viking landfall on that Arctic island corresponds closely to the saga's description of Helluland. The discovery of a small wooden carving of a priest on Baffin Island suggests that missionaries from Greenland may also have visited Canadian Inuit at a later date.

The earliest detailed information about European contact with Canada's northern people comes much later. In 1576 Martin Frobisher began a series of Arctic voyages from England in search of a passage to the Orient. He discovered iron pyrite or fool's gold in the strait that bears his name. Queen Elizabeth I was jealous of the gold-rich colonies established by her enemy, the Spanish, in South America. Frobisher manipulated the situation, brought prefabricated houses and experienced miners to Baffin Island, and planned to establish an English colony there. Terrible weather and battles with the Inuit forced him to drop his scheme.

In 1668, a small ship, the *Nonsuch*, entered Hudson Bay. This ship more than any other prompted developments that eventually brought aboriginal people in close contact with each other. The purpose of the *Nonsuch* was to establish the fur trade among Native people, not to seek a route to the East.

This was the beginning of the English fur trade in the Arctic and a key move in the struggle for an unchallenged English commercial foothold in the area we now call the Northwest Territories. In 1670, following the successful voyage of the *Nonsuch*, the Hudson's Bay Company was formed and most of what we call Canada today was given to the Company by a royal charter. It established a massive fortress called Fort Prince of Wales overlooking the point where the Churchill River enters Hudson Bay. For the first time northern Native people, both Dene and Inuit, were introduced to the world of trade and commerce. In exchange for the fur they trapped they were given European trade goods that would forever change their lives.

The Hudson's Bay Company has been closely associated with northern development since 1670 and every northern community has its HBC store, though it is a small department store today, the fur trade recently being only a small part of the business — and having been discontinued completely in 1991.

Between 1818 and 1880 the British Navy renewed its efforts to find a Northwest Passage to the Far East. Most of the exploration took place following the disappearance in 1847 of Sir John Franklin and his 128 men. The search for remains of his expedition lasted for more than twelve years. Over twenty sea expeditions were involved and much of what was learned about their fate came from Inuit. Despite the intense activity of explorers the contact between them and Native people was slight.

More than anything else, the fur trade formed the basis for further exploration. Samuel Hearne at Fort Prince of Wales used his base to extend the influence of the British Hudson's Bay Company and to search for further riches, including minerals. A rival Scottish company, the North West Company, had an even greater impact on Native people. It did not build great fortresses like Fort Prince of Wales and used no Native middle men. Its voyageurs left Montreal and spent years in the wilderness living much like Native people. Many Native people who carry French or Scottish names today — the Métis — are descendants of these hardy pioneers and are proud of their distinct cultural origin. Pre-eminent among the nor'westerners, as they were called, was a Scotsman, Alexander Mackenzie. He was the first European to discover the river that bears his name. He extended the fur trade up the huge river valley as far north as the Arctic Ocean. To commemorate the 200th anniversary of his discovery an international canoe race organized by Dene leaders using voyageur canoes took place in July, 1989. The 1,700-kilometre race began at Fort Providence, just north of Great Slave Lake, and finished at Inuvik.

The pattern of settlement in the Northwest Territories owes much to the fur trade. In the West the Dene and Métis settlements are on the large lakes, at the confluence of rivers, and near rapids or waterfalls or other natural stopping places for waterborne traffic. On the Arctic coast the Inuit settled around posts chosen by the Hudson's Bay Company or other traders because of good anchorage and shelter for their annual supply ships. Often the places chosen were not the best hunting and trapping areas. Today, many Inuit settlements find themselves with inadequate land for building, poor water supply, and air strips that must be blasted out of rock at great expense. The good land belongs to the trading company, the churches, or the police who settled there when Inuit were still hunting-camp dwellers and only came to the small settlements for short visits to trade.

Whaling

The whalers had a lasting impact on the way of life of the Inuit. Just as the fur traders introduced new ideas and new technology to the Dene, the whalers brought to the Arctic coast the methods of an industrial economy. Whaling had been carried on by the Inuit for hundreds of years using teams of kayaks. Thus, when commercial whaling reached its height between 1820 and 1840 with the arrival of English, Scottish, and American whalers, the better hunters were employed as harpooners and pilots.

In the eastern Arctic the main activity was around Pond Inlet on the northern coast of Baffin Island, further south near the present-day community of Pangnirtung in Cumberland Sound, and in northern waters of Hudson Bay. In the western Arctic the whalers, mostly out of San Francisco and Seattle, killed whales in the Beaufort Sea and wintered on Herschel Island.

The whaling era added much to the history and culture of the Inuit, since the whalers lived in close contact with them for over a hundred years. When they wintered over many took "sea wives" and produced children. Some eastern Inuit today trace their ancestry to English and Scottish whaling captains, some western Inuit to harpooners from Fiji, Samoa, or even the Cape Verde Islands.

Between 1857 and 1925 a Scottish whaling station established on Kerkerten Island near Pangnirtung was a major centre of the eastern Arctic whaling industry. So great was the impact of the whalers the government of the Northwest Territories has established a historic park on the island. Ironically, it is named after Angmarlik, a local chief who ran the station for over twenty years but who is best known among Inuit for his fight to retain the language and culture of his people in the face of the overwhelming forces of change.

In the western Arctic the whaling era brought many dramatic episodes into the lives of the Inuit. Whalers beguiled them with a bewildering array of trade goods and introduced them to alcohol. The social order of Inuit camp life was disrupted. Both the churches and the state were horrified when they heard lurid stories about debauchery on the whaling grounds and made plans to bring order and civility to this new frontier. Many of the young whalers who signed on in Seattle or San Francisco had little or no interest in whaling. At the first opportunity they intended to jump ship in Alaska and head for the Klondike gold fields.

Other crew members were criminals who simply wanted to escape into the wilderness. Whaling men did not represent what was best in Western civilization, yet this contact was for Inuit their first prolonged exposure to an industrial, commercial world that would eventually threaten their survival as a distinct culture and people.

The contact with whalers in the eastern Arctic was a little kinder; it has left a legacy of legends and memorable characters. William Duval jumped ship near Pangnirtung, early this century, settled among the people, and became a source of knowledge about the "outside" world. Today the most dramatic peak overlooking Pangnirtung fjord is named Mount Duval. When William Duval died the Inuit showed their respect by burying him in a coffin, not Inuit-style under a pile of rocks. The coffin had formerly been Duval's outhouse since wood was scarce and there was none available to make a real coffin. Another runaway was George Washington Cleveland. He'd been shanghaied in New England but jumped ship in Hudson Bay and settled in Chesterfield Inlet. Such was his skill he became known as Sherqaktie, the harpooner. He became a trader and opened up several trading posts along the western shore of Hudson Bay during the 1920s.

For many Inuit communities their first detailed knowledge of the outside world came from whalers. They were far more aware of life in Dundee, Aberdeen, and Hull than in Ontario. Several Inuit made the journey across the Atlantic in whaling ships and brought back stories of the wonders they had seen.

Religion

The Dene and Inuit had sophisticated religious beliefs before the arrival of Christianity. Some of the early missionaries were surprised to find similarities between the oral stories of Native people and Bible stories. Petitot, a Catholic priest (1838–1916), learned several Dene languages and discovered local legends about Creation, the Flood, and the Confusion of Languages. The Inuit also found much in the Bible that was familiar — nomadic lives of desert people, the importance of family, the family histories, the significance of names, the world of the spirit and the supernatural. Some Native leaders saw much that was familiar and saw no reason to change their old ways.

The conversion to Christianity was achieved through the efforts of some remarkable men, both Catholic and Anglican. In the eastern Arctic Edmund Peck established his mission on Blacklead Island near Pangnirtung in the late nineteenth century. He believed he could have a sobering effect on the excesses of the whalers, but he also had a carefully thought-out plan with far-reaching implications. He had adapted a syllabic system of shorthand writing originally developed for Cree Indians. Peck knew that if he could teach a few key people on Blacklead Island, they would in turn spread the writing system and the gospel along the coast. The Inuit turned their hands readily to whaling and, each summer, they were widely dispersed throughout Arctic waters — perfect vehicles for the mission.

The Catholic Church did not leave the eastern Arctic mission field to the Anglicans without a fight. From 1909, when the first Anglican mission was established at Lake Harbour on Baffin Island, the two churches played leapfrog — each attempting to establish a church closest to the North Pole. Legend tells us that an Anglican would arrive in camp, solemnly baptize everyone, and give warning about the evil men in black robes, dressed like women, who would soon arrive to claim them back for the Devil. One of the Catholic responses was to concede defeat on Baffin Island and to concentrate its effort on Hudson Bay. The Catholic Church built a hospital at Chesterfield Inlet and eventually an enormous school residence. The Catholic buildings so dominated the skyline that Chesterfield Inlet became known as "Vatican of the North." Priests from Europe spent their first year there to learn the culture and language of the Inuit.

The Catholic faith spread rapidly among the Dene communities in the western Arctic, where communications were much simpler than on the Arctic islands. The Mackenzie River was the highway linking the missions. Mission supply boats travelled from Fort Smith on the Alberta border to Tuktoyaktuk on the Arctic coast. Despite its powerful base on the western Arctic, the Catholic Church failed to make its long desired impact among coastal Inuit. Some credit for this must go to Isaac Stringer, "the two-fisted Bishop." The Anglican Church had decided to do something to protect Inuit from the excesses of whalers on Herschel Island, and Stringer was a large, powerful man, not easily intimidated. On the whole, the whaling captains co-operated with him. Some welcomed him and asked him to give spiritual support to their men. Occasionally, though, he made himself unpopular by smashing their stills and brew pots, and berating them for their immoral conduct.

The Catholic Church made one major attempt to establish itself among the Inuit when it sent two priests to establish contact with the Copper Inuit on the Arctic coast during the First World War. These two priests, Rouviere and Le Roux, were murdered by Inuit. It took five years before the assailants were brought to trial. Bishop Breynant was appalled at the justice system that gave the Inuit only two years' detention for their crime.

Sovereignty

Where the churches ventured to save aboriginal people from what they believed to be the despair of their pagan religion and the perils of moral disintegration on the whaling grounds, the police weren't far behind. The face of the state was the North West Mounted Police. The man chosen to bring law and order to the whaling grounds was Constable Fitzgerald, a gregarious, wild-eyed Irishman. It was also part of his job to deliver the mail from the coast to Fort McPherson, from where the NWMP winter patrol would take it to Dawson City in the Yukon. With so many American ships wintering at Herschel Island and the captains more or less law to themselves, it was this lone policeman's job to remind the Americans they were on Canadian territory and subject to Canadian laws.

A similar assertion of Canadian sovereignty was taking place on Hudson Bay at Cape Fullerton north of Chesterfield Inlet. In 1905 a five-man NWMP detachment was established to keep an eye on the New England and Scottish whalers who wintered among the Aivilikmiut Inuit. They also made patrols along the coast and onto the barren lands to report on the health of Inuit in their hunting camps.

The Events of 1921

In 1921 oil was disovered by Imperial Oil at Norman Wells. A stampede ensued as prospectors came up the Mackenzie River to make their fortune. Scenes reminiscent of the Yukon gold rush days were common as every boat in the river was pressed into service. This was the first oil discovery in western Canada and Arctic sovereignty took on a new significance. Canada had not signed a treaty with Indian people north of Great Slave Lake. If commercial activity was close at hand it was necessary to come to an agreement with the Natives; it was also necessary to reinforce the rule of Canadian law. This had been done in earlier days in the Klondike so that, unlike the California gold rush, developments would be orderly and peaceful. The Catholic Church was equally concerned about the impact of a wave of adventurers. The Catholic Bishop Breynant, still angry over the failure of the state to apply true justice to the murderers of his priests, pressed the police to enforce the law.

It is not coincidental that in 1921 the first Indian north of 60° was tried and hanged for murder. His name was Albert Lebeaux, who, finding his wife pregnant following many years of marriage, killed her believing a priest she had befriended was the father of the child. It seems the police pursued this case with relish. The bishop had demanded they be more vigilant in applying the full authority of Canadian law. This was a perfect opportunity. The trial took place at Fort Providence on the Mackenzie River just west of Great Slave Lake. Hundreds of Indians were gathered along the river bank in their tipis for the signing of Treaty 11, which the federal government believed would clear the way to exploitation of the northern oil fields. They were invited to attend the trial to witness the Canadian system of justice at work and, perhaps, to provide a warning that murder was a serious crime that would be severely punished. One can only imagine the discomfort of Bishop Breynant as the accusations in this particular case came to light!

Government

In 1870 the Northwest Territories included practically all the land in Canada west of Ontario. The federal government was reluctant to create new provinces out of this huge, sparsely-populated land mass it acquired when Rupert's Land and the Red River colony were transferred to the Dominion of Canada from Britain. The anger of the Red River colony about their absorption into the Northwest Territories led eventually to the creation of Manitoba and the rest of the Prairie provinces.

The federal leaders of the day were excited about the addition of the huge wilderness of Rupert's Land and the highly successful Red River colony to the Dominion of Canada and had every intention of running the entire area as a colony. They overlooked the fact that the colony had already achieved a high degree of self-government. From 1870 onward the political history of the Northwest Territories is about progress toward responsible government. In 1898 the region west of the Mackenzie Mountains was partitioned off to become the Yukon Territory. With the creation of Saskatchewan and Alberta as provinces in 1905 it seemed the potential for adding new provinces to the Confederation had been exhausted. What was left of the Northwest Territories was placed under a commissioner in Ottawa.

The move toward responsible government was delayed until 1967 when the seat of government was moved from Ottawa to the new territorial capital, Yellowknife. Although the federal government has officially stated its support for responsible government in the Northwest Territories, several factors have slowed the process down. The provisions of the Constitution Act (1982) were a partial success in blocking the admission of new provinces into Confederation. The Meech Lake Accord of June, 1987, although it ultimately failed to become part of the Canadian constitution, would have made the natural evolution of the Northwest Territories into one or more provinces very difficult since it required the unanimous consent of all ten provinces and of the federal government. The continuing demand of Native people for their own distinctive brand of self-government and the debate over the division of the Northwest Territories to give the Inuit their own homeland, Nunavut, have contributed to a cautious approach to the constitutional evolution of the Northwest Territories by the federal government.

During the period following the Constitution Act (1982) momentum began to gather toward some form of territorial autonomy short of provincial status but that gives province-like power to a responsible northern government.

Currently, there are twenty-four members in the Legislative Assembly of the Northwest Territories, which operates very much like a provincial legislature. Members are elected for a four-year term. What makes the legislature unique is the consensus-style of government. Members are elected as individual representatives, not as members of a political party. The twenty-four members meet in caucus and by secret ballot select a leader and seven other members to form the executive council or cabinet. The system is continually being modified since, despite its many weaknesses, the large majority of Native MLAs in the assembly (fifteen out of twenty-four) believe it is superior to the confrontational style of party politics and conforms more to the co-operative style of decision-making used by Native people.

In practice the eight-member executive council becomes a minority government and depends on coalition with other members of caucus, issue by issue, to survive. Survival is even tougher for the leader, who is chosen by the caucus but does not choose his own executive council. This makes leadership very difficult and government discipline practically impossible to achieve. The biggest problem, though, is the lack of accountability to the public, which is offered a choice of candidates every four years but not a choice of ideas. In the Northwest Territories the public does not elect a government. It elects politicians who then work out among themselves the kind of government the public will get.

Recent Developments

Since 1967, Canada's centennial, when the Northwest Territories began once again to quicken progress toward provincehood, several events have focused Canadian attention on

Canada's North.

During the 1970s the federal government began a process of transferring land and providing cash compensation to Native people for prior use of their land. The concepts of aboriginal title and aboriginal rights were discussed and explored. Instead of referring Native claims to the courts, negotiations with Native people were begun to supplement the rather outdated treaties of 1899 and 1921. Again, oil quickened the process. The oil crisis of 1973 made Canadians think of oil self-sufficiency and the potential of the Arctic frontier.

The appointment of the Berger Commission in 1974 to inquire into a Mackenzie Valley pipeline served only to heighten the debate about the Native need for a homeland under their own control and the need to develop the frontier for the benefit of all Canadians. In the commission's report, published in 1977, Mr. Justice Berger called for a ten-year delay in building a pipeline while Native people settled their land claims.

The debate also focused attention on environmental issues. Northerners began to demand more control over activities that closely affected their lives but were still under federal control. A process for the devolution of these powers to the Territories government was begun and Native leaders, wishing to be more heavily involved in the process, demanded work begin on examining new forms of northern government that would better protect their land, the rights of their people, and their way of life.

The growing awareness by all northerners of the Northwest Territories as a homeland, not as a national treasure house of oil and minerals, has helped focus their attention on the renewable resource base of the economy and the need to protect it. During the past decade fears have been expressed by all northerners about the increased militarization of the North with low-level bomber flights, cruise missile testing, nuclear submarines, and the North Warning System. In addition to military activity, there is widespread concern about uranium mining and the contamination of Arctic waters by PCBs and effluents, possibly from rivers in the Soviet Union. There is also a concern that the Arctic may increasingly be the recipient of airborne pollutants from southern Canada and other northern industrialized countries.

Today, the Northwest Territories faces a classic dilemma. It depends on the federal government for over 75 per cent of its budget but would like to become more responsible and independent. To become independent it needs to create more wealth and possibly risk greater damage to the environment. The North has the highest rate of unemployment in Canada. It is desperately attempting to re-establish its renewable resource base following the decline of the fur industry. Despite the need to create jobs at an increasingly rapid rate it's likely that northern leaders will pursue economic development with caution. They are aware the North is one of the vast wilderness areas in the world. They talk often about the responsibility they have toward future generations.

A major feature of northern development since 1967 has been the continuation of a colonial mentality within the public service in Ottawa. The devolution of powers to the territorial government has been slow. Despite the facts that fully two-thirds of the population of the Northwest Territories are Natives and that there is a fully elected government with a Native majority, the federal government still has a Department of Indian Affairs and Northern Development in Ottawa, a large part of which is devoted to promoting or protecting the rights of northern Native people. For twelve years DIAND has been attempting to negotiate a land claim with both Inuit and Dene that would make northern aboriginal people the biggest landowners in North America. The negotiations continue to break down since there has been disagreement about where the boundary should be between the Inuit and Dene claim areas. Also, the Native people would like to develop their own form of self-government. Although they control the current Legislative Assembly of the Northwest Territories they regard it as a neo-colonial institution with no roots in their own traditions.

It is likely the Inuit would settle for their own territory, their own direct relations with Ottawa, and the opportunity to develop a distinctive Inuit "homeland" since the Inuit are a clear majority in their claim area. The Dene in the West seem less certain of what they want but they do have a proposal for a western territory called Denendeh. The negotiations with the Dene have been difficult because most non-Native people or "others" live in the West. This is where the major developments in oil and gas and mining are likely going to occur and the Dene fear they could become a distinct minority with greatly reduced political power if a new western territory is created without some guarantees for Native political representation. The main proponents for division of the Northwest Territories are in the Ottawa bureaucracy, since they would have a new territory to "develop," and among the Inuit, who have a clear vision of an Inuit "homeland." The big problem for the politicians, both federal and territorial, is the cost of creating a new political division for the 20,000 Inuit and "others" of Nunavut, especially while the total cost of land claims and cash compensation for Native people is an added burden on a government already deeply in debt.

The development of responsible government in the Northwest Territories has been a constant theme in Canadian history since 1870. The current government of the Northwest Territories now has powers that are almost identical to those of a province. The Legislative Assembly is gradually developing a distinctive style that incorporates elements of traditional aboriginal ways of decision-making within the framework of parliamentary democracy.

When the territorial government was established with its new northern capital in 1967 it was hoped that Native people would be better served than under the "reservation system" that isolates Native people from society in the rest of Canada. Fully responsible government has not been achieved yet and several Native leaders are still seeking alternatives to both the "reservation system" and provincial-style government as they negotiate a land claim with the federal government.

In September of 1988, after twelve years of negotiations, the Dene-Métis of the western Arctic signed an "agreement-in-principle" on their land claim with the Prime Minister of Canada at Rae-Edzo, a major aboriginal community seventy miles west of Yellowknife. The chiefs of the bands in the claim area endorsed the agreement on April 9, 1990, in Yellowknife. Under this claim the Dene-Métis would become owners of 70,000 square miles of land, of which they would hold sub-surface mineral rights to 3,900 square miles. In addition, the federal government would pay the Dene-Métis $500 million over a fifteen-year period in compensation for past use of the land.

Since the signing of the agreement by the chiefs it has come under increasing attack because it contained no provision for self-government and extinguished aboriginal rights. As a result the agreement was rejected by the Dene-Métis General Assembly in July of 1990. Soon afterwards, the northern tribes in the oil-rich and mineral-rich areas of the Mackenzie Delta and Great Bear Lake withdrew their authorization for the Dene-Métis to represent them in claims negotiations and approached the federal government to negotiate regional claims. On November 7, 1990, the federal government announced it would proceed with regional claims. For the bands around Great Slave Lake in the southern part of the claim area, who have dominated the Dene-Métis movement for new constitutional arrangements within Canada, the move is a betrayal. They perceive regional claims as a threat to a unified Dene-Métis position to consolidate land claims and self-government within a new territory called Denendeh.

While events in the eastern Arctic have proceeded more smoothly, the timetable for the creation of Nunavut is still uncertain. The Legislative Assembly of the NWT unanimously approved the creation of Nunavut in October, 1989. A year later the territorial government and the Tungavik Federation of Nunavut (Inuit Constitutional Committee) formally requested the Prime Minister to consider a seven-year timetable for the creation of a new eastern territory. In light of current concerns in Canada about the size of government and the size of the national debt, current thinking places the creation of a new territory as much as ten years away.

Building a government has dominated northern development for more than twenty years. Because of the large presence of bureaucracies at the local, regional, and territorial levels, young people see government service as the main employment opportunity. In addition, each of the aboriginal organizations established to negotiate a land claim has become almost a parallel government providing a limited range of services to aboriginal people. As a result, young people with ability have been quickly absorbed into the political process and have not developed technical or professional skills needed for the advancement of northern society. The Northwest Territories continues to rely on obtaining medical, legal, and engineering staff from southern Canada.

Challenges

Many challenges confront the government of the Northwest Territories. The educational level in Native communities continues to be very low. The dropout rate worries many government officials, who observe the severe social problems caused by "walkabouts," young Native people who no longer have a real option for life as trappers or hunters, have limited employment opportunities in their community, and who have too little education to be able to find work outside the Northwest Territories.

The majority of small communities have limited economic potential. They developed around trading posts when the fur trade was the major economic activity. With the collapse of the fur trade they continue for the most part as heavily subsidized settlements with no clear alternative economy. Efforts are being made to re-establish a renewable resource base, to revitalize the arts and crafts industry, and to promote tourism.

Where there is mining or oil and gas development, companies have changed their employment strategy to accommodate the lifestyle of Native people. The old-style mining town has been replaced by mining camps where men work daily for two weeks on twelve-hour shifts, then fly home for a two-week break. Family life under this arrangement is no more severely interrupted than when a trapper or hunter leaves his family for a week or two. One gold mine near Yellowknife that began production in March, 1990, works closely with Dogrib people, providing work and business opportunities for nearby communities. Where there is open-pit mining and the use of heavy equipment in a very cold climate, the training and employment of local Native people may be the most economic approach to mining. Similar lessons are being learned in the Beaufort Sea, where Native people have become heavily involved in the oil and gas industry.

While the development of a responsible government and a northern society in which all ethnic groups can feel comfortable remains a major challenge, northerners have other visions. They wish to be more than a heavily subsidized society for the protection of Canadian sovereignty in the North. They would like to begin generating their own wealth and to be less dependent on the Canadian taxpayer. Most would like to see one or more territories taking their places as provinces in the confederation of Canada.

Living in a non-industrialized part of Canada, northerners are strongly aware of the high costs associated with economic development. Consensus is growing among northerners, both Native and non-Native, that the Northwest Territories and Yukon may represent Canada's best opportunity to show leadership in "sustainable development" and in the treatment of aboriginal people.

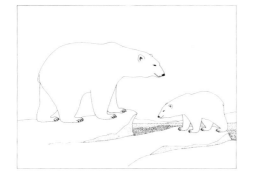

Eastern Arctic

Snow geese fly north along Baffin Island's east coast in spring to nest on the tundra of Bylot Island. *Barbara Brundege / Eugene Fisher*

The *Nanualuk* at Broughton Island can be used in the few months of the short Arctic summer only, when the sea ice has melted or drifted south. *Wolfgang Weber*

The eastern coast of Baffin Island, seen here between Clyde River and Pond Inlet, is characterized by countless fiords with glaciers and steep rock walls. Some fiords cut 50 to 100 kilometres inland. Few of the east Baffin fiords have ever been entered by white men. *Wolfgang Weber*

Early spring in scenic Pond Inlet, an Inuit community on the northern coast of Baffin Island. The area was one of the major centres of whaling in the last century. Archeological evidence suggests that Pond Inlet is among the most ancient Thule homesites.
Richard Popko

Roman Catholic church in
Pond Inlet, in the glow of a
northern early spring sky.
Richard Popko

Narwhals play "touch me"
in an open lead near Pond
Inlet. *John Ford*

23

Thick-billed murres — one of the most numerous seabirds in the northern hemisphere — nest on the sea cliffs of northeastern Baffin and of Bylot Island, as seen here. *Barbara Brundege / Eugene Fisher*

The long-tailed jaeger on the coast of north Baffin Island. *Barbara Brundege / Eugene Fisher*

King eider drake in breeding plumage. *Richard Popko*

Inuit youngsters study the anatomy of sea mammals in this rebuilt *qammaq* (whalebone house) from the Thule culture at Kekerten Island Historical Park near Pangnirtung, which once was a major whaling centre. *Mark Weidman*

Old grave of an Inuit shaman on one of the islands in Cumberland Sound, the coffin having been made from a Remington rifle box. *Mark Weidman*

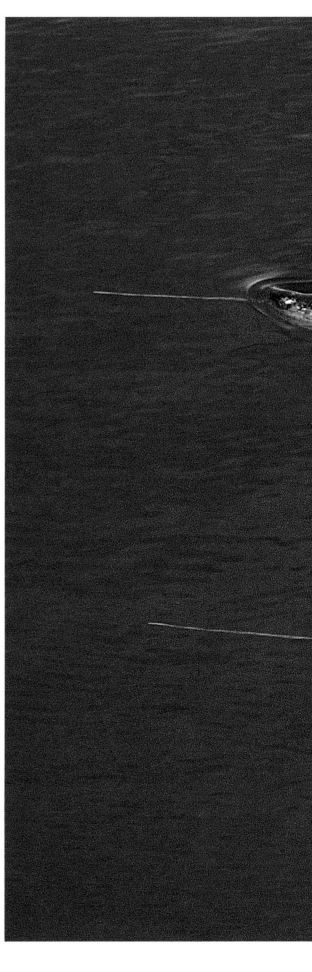

Four male narwhals,
accompanied by a female,
ply the summer waters of
Baffin Bay in Buchan Gulf.
John Ford

Springtime in Iqaluit. With more than 3,000 inhabitants Iqaluit is the largest Inuit community in the Arctic, and today it is the major regional service and government centre in the eastern and High Arctic. *Wolfgang Weber*

When the ice is gone, supply ships without keels can easily be unloaded at low tide in the "port" of Iqaluit.
Elke Emshoff

Air Inuit is a flourishing airline, serving towns and communities in northern Quebec and on southern Baffin Island.
Richard Harrington

Lena Evik-Twerdin and
Annie Naudlak playing
traditional string games.
Tessa Macintosh

Children learn the written
Inuktitut language with the
help of modern machines,
such as with this syllabic
computer program.
Tessa Macintosh

Modern housing in Iqaluit
being mounted on steel
frames due to permafrost.
Wolfgang Weber

Beluga whales are the most common year-round residents in eastern and western Canadian Arctic waters, seen here in Cumberland Sound.
John Ford

At Pangnirtung's annual
beluga harvest "festival."
Mark Weidman

Each family of this small
community gets its fair share
of the white whale.
Mark Weidman

Inuit hunters of modern time
still know how to use the
harpoon for whales and
walrus, as seen here with a
congregation of walrus on an
ice pan in Admiralty Inlet.
Glenn Williams

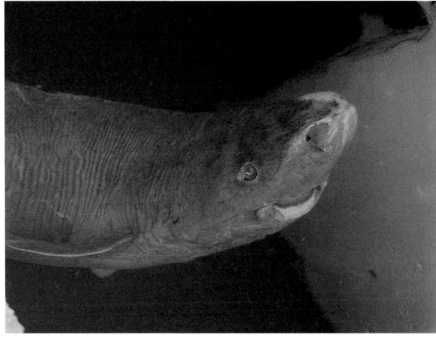

Tail fin of a bowhead whale north of Borden Peninsula. *Glenn Williams*

Greenland shark in the Arctic waters of Eclipse Sound. *Richard Popko*

Matheusie Akoomalik from Pond Inlet and his fan-hitched dogteam on thawing sea ice, looking for the right route. *Barbara Brundege / Eugene Fisher*

Mike, a young Inuk from Igloolik, on his way to hunt caribou. *Mike Beedell*

One of the forty-six sled dogs of Renee Wissink's Qitdlarssuaq expedition, waking up after a cold Arctic night. *Mike Beedell*

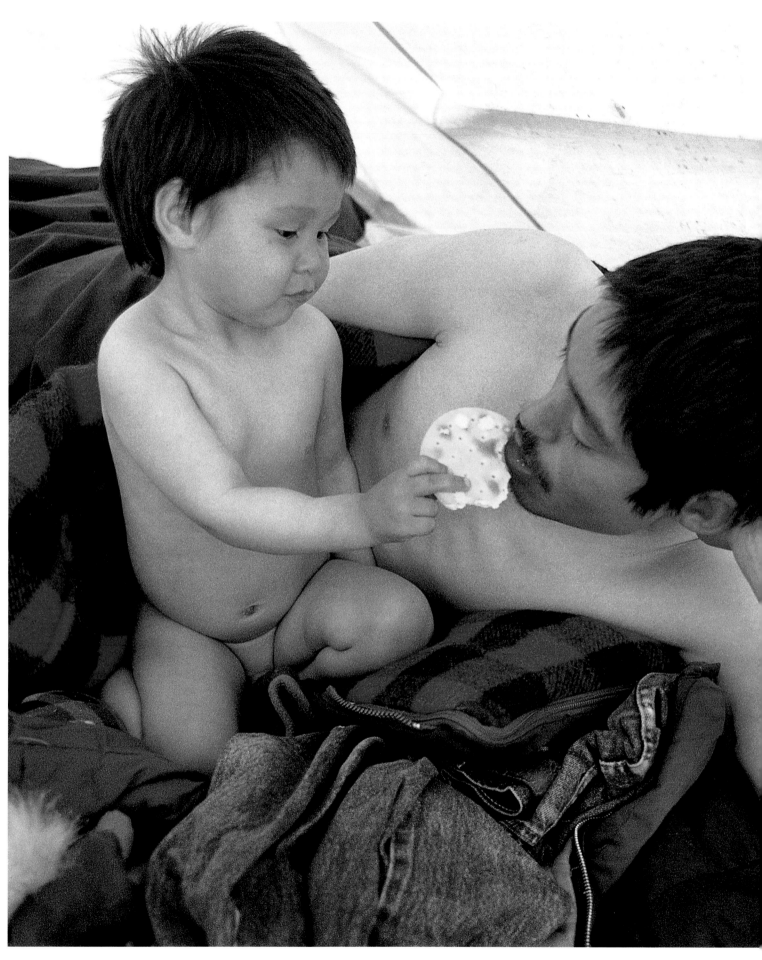

Daniel Qitsualik and son
Gabriel rest in tent on
hunting trip near Pond Inlet.
Barbara Brundege / Eugene
Fisher

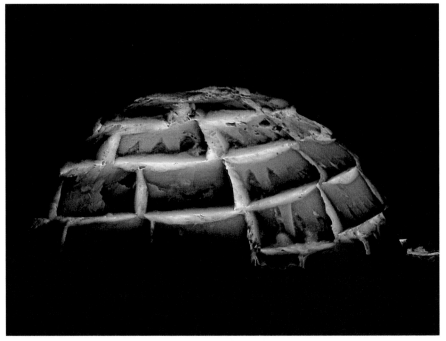

Snowhouse (*igloo*) on the
Borden Peninsula.
Glenn Williams

Traditionally, the Inuit used
seal oil stoves and lamps
(*kudlik*), such as this one.
Larry Dueck

Soapstone mask from Cape Dorset on the south shore of the Foxe Peninsula of Baffin Island. Contemporary Inuit sculpture is descended from the ancient craft of carving. The lives of a hunting people depended on the skill with which weapons and tools were made. Most objects traditionally made by Inuit were useful in very specific ways, but a few small art objects — earrings and decorated fasteners, intricate combs, dance masks, amulets, figures — have been handed down by early carvers. *Barbara Brundege / Eugene Fisher*

Marble carving by Luke Nuliayok of Spence Bay, the small Arctic community also famous for its "packing dolls," stuffed dolls of people, animals, and creatures often wearing an authentic miniature version of the woman's traditional *amauti*, and for its artistically decorated parkas trimmed with furs. *Tessa Macintosh*

Caribou antler carving, made by an Iqaluit artist. *Mike Beedell*

(Upper):
Master carver Simeonee Quppapik of Cape Dorset, the small settlement renowned for its outstanding stonecarvers and printmakers. *Barbara Brundege / Eugene Fisher*

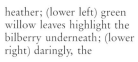

An Arctic tundra summer garden: (upper left) white lichens and purple saxifrage make a unique northern marriage bouquet; (upper right) the red bog cranberries and the black crowberries on a soft underlayer of moss are surrounded by the large red leaves of the *Arctostaphylos rubra* and by Arctic white heather; (lower left) green willow leaves highlight the bilberry underneath; (lower right) daringly, the bladder-campion blossoms in the windy Arctic. *Wolfgang Weber*

Tundra with blossoming willow herbs (fireweed) and prickly saxifrage along Adams Sound near Arctic Bay. *Glenn Williams*

Auyuittuq National Park on Baffin Island was created in 1972 to preserve a unique Arctic wilderness of perpetual ice, jagged mountain peaks, deep valleys, and spectacular fiords. Its Inuktitut name standing for "the place that does not melt," this park of 21,470 square kilometres is located just north of the Arctic Circle and is a luring temptation for hardy hikers and climbers as well as a paradise for nature lovers. Above the valley of the Owl River and Turner Glacier — nourished as all the other great glaciers by the huge Penny Ice Cap, a remnant of the last Ice Age — stands the Precambrian granite tower of Mount Asgard, reaching up to more than 2,000 metres. *Wolfgang Weber*

Wolfgang Weber and travel companion hiking in Auyuittuq National Park. *Wolfgang Weber*

Late spring melting waters dig tunnels into the metres-thick ice cover of Weasel River in the

Auyuittuq Park, seen here with Mike Beedell in the tunnel's opening. *Wolfgang Weber*

Hiking the rugged 97-kilometre-long route of Pangnirtung Pass through Auyuittuq Park in summer, with just a few shelters available. The Pass connects Cumberland Sound with Davis Strait, rewards the nature lover with spectacular views of mountain peaks, glaciers, and an abundance of wildlife. The route's highest point is Summit Lake, in the open water of which the peaks of Mt. Breidablick, Mt. Thor, and Mt. Odin are reflected. *Wolfgang Weber*

Baby ringed seal in summer.
Douglas Heard

Very young Inuk girl from
Arctic Bay. *Glenn Williams*

Matheusie Akoomalik with his son, in standard winter clothing. The relationship between an Inuk and his dogteam is not a "family affair," as this picture might indicate, but rather is a working relation. *Barbara Brundege / Eugene Fisher*

Ann Meekitjuk Hanson
Changes Within Memory

When my father and mother, Meekitjuk and Josie, were a young couple in the 1940s, they completely depended on the land and sea. They lived in an area called Piturqiit, a place outside of Lake Harbour on south Baffin Island. It was at the time when changes in the Inuit way of life were just about to begin.

When the Americans came to Lake Harbour during the Second World War, my father worked for them as a guide on the land, as a cleaner, and as a man for odd jobs. For us that was the beginning of a wage economy.

Since that time, there have been many changes in our lives. When my father was living, he hunted for animals on the land and the sea to provide for his family. The family moved with him wherever he followed the animals. My father was the leader in Piturqiit. Although the area is still called Piturqiit and is still considered to be Meekitjuk's homeland, it is no longer occupied.

In my father's time, each leader had an area of land in which people had their winter, spring, or summer camps. In the winter, several families would be together in one camp. Some were closely related and some not, but they were together because they wanted to make sure that everyone had enough to eat to survive. To survive, we had to travel. The animals did not come to us. My uncle Annowalk, as did other hunters, had a dog team. It was not a large team. My task was to put harnesses on the dogs. Sometimes it was very scary. When the dogs knew we were getting ready for a trip, they would get very excited and would fight with each other. Then my uncle would come and help, much to my relief. Sometimes I had to pretend that I was not afraid because we were told not to show fear around animals. Dogs are no exception. Once the dogs were harnessed, the long sealskin ropes were attached to one central loop that also held several ropes. One long sealskin rope, usually doubled for strength, was attached from the sled. The central loop holding several dogs made the dogs fan out so they would not crowd each other. The ropes were of different lengths, according to each dog's strength and ability. The lead dog always had the longest rope. The laziest dog or most disobedient dog always had the shortest rope. This way, the driver was able to keep an eye on the dog and discipline it accordingly. Once the dog was fully trained — that is, able to understand directions "to the left, to the right, stop, faster, slow down" — it was allowed a longer rope. Each driver made up his own commands for his dogs. I can still imitate my uncle's commands. Some commands were almost like songs, and the dogs knew their master's commands. My uncle seldom used his whip. When he did, it was only to alert the dogs by snapping the end of the whip above the dogs' heads.

Today, my uncle no longer needs me to help him before he goes on a hunt. Instead, he takes extra spare parts, tools, and gasoline because he now uses a snowmobile. The machine is cold and metallic compared to the warmth and dependability of the dogs.

When I think back, I remember the young men walked to hunt for small game. That was part of their education. Small game included ptarmigans, fish, foxes. My brother Egeesiaq used to walk. Sometimes he would come back empty-handed. When he came back with ptarmigans, they were shared by everyone in the camp. Years later, my brother candidly confessed that he sometimes pretended he was hunting. He would walk just outside the camp, sit down, observe the camp, have a rest. When he thought he had been gone long enough, he walked back to camp. Then he would relate his hunting "expedition" sorrowfully, saying "The ptarmigans were too timid today" or "There was too much wind." Today he says, "I was just being lazy!" in which case we bellow out with laughter.

When spring came, each family went its separate way to spend the spring and summer. They had to tell their leader where they would be. Each family had its favourite camp grounds.

If a family wanted to start its own winter homeland, it had to have permission from the leader. They had to agree that there was enough game to support the families. When agreements were in order, the man who asked for the winter homeland became the leader. He then looked for families who would be willing to share the new homeland under his leadership. It was very seldom that only one family moved away. People needed each other to survive.

Leadership was an inheritance. A person who was a good hunter, generous, wise, strong, and modest was considered to be the best leader. The sons and daughters of the leader were expected to follow the father and mother in the leadership role. If they were good people, they took over when the father got too old or became disabled. The respect and high regard for such a family was enormous.

I am writing this from experience. I was born when my people were completely on their own. I experienced the real Inuk way of life before it was assimilated with a new way. I feel very fortunate to have experienced the historical end of a nomadic way of life. It is not a fairly tale, nor is it a romantic way of life, because we went through hunger periods when animals did not pass our hunters' paths and when the weather was harsh for long periods of time.

I remember when my Aunt Mialee (Mary) and I were taken in by my mother's uncle Aupalutuq around 1954. His winter homeland was west of Lake Harbour, a place called Umiakuvik. My father had died. My mother had been taken out to a southern sanitorium because she had tuberculosis.

There were three families. I remember having just warm water to drink. There was nothing to eat. I don't know how long we survived like that, drinking just warm water. Then a man with a dog team came to our rescue. He was a member of the Royal Canadian Mounted Police. In those days the RCMP went around the winter homelands to check if everyone was okay. They often saved people from near starvation and sicknesses.

It is being debated among Inuit experts, governments, and intellectuals as to exactly how and when we, the Inuit, started to change our ways to fit the norm of the *Qalunaat*. I will speak from personal experiences, because the changes varied from region to region across the North.

I was born in 1946, in an era that my elders call "When people were still The People, The Inuit." Actually, the term they use is *Inuapiutidluugiit*, meaning "when they were the good people, the real people." When we say *Inuapiutidluugiit*, fond memories colour our whole view of the Inuit world. Thoughts of sharing, kindness, unselfishness, caring, and oneness with land and sea flow through our being. This is called *kajaanuqtuq*. There can be no proper translation in English. The closest translation is something like "a memorable beauty in time."

I started school when I was eleven years old. That was my first step into a new world. It was an exciting and frightening time. Exciting because it was something entirely new — I had never been in a classroom setting with many other children. Frightening because I could not understand the teacher — she was English and did not speak my language. We needed an interpreter for the first few months until we understood a few English words. We quickly learned not to speak our own language in the classroom. When we did, our hands were slapped with a wooden ruler. I remember being very silent. I would look into the eyes of my classmates and knew what they were thinking. Silently we were saying "I wish we could speak." We could not speak English because we had not learned it yet; we could not speak Inuktitut because is was forbidden in the classroom. We stayed silent. Only our eyes communicated.

Years later, I learned the reason why families were no longer living on the land. It was because we, the children, had to go to school. In my case this was 1958. Our reliance on the governments had begun.

I remember in my village, Iqaluit (formerly Frobisher Bay), there were many families. It was the first time we were together with so many people at one time. It was hard to remember who was who and whose family everyone belonged to. This was very strange.

My uncle Annowalk, as each head of family did, built a house out of scrap gathered from the local dump or wherever wood, tar, cardboard paper, or any usable material could be found. Since it was the new way of building a home, it was very cold the first winter. In our winter homeland, our hut had been made with materials from the land. Although the frames were wood, the insulation was blueberry bush. The hut was warmed by seal oil lamps. Our house in Iqaluit was heated by a homemade stove built out of a forty-five-gallon oil drum. I remember having to look for scraps of wood or hard paper. Every one in the village was doing the same thing so the whole area was quickly stripped of any usable items. To compensate, we used a kerosene oil stove. One of my chores was to make sure that there were enough burnable scraps for the homemade stove. I also got water, emptied urine pots, and looked after babies and toddlers. All my chores had to be done before and after school.

I remember some people got very poor. They did not have enough to eat or have heating in the house. Winters were especially unpleasant. Living in the village with many people created poverty within the people. When people were living in smaller numbers in winter homelands, they were able to help each other more readily by sharing. But here, it became altogether different. Close relations still helped each other, but there was just enough to go around.

Then the welfare system came in. People who were not able to care for their families were able to get help from the government. This was a new kind of help. Since all kinds of help are appreciated by the Inuit, because helping each other is survival, this was accepted as long as it was understood that it was temporary. In the winter homeland system, each family had been expected to contribute its share, no matter how big or small. For example, people who were not strong enough to hunt for bigger game were left in the camp to hunt for smaller game, such as ptarmigans, fox, or fish, and to do general handiwork. Young women and older people did chores that did not require a great deal of muscle strength — looking after children, cleaning or softening skins, mending clothing, or just keeping company. No one was useless.

In the 1960s, when we were new to community living with many people, it was hard to adjust. The hunters who had been able to leave their dogs to roam around the camp freely in their homeland suddenly found that their dogs were slaughtered by the police when they had inadvertently forgot the "new laws" to keep your dogs tied up. Without dogs the hunter was helpless. He could not leave town. He could not provide country food for his family. He had to turn to a wage economy and do his best during his days off to go hunting. Or he could go on welfare.

There were new diseases, skin infections, coughs, and sore throats. There was tuberculosis. There were sexually transmitted diseases that were "no-no" subjects. Then alcohol was added to the new problems. It was one of the most frightening experiences for my people because one was "out of control." As youngsters, we ran away from people who were "out of control" because they frightened us. Even their families, mothers, fathers, or grandmothers got out of their way until they were themselves again.

In the early 1960s the well-meaning southerners introduced a new way of governing the people. This involved what we call *niruaaq*, meaning selecting by preference. The people learned quickly to vote for a chairman or spokesman. The big meetings had to be translated. This process took a long time. The interpreters were uncomplainingly tired and most of the time they lost their voices. As this new way took over, the traditional way of leadership was quietly shoved aside. The younger people, who were more adaptable to new ways, were preferred by this system. Ever so innocently, quietly, and without a hint of the "you're no longer useful" attitude, the elders moved aside and a generation gap was born.

During this period the people were learning to make unilateral decisions in the *Qalunaaq* or southern way. When Inuit make a decision, it is by consensus. The decision has to be most agreeable to all concerned and ethically suitable. For example: when a childless couple want to adopt a baby from a relative or a friend, all concerned must agree. Not only the mother of the child, but all of her extended family. This agreement is made way before the child is born. When the child is growing up, the child knows his or her natural mother from birth. This law was ignored for several years after the new system was adopted. Now, it is being practised again.

The 1960s and 1970s are a haze to me. I was learning the *Qalunaaq* ways and ignoring my own culture. In 1965, I got a job that required using my language all day. I was a broadcaster for the Canadian Broadcasting Corporation (CBC) creating Inuktitut programming with my cousin Jonah Kelly. I like to think that we saved what was left of our language and culture. We encouraged our age group not to forget our language and learn more of what we did not know. I think we were on the way to reviving a declining language and culture.

Creating programs was not easy when you did not have any training. We learned as we went along. Often, we copied the *Qalunaaq* programmers from the radio, their interviewing techniques, story ideas, drama or music productions and put all that into Inuktitut. We interviewed our people for their life histories, adventures, legends, drum dancing, songs, and descriptions of everyday events. This was a big change to our advantage. By using the modern technology of radio, we passed on part of our life in our own language.

In the early 1970s, new Inuit leaders were emerging. People were starting to speak their mind. It was very exciting to be a broadcaster because for the first time we were able to interview politicians whose views were expressed in our own language. Before that we would just translate the views of politicians from Ottawa. At the same time we were learning to do current affairs programs that were relevant to our life.

I particularly remember the beginning of Inuit Tapirisat of Canada, the Inuit brotherhood, in the early 1970s. We had to explain the group, its goals, its purpose, and why it was started. The group's young leaders felt the same way we did. We were venturing into the unknown and not afraid of its consequences. Then more groups were started, such as the Baffin Regional Council. Its purpose was to aid municipal politics by having all the mayors meet and share common problems. Another was the Baffin Region Inuit Association. This group is directly under Inuit Tapirisat of Canada, serving on a community and regional level. Each northern region in the Arctic has Inuit associations that were started by Tapirisat. Education councils were created in each community. Health councils followed. Alcohol and drug councils were among the first groups formed. As the communities got bigger and more sophisticated in political development, regional boards were created to lobby the territorial and national governments.

At this time, we were receiving on-the-job training at CBC. We were taught how to do political stories, to be non-biased, impartial, and make good ethical sense. Much to our relief, we had been doing the right thing all along, even without training! We often laugh at ourselves in amazement.

I believe all the changes over the years have been harder to bear for those who understand what is going on. We, those who understand English, have to translate and interpret to our elders. We dare not leave them behind. The most difficult issues — land claims, constitutional debates, oil explorations, land rights, human rights — are treated with utmost care by our bilingual leaders. I know, our leaders go through a most difficult path, dealing with stress that is not in one language and culture, but two. It is no wonder some of them have fallen, but more often they have managed to pick themselves up again and continue their works.

Let me explain further: in previous generations, the leadership was shared in one language and culture. Everyone in the camp had a specific duty, usually shared. There were no strangers. Everyone knew each other's specialties and talents. Help and support was within reach. Concerns and issues were culturally and linguistically relevant to all concerned. Beliefs and values were strong, and they were practised. People were united in the common goals of survival, sharing, and gaining knowledge of the land and sea.

Today we practise all of the old ways but we are expected to know the new way as well. A leader who has inherited his or her father's leadership qualities serves the people *and* the new government well. These leaders are rare and overworked. Some of the new ways they have to learn are how to ask for help to understand complex issues from government documents without shame, to know who to trust, to make sense in both languages, and to travel long distances so that they often cannot provide country food for their families back home for extended periods of time. They have to learn meeting procedures and adapt them to our language and ways, invent new terms for computers, procedures, officers, and learn protocol for addressing government officials to suit their ways, dealing with civil servants through many referrals, writing letters, and keeping records, and they must endlessly read reports and documents. Such are a few of the procedures and things we have to get used to. When we do not do them well, we feel inadequate and ridiculous. Most of all we have to be good ambassadors to both cultures in order to serve our people.

I know we are not the only aboriginals in the world to cope with rapid change. What is unique is that we have used a lot of the changes to our advantage. When new things are brought to us — snowmobiles, motorboats, typewriters, computers, heaters, telephone, television, radio, and many other things that make life more comfortable — they quickly are given new terms in our language. In the last fifty years our language has grown because of new things. Each new item is given a descriptive name.

At the same time, old terms are still used in everyday language. Weather, for example, is *sila*. In regard to relatives, each cousin has a different term. *Silapiruuq* is greatgrand; *ananasiaq* is grandmother; *anna* is grandmother from the male side of family; *atata* is father; *anana* is mother; *angijuq* is older brother or sister; *nuukuq* is younger brother or sister; all uncles from father's side are *angakulook*; all aunts from mother's side are *ajakuluapik*. All the children of a family have different terms, too. When we use the terms for relatives, we know exactly which family they come from. This term is called *tusurautiniq*. Each region in the Arctic has its own way of *tusurautiniq*, according to the regional dialect. A landmark is an *inukshuk* — these are piled stones made to look like human beings. *Inukshuks* are used as guides to prevent people from getting lost. They were also used to confuse the caribou during the summer caribou hunts. When we are travelling, it is always comforting to see an *inukshuk* along the way because then we know humans have been here. There are many terms for the sea: *imavik* means, generally, the sea. We know right away that it means a body of natural saltwater. *Ikirq* means the sea without land or islands nearby. *Ingeeraniq* or *subbuq* is "the sea where there are strong currents." *Ikirasuk* is strait. *Tasiujaq* is an inlet or a bay. There is no one word for general health. Rather there are descriptions for state of health. For instance, *aniatailinirq* is "to stay healthy" and *anialik* is "in an unhealthy state." For the heavens, *qiilak* is the general term. *Qiilamitut* are the contents of the heavens — that is, the stars, the moon, and the sun. The general term for stars is *udloriat*. One star is *udloriaq*. The two stars that appear in the east during the night in the month of December are called *adjuuk*. *Adjuuk* were guides, calendars. When the *ad-juuk* appeared, it was an indication that the longer days were indeed on the way. People celebrated with great zest: drum dances, song contests, strength contests, games, feasts, storytelling. People were overjoyed because the ever present shortage of food would be eased by sunlight to hunt by. Animals would soon be more plentiful. Spring and summer would bring sweet roots, plants, flowers, berries, leaves to eat. *Singurii* is a summer star. It appears low in the sky in the south and shines very brightly. *Udlaaniit* are three stars in a row. *Udlaaniit* means "in a running order." *Sakiajuit* is a cluster of stars shaped like a human chest. That is why they are called *sakiajuit* — the chest is called *sakiaq*. These are just a few terms in our language. There are so many more to name. There is a myth, an ancient myth, about how the stars, the moon, and the sun came to be. It goes like this:

Many many years ago a young girl was alone in a snow house. She was in this snow house alone because of a superstitious belief of her time. She was menstruating. In that time, any female menstruating or having a baby was left alone in a snow house.

One night someone came to her snow house. There was a terrible wrestle. This person was much stronger than she. She could not fight back. The snow house was kept dark. She had to follow the belief and so she could not run outside for help.

The next night it happened again. And the next night. By this time she was angry and hurt that someone would take advantage of her. She thought for ways to find out who could be doing this to her.

This night she would be prepared. And so she waited patiently. At last she heard a noise. The person was coming in again! This time her resistance had a purpose. As she resisted, she rubbed her hands on the face of her attacker. She hoped it was the face!

After her attacker had left, she went to the giant *qaggiq*. *Qaggiq* is a huge snow house that held many people. It was a place for celebrations. There she waited. She looked at every face. A young man was entering the giant *qaggiq*. He stood up straight near the entrance. His face was marked with black soot! There he was. Her attacker!

To her horror, it was her own brother! The girl had smeared her hands with soot from her seal oil lamp. This way, she would know who her attacker was. The young man never knew he was marked.

She went to her brother and told him, "Come with me!" She led him to her snow house. There she cut off her breast and shouted, "My brother, my own brother, you want me so much. Here! Here, have my breast!" The brother was astounded.

The girl lit a torch from the flames of her seal oil lamp. She ran out. The brother lit a torch and followed after his sister. The sister ran around her snow house. The brother followed. They were running and running around the snow house. They were running so fast and for so long that they took off.

Once they were in the sky, the sister blew out her brother's torch. The half-lit torch became just ashes and became the moon. When the sister blew so hard the sparks from the torch scattered all over the heavens and became the stars. The sister never blew out her own torch and it became the sun. That is why the sun is always brighter than the moon and the moon can never seem to catch the sun. The sister is still running from her brother, the half-lit torch.

From this myth, we learn that our people had very strict beliefs, that touching your own sibling or kin is wrong and creates violence and anger.

These are just a few examples of our language. The old and the new. Through the legends, songs, myths, hunting implements, clothing, weather, food, and perhaps thousands of other ways, the language has survived by oral tradition. Like the myth I have told it has variations from region to region, but still it is the same, with same meanings.

The unpleasant side of the changes I have experienced are difficult to pin down because one person does not represent all aboriginals. I will talk about my personal experiences which may give some idea of what one person goes through in both cultures.

When I was a young girl I wanted to be just like a *Qalunaaq* girl. I wore makeup. I had my cousin Sarah cut my long hair short without consent from my aunt or uncle. I was so ashamed that I wore a scarf. Eventually I had to tell them. I was very embarrassed. Then I curled my hair. I spoke English to friends even though I knew my aunt and uncle did not understand me. This made me feel I knew more. I was so wrong.

When I came back up north in 1964 from Toronto, where I had been going to school, I felt very inadequate in my own language, in the Inuit way of life and, most of all, my Inukness had no depth. Underneath the makeup, curls, and nice clothes was a young lady with an identity problem. Fortunately, I was still close to my elders because of respect for them. They always accepted me as I was.

At the same time I was very close to my southern foster parents, Mr. and Mrs. Murray Cotterill of Toronto, who had saved me from total destruction during my transitional period. Mom and Dad Cotterill were the ones who encouraged me to retain my culture and language, even in Toronto. They would take me to Weston, Ontario, to see the Inuit patients so that I could speak my language. I would spend Sunday afternoons in the TB sanitorium there, visiting and conversing in our language. This helped me a great deal to stay in touch with Inuktitut.

The transitional period I am talking about is a period of self-realization: of knowing and accepting who you are. I know this sounds very easy to those who have not experienced it. There have been times when I have not been accepted by my own people because my ways had become too much *Qalunaaq*. That happened when I married a non-Inuk. In the 1960s, it was rare for Inuk women to marry outside the race. And there was a time I was not accepted by *Qalunaat* because I was not one of them. What can one do?

I had to work extra hard to prove to my people that I am an Inuk, no matter what. I speak Inuktitut, eat country food, sew from skins, and practise values that have been passed on through generations before me. It does not mean that I had to remind my people of my heritage. My Inukness is felt in the heart and people know it. There are no "how-to" instructions, unfortunately. The *Qalunaatitute* ways were easier because there are instructions. There is education in the schools. When I grew up, I learned to cook, shop, plan, and carry on conversation complete with acceptable opinions.

Transitional periods are the hardest to bear because one can turn to an undesirable route not accepted by either society — breaking the Western law, overindulgence in alcohol or drugs, stealing, telling lies, killing another human being, or just being a nuisance to everyone. This is called "must have strayed to bad ways of the *Qalunaat* and not listening to the Inuit ways," because we know that *Qalunaat* also have good ways. Inuit have bad ways, too. We used to call them "bad shamans."

Some people have adjusted well into both cultures and languages, because they must have experienced a good understanding during the transitional period. A good understanding of Inuktitut and the willing acceptance of *Qalunaatitute* good ways, mixed together, bring a very comfortable life. You are useful to both.

These are just a few things we have to go through as a bilingual, bicultural people in the North. There are many across the North who have had very interesting experiences. I know, because I have interviewed them. Some are sad because life just got too complicated and too heavy to bear. Death was the only way out for some of them. Others are so brave that they risk their own lives just to attend a meeting in another town. Some are humorous because people in the North like to laugh at themselves when they make mistakes or when funny things happen.

When visitors come from all over the world, we share our world with them. You are welcome to visit. But I must remind you that our life is very fragile right now. As you can see from the photographs in this book, nature is very delicate looking: it is us. We are a part of this nature. We may look very Western with our modern clothing but inside we are the Inuit who are practising the ancient values of our ancestors.

We have values. We have ethics. We have beliefs. We have convictions. Most of all, we have feelings. We are capable of understanding the most complex issues. We get a put-down feeling when all these are ignored and the *Qalunaat* ways are imposed on us. We accept readily because it is hospitable to make our guests feel at home.

All is not woe in the North. There are many people who are working hard to make life more pleasant. There are many Natives and non-Natives working together to prevent cultural and racial barriers from being raised and I applaud them. When there is no communication or understanding, racial and cultural stress sets in. I know, because I have been there. The majority of Natives are not racist. We just want to be heard when we speak. We want our hospitality to be observed and respected as we do when we visit someone else's home. I can say, when we visit the southern cities, we do not "take over" . . . but this is too trivially and crassly expressed. Instead, let me end my words with this: when we end our meetings, we say to each other *Inuqaatigisiaqta*, which means "Let us be good human beings to each other." After all, Inuk means a human being.

Renee Wissink
Ultima Thule: Adventure in the Arctic

"Oh my God! What have I done?"

The shock was immediate. Looking out the small window at the treeless expanse of rolling Arctic tundra — my new home — I was incredulous. As the Nordair jet taxied down the runway at Iqaluit (then known as Frobisher Bay), thoughts of adventure were the furthest thing from my mind. But why? Was this not the day I had dreamed of? Wasn't moving to the Arctic a long-sought-after goal? Was this not the land of my boyhood dreams? Of the Mad Trapper? Of White Fang? Of Sam McGee? No, this was a far different land. Its barrenness assaulted my southern sensibilities. It emanated an unconquered wildness, it beckoned in the way of a cocky challenger: "Just come try." Fear gripped the city boy in me — fear of the unknown. It was fight or flight. Stay or get the next flight south.

To me, the Arctic was as it is for most, a largely unknown land. Although it spans several million square kilometres from the Belcher Islands in Hudson Bay at 56° N latitude to Cape Columbia (the northernmost extremity of land in North America) at 83° N latitude on Ellesmere Island, it remains among the world's least known lands. It is a land of contrasts; contrary to popular belief, it is not just a land of vast, flat windy plains locked in perpetual snow and ice but also a land of mountain chains, of immense icecaps, and of productive arctic oases. It is a land rich in wildlife from the mythical exploits of the diminutive lemming to the continued existence of that ice-age remnant, the muskox. It is a land steeped in human history from the 4,000-year-old paleo-Eskimo culture to the modern-day Inuit; from the early explorers, traders, missionaries, and Royal Canadian Mounted Police to the present-day settlements with all the amenities of modern life: telephone, cable television, central heating . . .

Yet beyond the settlements the land is as wild as it has always been. The land is vast and the population, in comparison, minuscule. Iqaluit, for instance, with its population of a little over 3,000, is the largest of fourteen communities in the Baffin region. And for the Inuit majority, many of their traditions still live on. A generation ago they still lived their traditional nomadic hunting lifestyle. Only in the last thirty-forty years have they been catapulted headlong into the twentieth century.

The eastern Arctic is still in many ways the last frontier, an adventurer's paradise, a land with places where you can still place your feet and say, "I am the first living soul to have stood here." To the adventurer the Arctic is Thule, the mythical northland sought by the Greek explorer Pytheas 300 years before the birth of Christ. "Ultima Thule," that unquenchable drive for furthest north, has become the slogan of eastern Arctic adventures.

And so it was that the fear I felt upon arriving in Iqaluit was the first spark of adventure. For although adventure is many things to many people, its elements are the same. There is an element of mystery, of the unknown, of the thrill of discovery fuelled by our insatiable human curiosity. The mystery propels us on, the chance of discovery drives us. Even in the face of unknown dangers — another crucial element of adventure — we leave the security of our everyday lives and seek out adventure. Fear heightens our senses so that we feel as never before — Alive! Fear and adventure go hand in hand. I had come looking for adventure. I had left my home in southern Ontario — almost as far south as you can go in Canada — to come live in this strange new northern land. I would stay. It was the beginning of my own great personal adventure. It was "Ultima Thule or Bust!"

"Who the hell was Alfred Newlan?" I muttered, peering down into the cold darkness of the crevasse in an attempt to locate my lead dog. In the exhaustion of our eighteen-hour-day my thoughts and emotions were as tumultuous as the rising ground blizzard. Greenland our goal, had been clearly visible all day, a mere forty-five kilometres across Smith Sound, yet it seemed as far as the 2,700 kilometres we had already come — it may as well have been a million. We had progressed only three kilometres for all our effort that day and for the first time we faced potential defeat. The open water of Smith Sound, or the North Water as the whalers called it — the biggest *polynia* in the North American Arctic — cut off our sea ice route and forced us onto our last dubious option, Ellesmere Island's heavily crevassed Alfred Newlan glacier.

As leader of the Qitdlarssuaq Expedition the burden of responsibility weighed heavily on me. Dogs, as long as they did not slip out of harness, were relatively easy to extricate from a crevasse. But rescuing an unroped teammate or one of our 350-kilogram komatiqs was another matter. These crevasses hidden by thin snow bridges terrified me. I couldn't justify loss of life. But thoughts of defeat were equally troubling. The spring breakup was too advanced to even hope of returning along our outward route and our remaining budget precluded air support. Like Qitdlarssuaq, the powerful *angakok* (shaman) and leader of the last great Inuit migration from Canada to Greenland, whose sojourn of 130 years ago we were retracing, I wished that I could enter a shamanistic trance and send my spirit on a reconnaissance flight of the glacier ahead. Instead, I conferred with my teammates: Mike Beedell of Ottawa, and Inuit members Paul Apak, Theo Ikummaq, and Mike Immaroitok, all, like myself, from Igloolik, NWT. The consensus: make camp and proceed only when visibility improves, with two roped skiers going ahead.

Over the next eighteen hours of waiting my thoughts frequently wandered back to the original migration and especially to its controversial leader. The famous Danish Greenland-explorer and ethnologist, Knud Rasmussen, wrote of the migration: "It is the only example we met among the Eskimos of a group having undertaken a tribal migration implying a journey over several years from one polar region to another using their own methods and with no influence from civilization." Yet the qualities that Qitdlarssuaq — the great Qitdlak as the Greenlanders called him — possessed, inducing his clan of fifty to follow him, are not those we might esteem in our times. "We might even conclude," wrote Guy Mary-Rousseliere, OMI, renowned Arctic scholar and author of the most definitive work on Qitdlarssuaq, "that he was little encumbered by scruples and that a man's life was for him an affair of no great significance." But people are products of their times, Qitdlak being no exception.

Franz Boas, in *The Eskimos of Baffin Island and Hudson Bay*, relates that Qitdlak was forced to leave his native land of south Baffin Island after murdering another member of his tribe. The seemingly endless cycle of murder and revenge was not uncommon in Qitdlak's time. Having committed murder he could not rest easy. A man's male relatives, even his infant sons many years later, could seek vengeance. Life became a constant glance over the shoulder. But Qitdlak would not live like this. He longed for more peaceful lands. Along with a faithful companion, Oqe, they gathered up their family groups and left for the land of the Aqqurmiut, the inhabitants of north Baffin Island.

The move to north Baffin Island was to become only the first stage in this epic migration. Qitdlak's motive for new horizons is clear but how is it that so many were persuaded to follow?

Most would call pre-Christian Inuit superstitious. Their religion and their lives were centred on the belief in spirits. Evil spirits brought hunger, sickness, and death. Their omens were the harbingers of adversity. The helping spirits brought insight, bravery, good luck, and success. For instance, a predominant figure to Inuit mythology was Sedna, goddess of the sea. The cantankerous Sedna controlled the marine mammals the hunters depended on, and she easily withheld their bounty should any of the numerous taboos be broken. In this world of evil omens, spirits, and amulets the Inuit needed an intermediary, some way to control the uncontrollable and explain the inexplicable.

This job fell on the *angakok* or shaman. Through their secret language and soul travel they were able to enter the realm of the spirits and passify them. Sedna, because she had lost her hands, was unable to comb her long hair, which from time to time became entangled with filth and vermin said to be the accumulation of human wrongdoing. The shaman's soul would travel to the bottom of the sea, enter Sedna's abode, and soothe her mood by combing her hair. So appeased, she would release the animals and the hunters would again become successful. The shaman thus was both a feared and a revered member of each clan. Through his powers the spirits were controlled and the inexplicable explained.

The only other person in Inuit society who earned and commanded respect was the camp leader, usually an elder, who in an inconspicuous way dictated the rhythms of the yearly cycle. Normally each group had a separate leader and shaman. But I believe Qitdlak was both.

The stories that exist in the oral tradition attest to his supposed powers. Once, for instance, while out hunting polar bear far from land, Qitdlak and a young companion were overtaken by a severe storm. The ice was shattered and the open sea raged around them. Qitdlak ordered the young man to lay face down on the *komatiq* and not to open his eyes until so told. Having done so the young man felt the sled begin to move, and being both frightened and curious because he knew the open sea surrounded them, he opened one eye. Qitdlak had turned himself into a polar bear and his own dogs were chasing him. Wherever the bear trod, the sea turned to ice. But having opened one eye, the sled runner on that side began to sink into the sea. Terrified, the boy closed his eyes and did not reopen them until the sled stopped and Qitdlak ordered him to rise. Qitdlak was again a man and they were safe on land.

So is it any wonder that when this man — who could turn himself into a bear and raging seas into ice, and who it is said while travelling at night had a luminescent glow around his head — decided to leave, his people were so ready to follow. Their lives depended on him. He was, to them, immortal.

The idea of a long-distance dog-sled expedition had intrigued me since I first arrived in the eastern Arctic. When I learned of Qitdlarssuaq's great sojourn, I was hooked. My expedition would retrace the route of this eccentric rogue.

Preparation began in July, 1986, for an anticipated mid-March, 1987, departure — a mere nine months. Although I had no anticipated financing or committed team members, I dove headlong into the project. But progress was tortuously slow. By Christmas of 1986, my personal savings were exhausted, and I couldn't seem to get sponsors interested. Stubbornly, I forged on.

With assembling a team I was having more success. It did not take long to convince Paul Apak, an Inuit Broadcasting Corporation cameraman, or Theo Ikummaq, a former Department of Renewable Resources officer, to sign on. Both knew dogs and shared my zeal for travel on the land. But the greatest surprise came when I discovered that both were actually related to Qitdlarssuaq, being directly descended from his sister Arnatsiaq, who was also said to have been a powerful *angakok*. Next came Mike Beedell, whose reputation as a world-class photographer would prove instrumental to our success. Our last and youngest member was Mike Immaroitok. A recent high school graduate and nephew of Theo, he, like so many young Inuit in small communities, was unemployed with a bleak future outlook. The expedition would be a valuable experience for him.

The turning point came right after Christmas with an article published in the Toronto *Globe and Mail*. It gave us badly needed national exposure and loosened the purse strings of both government and business. Now with a full team and money in the bank, we began a flurry of preparations and training. March came around only too quickly and the stress of final outfitting bore down heavily. We worked almost around the clock.

Finally on March 9, 1987, we were under way. Leaving Igloolik with three teams consisting of forty-six purebred Canadian Eskimo dogs, we planned to retrace the main migration route by following the traditional trade route across north Baffin Island to the community of Pond Inlet (Mittimatilik); then west to Arctic Bay; northward from here for the crossing of Lancaster Sound, Devon Island, and Jones Sound to Grise Fiord; bypass the North Water by travelling up the east coast of Ellesmere to the north end of Smith Sound; turn east across Smith Sound; and finally travel south across the icecap of the Polar Eskimo communities in the Qaanaaq district of northwest Greenland. Our last stop would be the American air base at Thule for our proposed airlift home. It was an ambitious itinerary and many wagered against its success. It looked simple enough on paper. By the end of the second gruelling day even we started to have our doubts.

The major obstacle in our first two-week section from Igloolik to Pond Inlet was the constant battle with the cold. Temperatures never rose above −35° Celsius and often, with the wind chill, were considerably colder. Much coaxing and cursing went into lighting the stoves, erecting tents, and fiddling with other equipment with non-dexterous hands. Snow at these temperatures is as hard as concrete and our heavy sleds left almost no marks. The snow is also very granular and only iced runners slide easily over it.

Even the icing of the runners was not a simple task as it was important to ensure that a thin, even layer free of cracks was applied. The liquid for icing was two-thirds water, one-third urine; we supplied the urine by drinking copious amounts of tea at each break and applied it with a piece of bear skin. The water/urine combination provides a resilient ice layer that lasts considerably longer than freshwater ice. It is amazing the relative ease with which the dogs can pull extremely heavy loads on properly iced runners.

By the end of the first week we were beginning to settle into a well-practised routine. Up by 7:00 a.m. it took us two to three hours to break camp. We would travel eight to ten hours, interspersed with three to four tea and icing stops, then spend two to four hours tending to the dogs and making camp. If we could locate snow with the proper consistency and depth, and providing we were not too tired, we would build an igloo. Theo and Apak were masters of the art, and I marvelled at the ingenuity of the people that evolved this architecturally sound structure. Contrary to popular belief, igloos are extremely warm and very wind resistant. In one igloo, however, we failed to provide adequate ventilation and all received dangerous doses of carbon monoxide, first evidenced by bouts of uncontrollable and incessant laughter. Luckily, we realized in time that this was no laughing matter. Severe headaches were the only after effect.

Another morning I was awakened by Theo's shouts, "Grab all the skin clothing!" The dogs, many of which roam free at night, had broken through the igloo walls in search of food. Although we carried enough food for a daily ration, the dogs were always ravenous from the combination of hard work and extreme cold. Anything even remotely edible had to be kept from the dogs: sealskin harnesses and traces, caribou skin clothing, and all the food had to be taken into the igloo. Taking our eyes off an item for only a few seconds was all it took for a hungry dog to devour it. The loss of our caribou skin clothing to the dogs would have been a cold setback. Although we had micro-fibre undergarments, our outerwear was all of caribou skin, which is both light and extremely warm. It allowed us to travel comfortably during the severest cold, and without it, it is doubtful that the Inuit would have ever been able to exist in the Arctic.

In the extreme cold, over-exertion, which causes sweating and heavy breathing, became enemy number one. Heavy breathing could result in "Eskimo lung," a freezing of lung tissue due to improper warming of inhaled air, while cooling of sweaty clothing could encase you in a tailor-made, hypothermic set of armour. But in this regard, we soon learned that biologically the Inuit were also adapted to life in the Arctic. The Inuit members experienced almost no problems with sweat-soaked clothing. "No sweat in the Arctic" became our motto.

Another adaptation was the Inuit's lack of facial hair. Mike Beedell and I were frequently addressed as *Aiviq* (walrus) as large tusk-like icicles grew from our moustaches and beards. The ice accumulation became so dense that it was impossible to open our mouths to eat or drink. Using the scissors on a Swiss Army knife and a compass mirror, we crudely pruned back the growth.

Progress was slow in the first week. Across the almost featureless limestone plains of the area around Igloolik and north of Murray Maxwell Bay, the monotony was broken only by a few small rocky ridges. As we progressed north the rolling hills of the interior appeared. Signs of caribou were frequent but extremely disproportionate to the few animals we actually saw. One caribou shot by Apak in the first week would be the last of the entire trip. Although our success did not depend on hunting, the extra meat was welcome. Theo even used the stomach contents to repair his damaged sled shoeing, a trick he learned from his years in outpost camps. The Inuit are masters of using the meagre Arctic resources in myriad ways. "Sticks like Crazy-glue," he declared.

As we descended Phillips Creek approaching Milne Inlet, the topography quickly changed from the rolling hills of the interior to the mountainous terrain that would dominate much of the remainder of the trip. Navigation became easier. Well-defined valley systems and huge mountainous landmarks became our chief aids. Snowdrift navigation — an Inuit technique for determining direction of travel and maintaining a course using prevailing winds and their associated drift patterns — which we frequently used around Igloolik, was of dubious value her where winds were often localized and channelled by valleys. A sun compass and an RDF (radio direction finder), similar to those used in aircraft, rounded out our navigation system. Because of high declination and low horizontal intensity, magnetic compasses are unreliable at these latitudes.

As we passed Tununeq Mountain on the southwest coast of Milne Inlet, dog driving became just that. We were out of dog food, the dogs having pilfered our supply on two nights. They were quickly weakening. The next days were excruciatingly slow as the dogs had no will to pull; a slow walking speed is all we could muster from them. On the fifteenth day after leaving Igloolik — walking in front of my team while Mike pushed the *komatiq* from behind — we arrived in Pond Inlet.

The community of Pond Inlet embraced us wholeheartedly. We were taken in, fed, and treated as local celebrities. They even held a dance and feast in our honour. The next few days were spent feeding up the dogs, repairing the equipment, and catching up on our rest. We met with a group of local elders, all of whom had travelled extensively either in their normal hunting forays or as guides to the now famous RCMP patrols. Their advice and route suggestions would prove invaluable; I was amazed for the rest of the trip when weather and travel conditions would be exactly as they described. These were travelling men. The real Inuit. *Inummarit.*

The leg of the trip to Arctic Bay I denoted the "Great Detour." Our goal, Qaanaaq, is northeast of Pond Inlet but our route would take us west and sometimes even southwest. The detour was necessary because of the ice conditions in Lancaster Sound and the open water of Baffin Bay. Several Inuit muskox hunters had reported good ice north of Admiralty Inlet so it was here we would attempt the crossing to Devon Island.

Travel conditions over the sea ice of Eclipse and Tremblay Sound were ideal, enabling us to ride the sleds in an uninterrupted state of awe. My journal records the feeling:

> As we pass an island or a cape we have copious amounts of time to ponder its existence. I wonder about its formation, what caused this shape or that, what forces raised and deformed those striations. From today Curry and Emerson Island are well ingrained in my memory. But I suppose this is one of the beauties of dog-sledding, the long hours in which one can become lost within, either pondering oneself or your surroundings. The slow rocking movement of the *komatiq*, the creaking of its runners, the squeak of the snow beneath, and the rhythmic movement of 56 canine feet all add to the hypnotic effect. Often I will be jolted from these trances by a differing movement or sound — the *komatiq* hitting a large snowdrift, a quarrel amongst the dogs, or Mike speaking to me. The effect is like awakening from a sleep; although always conscious I must reorientate to my surroundings and the task at hand. I often look back at terrain covered but harbour no memory of having covered it.

As we passed under the Precipitous Mountains, deeply incised, truncated, plateau-type escarpments with extensive talus slopes, Theo searched for the subnivean birthing caverns of the ringed seal. The seal pups are considered a delicacy. Morale is high and as an April Fool's prank Mike strips naked and streaks about in the snow. A new form of Arctic hysteria, indeed!

For the crossing of the Borden Peninsula the tempo returned to "bump and grind." In some places soft snow or long uphill climbs slowed progress, while in others boulder fields and a dearth of snow reverted us to what we called the RAT patrol (Rock Aversion Technique). On the Magda Plateau we became lost, until we found the Fleming River and the unnamed stream that drains into Adams Sound. This stream proved to be one of the most exhilarating rides of the trip. It started out gently enough but as we progressed it became rockier and steeper until we had to proceed over a completely windswept rock garden between steep canyon walls. The huge boulders were like many immovable ball bearings that the komatiqs bashed their way over. The dogs worked hard and we all sweated profusely despite the high head winds and blowing snow — an incredible adrenaline rush as we scurried from side to side steering the *komatiq* and commanding the dogs, the whole time remaining nimble enough to avoid being crushed by the lurching *komatiq*.

Almost the entire population of Arctic Bay (400) turned out on the ice for our arrival. Snowmobiles raced around us, hordes of children jumped aboard, and when the dogs gladly collapsed on the command to halt, the questions came in rapid fire and the mandatory shaking of hands seemed endless. The community is named for the ship *Arctic*, which, captained by Joseph Elezear Bernier, wintered there during 1910 and 1911 as part of the Eastern Arctic Patrol, a campaign by the Canadian government to assert its sovereignty in the North. Within sight of the community and at the foot of the St. George Society Cliffs is Uluksan. It is from this now abandoned camp that Qitdlarssuaq, after spending many years in North Baffin and after still experiencing problems with reprisals, decided to leave for Tutjan, the islands north of Lancaster Sound.

On the morning of our departure from Arctic Bay I was growing increasingly apprehensive. Lancaster Sound has a nasty reputation. During most winters the sheer zone — separating the solid from the moving ice — is located near or west of Prince Leopold Island. Most of the sound is a mass of moving, grinding, and overriding ice propelled by a number of alternate and gyrating currents. To add to this was Lancaster's reputation as a polar bear haven. Two thousand bears, perhaps one eighth of the Canadian total, roam the area.

Although many considered our timetable to be too late, our crossing of Lancaster in early April was not unplanned. Previous discussions with elders indicated that during April there is a window of time when the ice movement ceases. Arriving at Cape Crauford, we found that this was one the few years that Lancaster had frozen solid, the flow edge being far to the east, north of Navy Board Inlet. But being stationary did not make it easy. The slabs of moving ice had frozen in a chaotic jumble of hummocks and pressure ridges, some as much as fifty feet high. Our job was to find a route through this maze. We weaved in and out, we laboured up and over. It would take five and a half gruelling days.

The dogs sensed the closeness of the bears in many of the sets of tracks we crossed daily. Maybe they had passed hours ago, maybe only minutes. We all knew it was just a matter of time until one came to visit. We slept with loaded guns under our sleeping skins. Since a bear will always approach from downwind, we placed our camps in the lee of large ice ridges with the best bear dogs chained in a semicircle on the downwind side of the tents. The rest of the dogs roamed freely.

On the morning of the fifth day in Lancaster, our first of several visits came.

> Somehow I sensed a bear would come during the night. I was awakened about 6:30 by a strange howling from the dogs. I knew immediately it was a bear and a quick glance out the tent door confirmed this. A young bear stood just beyond the dog line. He rocked the front part of his body back and forth slowly and gazed past the dogs at the tents beyond. It was as if he was attempting to decide what to do. A strong ground blizzard had risen during the night and what

a fine sight the bear made swaying in the blowing snow. The focus of all 42 dogs was upon the bear. They were all facing him, the wind to their backs, their long manes flowing forward. The bear made a move to advance between the chained dogs, but as if violating a defended territory, the loose dogs rushed him and drove him back into the rough ice.

The bear advanced a second time, but this time met with an unpleasant surprise. Theo had our polar-bear deterrent gun ready, a 12-gauge pump-action shotgun loaded with rubber slugs. Backed by Apak and me, armed with deadlier ammo, Theo fired two shots. The first missed; the second did not. The bear bolted with a few dogs in hot pursuit. They would return a short time later. The bear never did.

Lancaster relinquished us very reluctantly. The last kilometre was one of the most hellish of the crossing. With bruised bodies and battered komatiqs, we at last entered the smooth ice of Maxwell Bay. Our rough ice problems were over, at least temporarily, but bears plagued us yet. One came to within 100 metres and sat sniffing the air for an entire tea stop. Another was educated when it wandered into camp when all forty-two dogs were loose. Two days later Theo and Apak had to track the last seven dogs twenty-five kilometres to where they still held the exhausted bear at bay.

The crossing of Devon Island was an eye-opener to the High Arctic's meagre populations. Over vast areas the land was devoid of life, even lichens being locally sparse. Areas of exposed rocks, their pocked surfaces reminiscent of coral, badly abraded our runners. A few Arctic hares found grazing among the rocks made up our total faunal count. Other areas of Devon, such as the Truelove Lowlands, are lush oases where life abounds.

It took a whole day to descend the long river valley leading into Sverdrup Inlet. Its valley walls rose hundreds of feet and were lined with isolated pillars and massive cores of hard rock, remnants of once lofty mountains ravaged by time and her allies — wind, water, and frost.

Reaching Sverdrup Inlet, we now were into the twenty-four-hour light. To avoid overheating the dogs and to take advantage of the firmer snow conditions, we switched to travel at night, sleeping during the warmer daytime hours. The transition played havoc with our biorhythms. Time began to slur, days muddled. At one camp we argued as to whether the present time was a.m. or p.m. We concluded by agreement that resolution was irrelevant. In the Arctic spring, who cares.

We followed the coast of Jones Sound to Cape Sparbo, where Dr. Frederick A. Cook is said to have spent a desperate winter in a cave on his return from his controversial polar attempt in 1908. From here we struck out for what would be a seventeen-hour crossing of Jones Sound. We took turns skiing to quicken the pace but the last several hours we all rode, desperately fighting sleep.

In Grise Fiord (Pig Fiord in Norwegian) the Inuit team members were amazed to hear some of the people here in Canada's most northerly community speaking the Quebec dialect of Inuktitut. In order to establish a resident population on Ellesmere — a major premise for proving sovereignty — the Canadian government moved several families from Port Harrison, Quebec, and Pond Inlet to near the present site in the early 1950s.

On the evening of May 2, we left Grise Fiord on the final leg. I was extremely anxious. We had received reports of bad ice in the vicinity of Pim Island. A Japanese adventurer attempting to walk from Resolute Bay to Oaanaaq had recently gone through the ice near Pim Island and had to be airlifted out. How could we hope to pass with our heavy sleds where a lone man had broken through?

Our route took us overland to a small lake near Makinson Inlet. After spending six years in Greenland, Qitdlarssuaq and most of his people attempted to return to their homeland. This small lake was their furthest point of return. Here a great human tragedy was played out. Caught unprepared by the advancing winter, many starved. Others reverted to murder and cannibalism. We found remains of several *qammaqs* (sod and whalebone houses), and I wondered if these belonged to the migrants or some other inhabitants of Ellesmere whose settlement pattern is poorly known. Only five survivors returned to Greenland, never to attempt the journey home again. Ever since that time Makinson Inlet has been called Perdlerarvigssuaq — the place of the great famine.

It is near here also that we find muskoxen. It is impossible not to be impressed by these animals: a box wearing a shag carpet, stocky in stature with a long coat reaching near the ground. Muskoxen are supremely adapted to living on the meagre resources and harsh climate of the ice edge. The muskox clings tenaciously to existence.

At the mouth of Makinson we entered Baffin Bay. Although Qaanaaq, our goal, was almost directly east of us, our route turned north to avoid the North Water which extends from Baffin Bay through to the north end of Smith Sound. Our route was along the east coast of Ellesmere, an almost continuous ice cap with a few rocky bluffs, capes, and nunataks being the only visible land. Legions of calved icebergs, their progress temporarily halted by winter, extend as far as the eye can see. Bears are also numerous here, but well fed on the rapidly growing but susceptible seal pups, they ignored us.

On May 8th, still two weeks out of Qaanaaq, we fed our last dog food. To lighten our load and quicken our pace in the rapidly advancing spring season we opted to rely on hunting. It was then the time of year that seals enlarge their breathing holes (*aglu*) and haul out onto the ice to sun themselves. These would have to sustain the dogs for the remainder of the trip.

Reaching Orne Island (Ingersarvik) we felt close to the original migrants and the excitement of potential success began to swell. Easily overlooked by the majesty and grandeur of the mainland, this small inconspicuous rocky island was a pivotal landmark, being used on three separate occasions by the migrants on their outward journey and the unsuccessful attempt to return. It was the richest hunting ground along the coast. Walrus, seals, polar bears, and foxes can all be caught here. Without Orne Island, it is doubtful the migration would have succeeded.

The next five days proved to be the most trying of the trip. Three headlands — Cape Dunsterville, Cape Isabella, and Cape Herschel — extend right into the open water of Smith Sound and forced us to travel overland across glaciers. The crossings of Cape Dunsterville and Cape Isabella were accomplished without mishap. Reaching the top of the glacier on Cape Isabella, however, our hearts sank — open water in every direction as far as the eye could see, right to the Greenland coast now clearly visible. Polar bears, crevasses, katabatic winds, lack of dog food, and intense cold — these we could deal with. But open water!

We dropped down into Baird Inlet and followed a lead along its mouth. Open leads and treacherously thin ice disguised by thick snow plagued our route. We crossed the leads, forcing the dogs to swim, and avoided the thin ice by zigzagging along on pans of multi-year ice. A kilometre from Cape Herschel our forward progress was halted altogether. A tongue of open water right up to the toe of heavily crevassed Alfred Newlan glacier was an insurmountable obstacle. The realization was shattering. Only wings could save us now.

Pulling ourselves together, we decided to backtrack laboriously in the hope that we could find a route onto a glacier, around the crevasses and Cape Herschel, and down onto Rosse Bay, where we hoped we would find good ice. It was a desperate last hope.

A small bay near Cape Herschel is known as Qitdlaqarvik, Qitdlak's place, so named because it is said to be the burial place of the great shaman. Soon after the departure for the return journey, the aged leader died of severe abdominal pains, which his followers believed was the occult vengeance of Avatannguaq, a Greenlandic shaman Qitdlak had murdered on the request of his people. Some claim that his burial cairn can still be found there. It was not hard to imagine the spirit of Qitdlak warding us off — "This place is not to be visited."

Two days later we stood at the 1,000-metre level on the glacier, having successfully bypassed the crevasse field, and looked down at a beautiful site in Rosse Bay — a solid sheet of ice. The descent was an incredible ski. Mike carved an endless series of graceful telemark turns while my attempts left an erratic line punctuated from time to time by snow angels. The dog sleds followed; chains and climbing ropes twisted around the runners retarded their rate of descent to a controllable speed. It took us only two hours to reach the sea.

As we entered Rice Strait, the narrow channel between Ellesmere and Pim Island and now very close to where we anticipated we could traverse into Greenland, our morale was high. Apak managed to kill a seal, the first feed for the dogs in five days.

From our camp at Cocked Hat Island on the 16th of May, we began the crossing of Smith Sound. We headed in a north-easterly direction into southern Kane Basin, stopping frequently to stock seals or to climb icebergs in order to reconnoitre the rough ice ahead. Old *komatiq* tracks headed in the direction of Alexandra Fiord were our first sign of Greenlanders. They frequently cross into Canada in search of the highly prized polar bear. A short while later, from atop another berg, Apak shouted, "Qimmuksiit, Qimmuksiit!" ("Dog teams, dog teams!") and lifted me off the ice in an enormous hug.

As they rapidly closed on us, following our fresh trail, I thought of Qitdlak's first meeting with the Greenlanders not far from here. Qitdlak had met a man called Arrutak, who had lost his leg in a rock fall and had a wooden substitute. On seeing his approach Qitdlak's clan believed they had arrived in the land where all people had a wooden leg.

As the Greenlanders neared I was impressed that these were real dog men. The way they handled their dogs and sleds looked smooth and harmonious. Even the way they communicated with their dogs in a continuous series of whistles and guttural calls was melodious. The two Greenlanders were the brothers Aron and Angu Tuneq, fittingly, also descendants of Qitdlak. Hearing of our imminent arrival, they had set out to greet us. The meeting was very joyous; we had tea and traded foods. The exchange of information began immediately — which route, how many weeks, etc. The thing that impressed me most about them was how light they travelled: their loads looked minuscule compared to our long, heavily laden sleds. They took part of our loads and our little expedition had grown to seven people on five sleds pulled by sixty-three dogs.

The Greenlanders led us through several kilometres of tortuously rough ice before exiting onto a flat shelf of newly formed ice between the rough ice and the floe edge. We had anticipated an extremely rough crossing but this shelf provided some of the best conditions of the trip. Narwhal by the dozen cruised the floe edge and basking seals were numerous. It was a happy time. No one anticipated the problems of the next few days.

Crossing the Greenlandic border we met Qaordluktoq Miunge and his wife — again, both in the Qitdlarssuaq family tree — who had been out for fifteen days on an unsuccessful bear hunt. Over tea and much joviality, Qaordluktoq indicated that he had pains in his lower abdomen. None of us thought much of it at the time. Later that day, however, it became obvious that the pains were becoming worse. We stopped when Qaordluktuq could no longer drive his team. Unsure of what to give him, we radioed the nurse in Grise Fiord. We ruled out most ailments, including appendicitis, and decided on a course of action. We made camp but Qaordluktoq's condition continued to deteriorate. The pain became unbearable and we radioed Grise Fiord to arrange a medivac from Qaanaaq.

It's hard to express our feelings of helplessness. Mike spent hours assisting his wife in attempting to comfort him the best they could. At one point, Qaordluktoq made an unsuccessful attempt to take his own life. All we could do was hope for an early arrival of the helicopter. Four hours before it arrived, Qaordluktoq died.

We broke camp immediately after the helicopter's departure. None of us wished to stay in that cold death camp on the ice. As we departed camp, Qaordluktuq's hunting equipment piled and burning on the ice — one of his last requests — I reflected on the almost eerie similarities between Qaordluktoq's and Qitdlak's deaths. Both had died of abdominal pains, and Cape Herschel — where Qitdlarssuaq had died — was clearly visible directly opposite in Smith Sound. To add to the mystery, an autopsy performed in Qaanaaq failed to find anything wrong.

Four hours after leaving the camp we set foot for the first time on Greenland at the south end of Hatherton Bay, near Littleton Island. On May 20, 1987, seventy-four days after leaving Igloolik, we had reached our goal. We all shook hands and congratulated each other, but our joy was overshadowed by the events of the past twenty-four hours. No celebrations, only food and sleep. Three hundred kilometres of sledging still lay before us.

We travelled overland to Foulke Fiord, where the abandoned settlement of Etah is located. It was here that Qitdlak had first met the Greenlander Arrutak. When Qitdlak's clan arrived they found the estimated 120 Polar Eskimos populating this coast living in a precarious state of existence. For a variety of reasons, including climatic fluctuations and an epidemic that is said to have carried off all the adults, the Polar Eskimos had lost certain important technologies. They lacked bows, without which they were unable to obtain caribou for food or clothing. Some had even come to consider the meat inedible. Kayaks were also unknown. The Greenlanders were mostly hunters of the ice, having no way to pursue the sea mammals into open water. Their rivers teemed with char, but having no *kakivaks* (spears) this resource also remained untapped.

The Baffin Islanders reintroduced all three. The kayak allowed for the extension of the hunting season for marine mammals, while reintroduction of the bow and *kakivak* diversified the Greenlanders' diet. They also taught them to make igloos of the kind with a long sunken entrance, a warm substitute to their sod and stone huts. The migrants also injected fresh blood into this small isolated population. Today one-third of the area's 800 inhabitants can trace their ancestry to the original migrants.

Over the glare ice of Foulke Fiord, blown clear by katabatic winds, we passed abandoned sod houses. At its end, our route ascended the Brother John Glacier to the Greenland Ice Cap. Looking back, I saw our procession of six dog teams, Foulke Fiord, the North Water, and Ellesmere Island combined in an array of shapes and colours to form the most beautiful view of the entire trip. The south-facing slope of Foulke Fiord is covered in bright orange lichen after years of fertilization by millions of dovekies. These incredible swarms of birds, which return each spring to nest along the coast, were the Polar Eskimos' secret to survival in the face of all their losses. From rock blinds and using long-handled nets, thousands of these little birds are easily gathered and cached. Several hundred, for instance, packed inside a seal skin with the fat left on and stored under the rocks for several months, produces the fermented local delicacy called *kiviaq* — kind of a combination of vinegar and blue cheese.

As we reached the ice cap the winds began to rise, and soon we were proceeding into a driving ground blizzard. Using the sun as our navigational aid we attempted to advance. It began to snow and soon even the sun was blocked out. The conditions deteriorated to total white-out. Mike Beedell, Angu, and I became separated from the others. We wandered around aimlessly. Without the sun we lost our sense of direction and as the whiteness fell we lost all sense of spatial perception. It was like life in a cup of milk — white everywhere. Ground became indiscernible from sky, and the only way to tell if we were going uphill or downhill was by the speed of the *komatiq*. Even trying to walk proved difficult as the eyes and inner ear sent conflicting messages to the brain. We soon concluded that continuing was futile. We didn't relish the thought of wandering into a crevasse field. We had no choice but to make camp and wait.

The next day conditions improved and we moved on. After going in circles and after getting glimpses of the sun now and again, Angu suddenly realized our location. We began the long downhill journey to the sea, finally exiting at Neqe where a small squalid house provided us with a place to rest until the others caught up the next day. They had come down to the sea on another route to Pitorarvik, where many people had gathered to hunt walrus.

From Neqe it was only a few hours to Siroapaluk. A dozen colourful houses, none with electricity, sheltered the seventy inhabitants. A small store provides basic goods but most are subsistence hunters who still live close to the land. The Polar Eskimos are proud of their culture. Dogs and kayaks are an everyday part of life. Even though restictive legislation and high gasoline prices make snowmobiles impractical, it is doubtful that if they could they would switch now. A Polar Eskimo, once asked for a definition of happiness, replied, "Being out bear hunting, spotting a bear, and being the team out front." Unlike the Canadian Inuit, which have for a number of reasons become highly dependent on modern technology, the Polar Eskimos are content with the old ways. When I asked, for instance, why no one carried radios similar to the one we carried for emergencies and which allowed us to alert Qaanaaq about Qaordluktoq's plight, I was told that they did not want them. Not only were they expensive and an additional weight, but they were unnecessary. They realized the risk inherent in their lives on the ice and did not expect anyone to come and get them should disaster strike. Qaordluktoq was a hunter of the ice. I'm sure it's where he would have wanted to die.

After a brief stay in Siroapaluk, we set out for Qaanaaq (pop. 400), the regional capital. Notified of our imminent arrival by Siroapaluk's only phone — located in the store — a convoy of about twenty dog teams set out from Qaanaaq to greet us. We met about midpoint and a giant tea party ensued. After tea, as the convoy approached Qaanaaq, I felt sad. My dream would soon be realized. It was now a time for new dreams and new phases in my life.

We stayed in the area for two weeks, going on endless rounds of visiting and tea drinking in Qaanaaq, hunting seals and walrus north of Neqe, and netting dovekies at Siroapaluk. Wherever we went we felt welcome. The Qitdlarssuaq story is well known here and many people bear names passed down from the original migrants. As we prepared for the final 120-kilometre leg to the Thule air base, where we would catch our Canadian Armed Forces airlift home, I compared the two expeditions. I thought of Qitdlak. I thought of myself. Why did he come? Why did I? We were from different times and different cultures. We appeared to have little in common. But then I remembered a quotation attributed to him and I found the link: "Do you know the desire to see new lands? Do you know the desire to see new people?"

"Is the ice safe to land on?"

The apprehension showed clearly on the face of my twelve-year-old son Jason. I looked at him and smiled in an attempt to ease the tension — my own as much as his. Below us and spreading from horizon to horizon was the tangled ice mass of the Arctic Ocean. We were more than 700 kilometres from the nearest land. Everywhere were high pressure ridges, while here and there dark patches, indicating leads of open water, loomed ominously. It did not look like a very inviting place. What madness had brought me here to this indistinguishable spot in the middle of nowhere?

Our chartered Twin Otter aircraft continued to circle the spot on the ice we had been seeking. The plane's satellite navigation system attested to our success; as we circled, the latitudinal reading on the panel changed only slightly while the longitudinal readings were a blur of changing numbers. Canada, Denmark, Norway, Russia, the United States — each few minutes we were flying around the world. Below us lay that elusive goal of so many polar explorers, the goal for which hundreds of years of effort and numerous lives have been spent — the Geographic North Pole.

After what seemed an eternity of circling the world, the pilots made one final low pass over a likely stretch of ice. It looked good — flat and solid. A few minutes later the skis touched down and the plane's engines roared as the pilots reversed the pitch on the props and brought the aircraft to a halt. We were jubilant and a round of applause erupted in the crammed cabin, which my tour group shared with extra drums of fuel and a mound of sleeping bags and other survival equipment. We had arrived!

I was first out. Jason followed, and as he stuck his head out the door his eyes quickly surveyed the surrounding ice as if expecting to see something magical and unusual. He was followed by the rest of my international crew, with representatives from Germany, Venezuela, Japan, the United States, and Canada. The pilots left one engine running. We would only be allowed an hour on the ice before we would have to begin the arduous journey home.

First on the agenda were rounds of handshakes and congratulations. Then out came the flags and the champagne. Cameras clicked endlessly as each tried to make the most of his brief time at the pole. And then, as if on cue, everyone dispersed to find a spot to be alone with his thoughts at the pole.

Jason and I wandered off to the nearest pressure ridge to take a series of sun shots with a sextant. As we shot the sun, I reflected on my time in the North. It was just little more than ten years ago that I arrived in Iqaluit, slightly fearful of an unknown land. Now it was my home and I felt comfortable here. My search for "Ultima Thule," both symbolically and literally, had taken me on many adventures: the Qitdlarssuaq Expedition; a trek across the ice of Eureka Sound to Axel Heiberg Island in the High Arctic; now the Geographic North Pole. These had been just a few — there had also been cross-country ski adventures; first descents of wild, whitewater rivers such as the McKeand on Baffin Island; other hiking trips to the Auyuittuq and Ellesmere Island National Park reserves. Even now as I stood at the summit of the world, the ultimate "Ultima Thule," I knew it was not the end. As I stood at the pole with all directions being south, I knew that "Ultima Thule" was south of me now.

High Arctic

Alluvial lands of the Very River at the western end of Lake Hazen, the most northerly thermal oasis, with the protective Garfield Range to the northwest. Lake Hazen is part of the large Ellesmere Island National Park Reserve, the most northerly point of which, Cape Columbia, is less than 800 kilometres from the North Pole. *Wolfgang Weber*

A supply plane fuels up at a depot alongside Tanquary Fiord on northern Ellesmere Island. In the background are the steep ridges of the Osborn Range in the southwestern corner of the new national park reserve.
Wolfgang Weber

Bush pilots are the taxidrivers of the North. They fly to any desired place at any time. Chuck Montgomery, however, has recently changed to flying 727s for First Air.
Wolfgang Weber

Miners board Twin Otter at Resolute for ferry flight to Little Cornwallis Island's Polaris mine, 110 kilometres to the northwest. For northern mines such as this operation, the nine to ten months of harsh climate is a cost factor but not a physical barrier. *Erik Watt*

Polaris is the world's most northerly metallic mine, producing zinc and lead. Ore concentrates are stored in the huge warehouse during the long winters and can only be shipped out in deep-sea bulk freighters during the few weeks of the summer navigation season.
Wolfgang Weber

The yearly supply ship has docked at the pier of Resolute Bay.
Wolfgang Weber

Bezal and Terry Jesudason's
"International Explorers
Home" in Resolute: the start
of a snowmobile-driven
expedition to Grise Fiord;
one week on the ice requires
sufficient equipment and
supplies. *Wolfgang Weber*

Scientific summer camp on
Bathurst Island.
Catherine Young

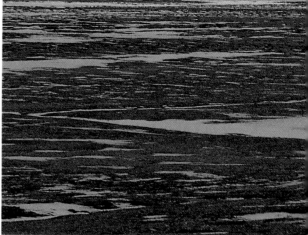

Resolute Bay on the southern coast of Cornwallis Island is an important staging point for other islands of the High Arctic, for the North Magnetic Pole, as well as for the geographical North Pole. For many years it has been the High Arctic headquarters of the huge scientific Polar Shelf operation of Canada. The village was named after HMS *Resolute*, one of the many nineteenth-century ships that searched for Sir John Franklin's expedition. *Elke Emshoff*

Ice crystals in the atmosphere are responsible for the appearance of halos around the sun and moon and for "sun dogs," or parhelia, as seen here over smooth sea ice on an Arctic expedition. As many as eight bright spots of light may appear to radiate from the sun. *Wolfgang Weber*

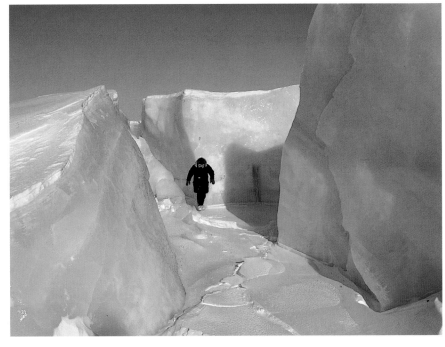

Tokilkee Kiguktak is building a snowhouse on Cornwallis Island. Around some communities of the North, igloo-building contests are held every year. The record for speed is twenty-nine minutes.
Wolfgang Weber

Movement of Arctic currents creates pressure ridges of ice, seen here north of Devon Island, that can reach up to thirty metres.
Wolfgang Weber

Weldon W. Phipps — "Whiskey, Whiskey, Papa" to most aviators in the Arctic — is surveying north of latidude 80° N on Axel Heiberg Island in 1959. His Piper Supercub wears oversized, underinflated, and self-adapted DC-3 tires suitable to land on snow, rocky beaches, and muskeg, prototype of the so-called tundra-tire used around the world today in areas without airstrips. *Weldon Phipps*

Wolfgang Weber stands on the spot to which all magnetic compasses of the world point. The location of the North Magnetic Pole shifts continuously. *Wolfgang Weber*

In earlier times, such as in 1961 when this picture was taken at −45°C, mechanics threw a tarp (nose tent) over the engine to shelter themselves during their maintenance and repair work. These Sikorsky S-55 helicopters worked out of Isachsen on Ellef Ringnes Island for exploration crews. Even in summer, Isachsen is usually unreachable by ships because of ice. *Erik Watt*

The morning sun of late summer illuminates steep rock walls and inlets that mark large parts of the southern coastline (along the Northwest Passage) of huge but unpopulated Devon Island. *Mike Beedell*

Expedition camp on the sea ice of Wellington Channel between Cornwallis and Devon islands. *Wolfgang Weber*

Beechey Island just off Cape Riley on the southwest corner of Devon. Graves mark the location of the last

known winter camp of the lost Franklin expedition in search of the Northwest Passage. *Wolfgang Weber*

Abraham Pijamini from Grise Fiord hunting at South Cape. *Wolfgang Weber*

A dogteam is pulling the *komatiq* (Inuit sled), or *qamutik* in some dialects, in the traditional eastern and High Arctic fan-hitched harness. In the western Arctic, where there are trees and more vegetation, dogs are harnessed and run in a row. *Wolfgang Weber*

Nanook, the polar bear, is the uncontested ruler in the ice of the Arctic.
Wolfgang Weber

"Glacier parade" at Glacier Fiord, being nourished by the Steacie Ice Cap on southern Axel Heiberg Island. In the northeast of this huge island, James Basinger of the University of Saskatchewan and Jane Francis of the University of Adelaide in 1986 discovered petrified trunks and stumps of a prehistoric redwood forest, aged at 45 million years. *Wolfgang Weber*

Looti Pijamini of Grise
Fiord and his family on a
picnic on Ellesmere Island.
Looti Pijamini

Polar bear furs,
frame-stretched for drying
and tanning, can be found in
all settlements of the High
Arctic during spring.
Wolfgang Weber

Late winter in Grise Fiord on the shores of Jones Sound, on which pressure ridges of ice abound. This small Inuit community with little over 100 inhabitants, most of whom still subsist on abundant wildlife, is the site of ancient tent rings, stone houses, and fish weirs of bygone cultures.
Wolfgang Weber

Grise Fiord's co-op store is
supermarket, post office,
and news centre all in one.
Wolfgang Weber

Mike Floyd of the RCMP
represents the law at the
Canadian end of the world,
as well as standing for
Canadian sovereignty in the
High Arctic region.
Wolfgang Weber

Summertime in Grise Fiord
on southern Ellesmere
Island. The most northerly
community in North
America, it lies 1,500
kilometres south of the
North Pole. *Wolfgang Weber*

Arctic hares under the midnight sun on a tundra slope of Ellesmere Island. They experience population cycles, the high point of which is extremely obvious, as the hares herd together in groups of 100 or more. *Jim Brandenburg*

Lemming — watch out for birds of prey and foxes! *Richard Popko*

Rock ptarmigan are one of the few overwintering land birds in the Arctic. *Richard Popko*

(Upper):
Arctic fox on Ellesmere, searching for food under the snow and ice cover. Lemmings are their main diet. *Jim Brandenburg*

The Arctic wolf is a large,
white, uniquely Canadian
sub-species and inhabits the
High Arctic islands.
Jim Brandenburg

An Arctic wolf at its den,
Ellesmere Island.
Jim Brandenburg

Arctic wolves target the three muskoxen calves guarded by eleven adults, whose hooves could crack a wolf's skull.
Jim Brandenburg

Ann Meekitjuk Hanson
The Art of Storytelling

Storytelling was done when people were laying down trying to sleep. The stories were mostly told to children and young people.

I did not hear any stories from my parents or grandparents because by the time I was born (1946) storytelling or singing old songs was discouraged by Christian ministers. Some ministers thought telling old legends and singing songs was practising shamanism or promoting it. So my people in southern Baffin stopped telling legends. They just kept the legends and old songs inside their minds.

When I was going to school in Toronto in the early 1960s, I learned to read and write English. I read some books about my people. I was perfectly literate in my language — reading and writing syllabics. I just did not know any legends or songs. I was fascinated by the legends. I tried very hard to remember if one was ever told to me. None came.

When I got older, in my early twenties, it bothered me not to know part of my culture. I was missing the original art side of my own culture. It was all very secretive and mysterious. I knew my people had original songs and that storytelling was once very special.

The Canadian Broadcasting Corporation (CBC) is an institution promoting Canadian culture. I had worked for CBC on and off between having babies for many years. In 1965 I was hired by CBC as a secretary, then became a broadcaster. My cousin Jonah Kelly was there also. Together we started to record and air our elders' stories. At first it took much encouragement on our part because people were almost superstitious, and they were sceptical that it was okay. We assured them it was very much okay. Jonah and I told each person, "If we don't record and tell our legends or sing our old songs, we will lose part of our culture, part of our language, part of our art." People were very receptive and helpful after learning of all the possible consequences. Now, CBC here in Iqaluit has a huge collection of tapes containing every aspect of Inuit life.

The story I am going to tell is popular all over the eastern Arctic. The story has different versions, region to region. This particular version is from southern Baffin. It was told by one of our great leaders, Arnitook Ipeelie, and is taken from CBC Iqaluit's collection with permission of Production Manager Simon Awa. I translated the story and the songs.

The story is about the magical adventures of Kiviuq. Kiviuq went all over the world by kayak. Along the way he meets different monsters and animals possessing, as he did, shamanistic powers. Events and characters are made to appear incredible to expand the imagination, to stir wonder and awe, therefore, differentiating reality and the art of creating a story.

Adventures of Kiviuq
(a song)

> It is known,
> This Kiviuq,
> He is capable of coming back,
> He is capable of sitting,
> He is capable of feeding,
> Take a piece of flat rock,
> put it on your upper abdomen,
> Then try to sleep,
> Ai ja ja . . .

A long long time ago a grandmother and her granddaughter were living by the shore in a snow house. It was almost spring when snow houses were in their last usefulness.

There were many other people living in this camp. It was a beautiful calm day. The waters near the floe edge were shining like that of oil. On the land, the people were playing ball. They were having a good time.

A little girl went down to the people playing ball to watch. One of the ball players came, grabbed her by the hood, and then cut off the tip of her hood. The little girl got frightened and ran to her grandmother holding her severed hood. The grandmother sewed the tip back to her hood. The little girl went back to the ball game. Again, the tip of her hood was cut off. She went back to her grandmother. The grandmother sewed it back. She returned to the ball players. Sure enough, the tip of her hood was cut off. Back she went to her grandmother.

This time the grandmother got annoyed. She told the girl, "Go to our waste (dump). Look for a skeleton of a young seal's head. Bring it to me." The girl obeyed her grandmother without thinking why she had to bring a skeleton of a young seal's head.

The little girl handed the head of a young seal to her grandmother. The grandmother said, "I am going to change your head into the head of a young seal. Once this is done, you will become a young seal. You will surface near the people who are playing ball as a lovely young seal." The girl nodded obediently.

Near the snow house there was a hole in the snow where urine waste had been dumped over and over. The urine waste had made deep holes. The grandmother sank the girl into the hole after she had turned her into a young seal. The girl disappeared.

After a while the girl reappeared as a seal near the people playing ball!

One of the ball players sighted the seal and shouted excitedly, "Seal!" The ball players stopped their game and scattered in every direction in pursuit of their kayaks.

There were many kayaks chasing this seal. The seal was heading toward the deep waters where there is no land. The ball players followed in their kayaks.

When they were far away from the land out at sea, the seal sat up on the water and said, "Where is my sky? Where is my sky?"

Soon, the seas turned into torrential terror! The many kayaks were overturned and were lost! Only one survived. Kiviuq.

When Kiviuq was a boy, he had followed and obeyed the traditional laws of his people. The boys were always told by their fathers: "When you get your first kayak, you must put a skin of a bird, a tern, on your kayak. This will protect your kayak from sinking in the seas."

Kiviuq was the only survivor because he had applied a piece of a bird onto his first kayak.

This was the beginning of Kiviuq's adventures.

Kiviuq paddled his kayak without seeing any land for many days. When he would get on top of yet another huge swell he exclaimed, "What looked like a land, it disappears again!"

At last Kiviuq saw land for real. At this time he was very sleepy. He paddled with renewed energy. He landed his kayak and got off.

He walked the land and saw the land had been occupied by humans. There were bones on the land. The grass had grown over the bones in some areas.

Kiviuq was walking around and looking over the land. Suddenly a voice in a song talked to him:

> It is known,
> This Kiviuq,
> He is capable of coming back,
> He is capable of sitting,
> He is capable of feeding,
> Take a piece of flat rock,
> Put it on your upper abdomen,
> Then try to sleep,
> Aii ja ja ja . . .

As instructed in this song, he found a piece of flat rock, put it on his upper abdomen, laid down, and tried to sleep.

Kiviuq tried to sleep but could not. Beside him, he saw a woman sharpening the end of her tail. She was a monster. Kiviuq pretended to sleep. After the woman had sharpened her tail, she mightily pierced her tail into Kiviuq's upper abdomen. But there was only a sound of a loud snap! The tail broke when the woman hit the flat rock. The woman wailed, "Oh, my poor tail, unna, unna, unna. Oh my poor tail, unna, unna, unna . . ."

Then, without movement, Kiviuq was inside of a house.

The house belonged to the woman with a tail.

When Kiviuq looked around, his boots, socks, and slippers were already on drying racks. Kiviuq was sitting on a bed platform. On the bed, sharp knives were appearing and disappearing in and out. Kiviuq saw that they were very sharp. Kiviuq told the tailed woman, "These knives are appearing and disappearing in and out on the bed. Give me my boots!" The woman only replied: "I put them on the rack to dry. You get them yourself!" When Kiviuq tried to reach his boots, the drying racks moved upward each time on their own. Once again, Kiviuq told the woman, "Look. Each time I reach for the drying rack, it moves upward!"

Kiviuq, not having any success in retrieving his belongings humanly, resorted to his shamanistic powers and shouted in a song:

> "My bear, my bear,
> Come, Come,
> Come, maul and eat this woman . . ."

In no time, the movements of a bear outside the house were heard. The woman was so afraid of the bear. She rushed to retrieve the boots, socks, and slippers off the drying rack saying:

> "Here are your boots, nana, nana, nana,
> Here are your socks, nana, nana, nana,
> Here are your slippers, nana, nana, nana."

The woman was in such a rush that she was fumbling and falling.

Kiviuq hurriedly put on his boots, socks, and slippers so he can get out of the woman's house. When he tried to get through the door, the door shrank to a small size. He could not get out. This happened many times. Kiviuq tricked the shrinking door by entering into it before it had a chance to shrink. He was out! He ran to his kayak. The woman followed.

Kiviuq got into his kayak. Kiviuq started to paddle away. The woman went for the point of the kayak to grab. She touched the tip but could not get the proper grip. Kiviuq got away from the shore and paddled hurriedly.

Once Kiviuq was safely away from the woman, paddling his kayak, he started to sing:

> Woman,
> You are beaten,
> I am thankful,
> You grabbed the tip of my kayak,
> When I tried to harpoon you,
> you rang like a piece of ice.
> Oh. It was piece of ice.
> Oh, it was piece of ice.

The woman's *ulu* (knife) had become a piece of ice.

Kiviuq paddled for many more days. He did not know where he was heading to.

Kiviuq finally met with two people. They were both women. They were mother and daughter. They were all alone. The daughter was a beautiful girl. The mother was married to a dead tree. The stumps of the tree were full of caribou hair!

The mother would send the tree with a rope tied to it out to the sea. The tree always came back with seals.

Kiviuq lived with these women and married the young girl. Kiviuq hunted for seals. When he would return, his wife waited for him on the shore. She would grab the seals by the flippers, swing them onto her shoulders, and carry them that way. She was very strong.

Kiviuq's wife made him beautiful clothing. She made beautiful boots, mittens, and slippers. Each time she made clothing, Kiviuq told her to make some more because he kept losing them. What really happened was, Kiviuq was hoarding the clothing in a hiding place because Kiviuq knew he would be leaving the women to look for his real home.

One day when Kiviuq was out hunting as usual, the mother told her daughter, "Daughter, come. I will pick out your lice out of your hair." The daughter obeyed. When the daughter laid her head on her mother's lap, the mother took a *taaqut* (a piece of wood used to flick and even out the flames of a seal oil lamp) and pierced it into her daughter's ear. She killed her. The mother did this so she could marry Kiviuq, a human being.

The mother exchanged her head for her daughter's head. She had become her daughter.

The daughter always met Kiviuq at the shore to help when he returned from a hunt. The mother did the same. She knew she looked exactly like her daughter.

Before Kiviuq had a chance to unload his seals, the woman said, "My mother died today."

As Kiviuq had done many times before, he tossed the seals to his wife so she could flip them onto her back. But she could not even lift the seals!

Kiviuq knew right away this woman was not his wife! He paddled away out to sea.

Kiviuq travelled many more days keeping close to the land. He heard a voice coming from the land: "I cannot climb up. Come. Come help me to climb up."

Kiviuq landed his kayak and started to look around. He did not see anyone. All he saw was a small lemming stranded on a rock surrounded by water. He lifted the lemming and put it on the mainland. Kiviuq continued his journey.

Once again, Kiviuq heard a voice coming from the land: "Come. Come. I have something in my eye. Come and remove the dirt from my eye." Kiviuq landed his kayak and walked around. He could not see anyone. He was getting into his kayak when he saw an old seal hip bone. There was

dirt in the bone so he removed it.

Kiviuq travelled looking for his homeland. At last he recognized his home. He had been travelling for so long that no one knew how to measure the length of his absence.

Kiviuq had a special song he sang when he was arriving from a hunt before his adventures. When he recognized his home he started to sing: "Assigii, Assigii, Assigii . . ."

But before he could finish his song, his wife heard his familiar song. She responded by singing:

> "Only my husband,
> Only Kiviuq sings Assigii
> As he arrives.
> Assigii, sigii sigii
> Assigii, sigii sigii . . ."

The wife ran to her husband's kayak and jumped to get on. She missed. Kiviuq had finally come home but his wife died when she missed the kayak.

That is the end of the story.

Jonquil Graves / Anne Gunn

Fauna of the North

The Arctic region of Canada is a forbidding place in winter. At the highest latitudes, the sun disappears in November and is not seen again until it returns for a few minutes in the eastern sky in mid-February. The land is shrouded in darkness and seems devoid of all life; the temperature hovers at −40° Celsius; the only sound is the wind.

But suddenly there is movement, and there are shapes — dark, prehistoric shapes materializing out of the gloom. A herd of muskoxen is grazing along a slope. Pawing at the wind-hardened snow to reach the willows and sedges, the shaggy beasts move slowly across the horizon. Muskoxen are superbly adapted for cold weather with a long coarse outer coat covering a warm underlayer of soft fine wool, as well as habitually energy-conserving behaviour. Their sense of smell directs them to food in the winter darkness while their excellent hearing and eyesight keep them alert for potential enemies. During the winter muskoxen herd together in groups of sixty or more animals, perhaps to protect themselves from wolves. They are active at all times throughout the year, but in blizzards they may lie down for hours and allow the snow to cover them.

In the nineteenth century severe weather and unregulated commercial harvesting combined to decimate the muskox populations. By the 1900s so few animals remained that in 1917 the Canadian government banned muskox hunting. Hunting was prohibited until the late 1960s, when biological surveys documented the recovery of the herds. Today there are about 80,000−90,000 muskox in Canada, ranging from the Arctic islands south to the Thelon Game Sanctuary and the coast of Hudson Bay. Muskox hunting is now restricted by a quota system that allows Inuit communities a limited muskox hunt every year.

Spring in the Northwest Territories and Yukon arrives around the beginning of March. Although temperatures may still lurk at −40° and −50° Celsius, northerners call it spring because the sun feels warm and the hours of daylight are rapidly overtaking the hours of darkness.

The animals of the North are quick to respond to the changing daylight hours. Along the Arctic coast, female polar bears lead cubs from their dens at the end of March or early April. Born between late November and January, the helpless cubs, which at birth weighed about 0.7 kilogram, are now active and white-coated, weighing about ten-fifteen kilograms. They are still wobbly on their feet but after a few days of sliding down snowbanks and playing under their mother's solicitous care, they are ready to begin their journey to the sea ice. Inuit call the baby bears "ah tik tok," which means "he who goes to the sea."

The sea ice may be only a few hundred metres away, or in the Hudson Bay area it may be 100 kilometres or more distant. Whatever the distance, the female bear, who has not eaten for five months, must lead her cubs there to feed on seals. Five species of seal are found in Arctic waters but the most common is the ringed seal, the mainstay of a polar bear's diet. The seal pups are born in snow dens on the land-fast ice between mid-March and mid-April. Bears hunt the defenceless pups by scooping them out of their snow dens. In some years unusual ice conditions cause failure of seal pupping and the bears and their attendant scavengers suffer food shortages.

After finishing their meal the mother and cubs move on to the next seal den or "aglu." But the remains of the seal carcass do not go to waste. An Arctic fox has been following the bears and quickly cleans up whatever carrion is left behind. Arctic foxes are active year-round, tirelessly loping across land and ice in a never-ending search for food. Arctic foxes that follow polar bears are easily recognizable by the yellowish staining on their white winter fur caused by eating seal blubber. Inland foxes, which depend on lemmings, remain white until summer, when they shed the white coat for a brown summer coat.

On the mainland, Arctic foxes range throughout the barren-lands and when populations are high the foxes travel south of the treeline. Arctic foxes are prodigiously productive, raising up to twenty pups in a single litter, but the populations sharply decline a year after the disappearance of lemmings, the mainstay of the fox's diet.

Brown lemmings and collared lemmings are mice-sized rodents found throughout the Arctic tundra and most of the Arctic islands. They are active year-round but because their small size does not allow them to generate enough heat, they spend the winter tunnelling about under the snow. Lemming populations dramatically peak every three or four years with numbers of lemmings reaching up to 50−100 per hectare of tundra. Foxes, ermine, wolves, wolverines, owls, hawks, falcons, gulls, and jaegers all prosper when lemming numbers are high. But in other years, when the populations crash and lemmings almost disappear, the animals that depend on them either change their diet, face starvation, or move elsewhere. Foxes, for example, may briefly turn to goose eggs, and biologists are beginning to find a correlation between lemming and goose populations with the Arctic fox as intermediary.

As spring advances in the North many species begin migrating north to take advantage of the long daylight hours and the accompanying productivity of food sources. Several species of whales migrate from southern waters to the Arctic Ocean in summer, and the three species that remain year-round in Arctic waters move further north from their ice-free wintering areas.

The beluga or white whale is the most common year-round resident. Belugas occur in both eastern and western Canadian Arctic waters. In winter the eastern populations migrate to the west coast of Greenland and Hudson Strait, while western belugas winter off the coast of Russia in the Bering Sea. Belugas are usually found in small groups of about twelve animals except during migration, when herds of several hundred travel to shallow coastal waters in summer and return to deep open water when the bays freeze over in September. Narwhal are unusual in that the males have a long, spiral tusk, a front tooth projecting through the upper lip. In the female, the tooth usually remains embedded in the gum but occasionally a short tusk may form. The reason for the tooth is a mystery although it is generally believed that the males with the largest tusks are the dominant animals. Like belugas, narwhal are migratory. During the summer they are found throughout the eastern Arctic but in winter they leave the areas of fast ice for the pack ice of Baffin Bay and northern Davis Strait. Narwhal have always been highly valued by the Inuit, who used narwhal oil in lamps and made the hides into coverings for whale boats and boot soles. Today narwhal are hunted primarily for their tusks, which are sold to tourists, and for *muktuk*, the outer skin with a layer of blubber that is eaten raw, boiled, smoked, or dried. Only Inuit may hunt narwhal and only a certain number are permitted annually.

The bowhead whale is also known as the Greenland right whale. It is by far the largest Arctic whale, reaching twenty metres in length and up to 50,000 kilograms in weight. Its immense head contains 600–700 baleen plates, some up to four-and-a-half metres long. The early whalers considered bowheads the *right* whales to hunt because they were slow swimmers, they floated when killed, and their enormous size provided large amounts of oil and whalebone. This, unfortunately, contributed to their near demise. Before the arrival of the whalers, bowheads existed in vast numbers, but in less than 100 years they were reduced from tens of thousands to fewer than 3,000 in the entire Arctic. Today bowheads are listed as an endangered species.

As the whales are moving north in the oceans another spectacular migration is taking place in the forests and tundra. The barren-ground caribou are beginning to travel northward from their wintering grounds.

There are four sub-species of caribou in northern Canada. Woodland caribou, which are the largest, inhabit the boreal forests of the Yukon and western Northwest Territories. Grant's caribou is found mainly in Alaska. One herd of Grant's caribou, the Porcupine herd, winters in Yukon and sometimes crosses into the Northwest Territories. Peary caribou, which are the smallest, are a uniquely Canadian sub-species found only on the Arctic islands. The fourth sub-species, the barren-ground caribou, is the most abundant and most important culturally and economically. Barren-ground caribou range over the tundra from Hudson Bay to the east end of Great Slave Lake and north from Great Bear Lake to the Arctic coast. There are over one-and-a-half million caribou spread among four large herds and several smaller ones. The herds are named according to the areas where they calve every year.

Most barren-ground caribou spend the winter in the forested areas of the Northwest Territories and Yukon. But every spring they are drawn northward to the barrenlands. Led by cows and their last year's calves, the caribou make their way in long files over the still-frozen lakes and rivers until they reach their calving grounds, sometimes as far as 700 kilometres away, where they themselves were born and to which they return every year. Almost all the calves in a herd are born within a few days of each other. This is a defence against predators, for such a glut of potential prey appearing all at one time seems to overwhelm the attendant wolves and marauding grizzly bears and prevent them from taking too many calves.

Caribou are one of the most important animals to the people of the North. Traditionally both Inuit and Dene as well as Yukon Indians relied on caribou for the necessities of life: they used the meat for themselves and their dogs; hides became clothing, sleeping robes, dog harnesses, and tents; bones became needles and utensils; antlers were fashioned into tools. When the caribou were plentiful the people prospered. But when the caribou changed their migration routes or declined in numbers, the people starved. Today the caribou are no less important. Most northern people still prefer caribou to any other meat and they still make clothing from the hides. Although snow machines instead of dogs now pull their toboggans, caribou skins serve as warm blankets in the toboggans and line the floors of their winter tents.

In the past, caribou populations have fluctuated. Only ten years ago the herds had declined so severely that it looked as though they would never again approach the early explorers' descriptions of them as "endless flowing rivers of animals." Today, however, the herds have recovered and have increased in size.

As the caribou migrate north in the spring and return to their forest wintering grounds in the fall, they are accompanied by wolves. Those wolves, which remain with the caribou all year, are called *tundra* wolves. *Timber* wolves live south of the treeline and *Arctic* wolves, a large, white, uniquely Canadian sub-species, inhabit the High Arctic islands. Tundra wolves feed mainly on caribou, but lemmings, birds' eggs, and even berries are not scorned. South of the treeline, the timber wolves, which are more territorial and form traditional wolf packs, hunt bison and moose. Beaver, geese, and mice are also acceptable fare. In the mountainous areas in Yukon and the western Northwest Territories wolves prey on mountain goats and Dall's sheep. In the High Arctic, muskoxen and Arctic hares are alternate prey for wolves when caribou are not available.

Man has long had an ambiguous relationship with wolves, torn between respect for this social hunter and fear of its competitive ways. In most parts of the world wolves have long since disappeared as humans encroached on their habitat. But in northern Canada, where most of the land remains undeveloped, wolves still range throughout both territories, their numbers flowing and ebbing with the numbers of their prey. In the past localized wolf control programs were instigated to help stop declining caribou, bison, and moose populations. Today deliberate wolf control programs are no longer carried out, but wolves are actively hunted and trapped for their luxuriant fur.

One of the prey species of wolves is bison. Wolves can seriously affect calf numbers and overall population of bison herds, but if no other conditions such as hunting or poor weather occur a balance between prey and predator is usually maintained. When wolf control programs were introduced on the bison range of the Northwest Territories, bison populations were already in serious trouble.

The great herds of plains bison that ranged from Mexico to northern Alberta had, by the end of the nineteenth century, been reduced by hunting to a few scattered herds. Wood bison, a slightly larger sub-species that inhabited the forested areas of northern Saskatchewan and Alberta and the southwestern Northwest Territories, were less accessible to hunters. However, by 1840 they, too, began to decline and in 1897 a federal law was passed to protect them from hunting.

In 1906 the Canadian government, in an effort to save the plains bison, shipped a small herd north from the United States and later moved them to the newly created Wood Buffalo National Park on the Alberta/NWT border. The herd grew and interbred with wood bison. By the mid-1930s there were about 12.000 animals from the original herd but they were all hybrid bison and it was thought that wood bison were extinct. It was not until 1957 that a herd of 200 pure wood bison was found in an isolated area of the park. To protect those animals from hybridization and also from disease, which had been inadvertently introduced into the park, a number of animals were moved to a new area, the Mackenzie Bison Sanctuary, on the northwest side of Great Slave Lake. That herd, which has grown to more than 2,000 animals, is the largest population of free-roaming wood bison in the world.

The wood bison herd is free of disease, but about half of the hybrid herd in Wood Buffalo Park, which is now reduced to about 3,000 animals, is infected with brucellosis or bovine tuberculosis. Fearing that cattle in the area would be infected, ranchers, supported by health and agriculture officials, recommended that the infected bison herd be slaughtered and the park restocked with disease-free wood bison. Native people from communities in northern Alberta and southern NWT, however, rejected the proposal for a wholesale slaughter and a new plan has been introduced.

The Native people wish to salvage healthy animals from the herd, and they are now being supported by the Canadian government and the governments of the NWT and Alberta. A steering committee of government representatives and two Native representatives has been formed to develop terms of reference for a Buffalo Herd Management Group. This group will work to develop a management plan for creating a healthy bison herd. Although it is generally agreed that a test and slaughter program will be very difficult to carry out, this is what the Buffalo Herd Management Group will now try to evaluate.

Toward the end of April when the days are long and sunny, northerners begin to listen for the excited calls of skeins of geese, swans, and cranes winging their way overhead to their nesting grounds. Just as the flowing lines of caribou are a characteristic of the northern tundra in spring, so are the myriad waterfowl that annually return to nest and rear their broods. Tens of thousands of lakes and ponds dot the tundra and the abrupt return of warm temperatures and twenty-four-hour daylight trigger a burst of productivity of detritus-feeding insects and plant growth. Hundreds of thousands of geese graze the grasses and sedges in the wetlands while the ducks and loons surfeit themselves on the countless insects or on the fish that reap the benefit of the insects. The clouds of mosquitoes and blackflies that drive the human inhabitants and wildlife to distraction are the same insects that make the tundra rivers and lakes a fisherman's and birder's paradise.

About thirty species of ducks, geese, loons, and swans nest in the Canadian North. These include the common tundra swan and the rare trumpeter swan now making a comeback in the western part of the Northwest Territories as well as in the Yukon. The abundant and well-known Canada goose, the snow goose, and the smallest and rarest North American goose, the Ross's goose, all nest in noisy, garrulous colonies, while the shy white-fronted goose and the Brant goose are more solitary. Seven dabbling ducks, five diving ducks, and ten sea ducks also nest in the Arctic.

Most aquatic Arctic birds are primarily white, or black and white. In startling contrast are the male harlequin duck with its bright chestnut-coloured sides and the king eider drake with a red-orange bill and an orange knob on its forehead. The oldsquaw duck is one of the most common and noisy ducks of the North. Its distinct yodel-like whistle is a familiar sound in the summer on tundra lakes. The king eider and oldsquaw ducks are the most northerly summer ducks, travelling as far as northern Ellesmere Island to breed.

The steep cliffs of Arctic islands provide sites for some of the largest nesting colonies of sea birds in the world. Nesting colonies of northern fulmars on the eastern Arctic islands have as many as 100,000 pairs. The thick-billed murre is one of the most numerous seabirds in the northern hemisphere — some 1.5 million of these nest on the sea cliffs of northeastern Baffin Island, of Bylot Island, and of the smaller islands in Baffin Bay and Davis Strait.

With twenty-four-hour days and dramatic rises in temperature, spring can occur almost "overnight" in the Arctic. Ravens and gyrfalcons anticipate the arrival of spring and competitively joust for cliffside nest sites almost a month before the arrival of other birds. When the migratory birds arrive, in large, noisy flocks, they, too, begin immediately to claim territories and start nesting activities. Geese and ducks, notably, of course, the eider ducks, build warm nests insulated with down from their own bodies. The nests of many sea birds and waders, however, are simply depressions in the ground, lined with moss or leaves. Some cliff and rock dwellers dispense with all nesting frills and just lay their eggs, or egg, on the bare ground.

Spring temperatures are still low, and the birds begin incubation of their eggs as soon as the first one is laid. If the eggs are laid at intervals, the families have young at various stages of development. This strategy, which is practised by birds of prey, is an adaptation for an environment with a variable food supply. In years when food is in short supply, the firstborn and therefore largest chick can successfully monopolize the parents' meagre pickings.

Most small Arctic birds, such as the Lapland longspur, redpoll, snow bunting, northern wheatear, and horned lark, have brief incubation periods, from ten to fourteen days, and the young hatch at a time when seeds and insects are most abundant. Incubation for larger species may be slightly longer, but all birds in the Arctic are hatched and many are fledged by the end of July.

Breeding success depends on complex interactions between weather and the food supply. In a good year small birds may raise six or seven chicks. However, a late or cold and wet spring may destroy the eggs or fledglings. There is rarely time for a second brood, although some sanderlings raise two broods simultaneously. The female leaves her mate with the first clutch of four eggs while she lays another clutch and raises the second family herself. Swallows, falcons, and some waterfowl may also attempt a second brood if their first clutch is lost.

The northern summer is short, especially in the High Arctic, and to escape the onslaught of freezing, wintery weather, decreasing daylight, and a diminishing food supply, migration begins early. One of the first birds to leave, as well as being the last to arrive in spring, is the phalarope. Two species breed in the Arctic, the northern phalarope, which nests primarily across the low Arctic and subarctic tundra, and the red phalarope, which is found in coastal regions on the mainland Northwest Territories and on most of the High Arctic islands. Phalaropes are unusual in that the female is the more brightly coloured and she initiates courtship. After she lays hers eggs, she flies off southward, leaving the male to incubate the eggs and care for the chicks. Other birds are not quite so carefree and hasty, but many begin to flock and start travelling south almost as soon as fledging and the annual moult of their plumage is complete.

Spectacular migrations between breeding grounds and wintering areas are characteristic of Arctic birds. The red knot, a medium-sized sandpiper, breeds on the High Arctic islands. As soon as the chicks are fledged in early August, the adults leave, followed about two weeks later by the young. The knots from Ellesmere Island fly across Greenland and Iceland and then continue on to Britain and Holland, where they spend the winter. Knots from the lower and western Arctic have a different route, which takes them across Canada and the eastern United States over the ocean to Surinam and across Brazil. They winter along the eastern coast of Argentina as far south as Tierra del Fuego.

Lesser golden plovers also nest on the High Arctic islands and fly non-stop over nearly 8,000 kilometres of open sea to Surinam and on to southern South America. The small northern wheatear migrates from its nesting grounds on southern Ellesmere and Baffin Island to its winter range in central Africa. The long-distance record, however, is the 30,000 kilometres covered by the Arctic tern every year. This graceful black and white sea bird nests near salt or fresh water throughout the Northwest Territories and Yukon. In the fall the terns leave their nesting grounds when the daylight hours decrease in August and fly across the oceans to winter for a short time on the pack ice of the Antarctic. In spring, the terns start their return journey up the Atlantic and Pacific coasts following the sun as it returns north.

It is sometimes difficult to connect the world's tropical forests to the ecological balance of the treeless Arctic barrens, but with the migrations of the birds the fate of the tundra's unique ecology is inextricably bound to man's depredations of the rain forests. Tragically, the vast size of the Arctic means that the loss of wintering habitat in tropical forests and the consequent reduction of the bird populations will be well under way before it is detectable on the breeding grounds.

Not all birds migrate to warmer climates, and a surprising number withstand the harsh winters of the North. Beyond the treeline, the only overwintering land birds are rock and willow ptarmigan, snowy owls, ravens, and gyrfalcons. In fall the ptarmigan moult to winter white plumage and grow a dense mat of feathers on their toes to enable them to walk over the soft snow. In the coldest weather they keep warm by burrowing into the snow. The snowy owl is protected from the cold by facial feathers that nearly cover its beak and thick feathering on its feet and toes. Ravens also have protective feathering around their beaks, but their legs and feet are bare. This is compensated for by the raven's extremely high metabolic rate, which keeps it warm even in the coldest temperatures.

The same upwelling Arctic Ocean waters and currents that concentrated nutrients for the summer breeding of birds also play a critical role in the winter ecology of resident sea birds. The currents keep some water free of ice all year. These patches of open water, called *polynia*, are a magnet to sea life. Dovekies, black guillemots, thick-billed murres, black-legged kittiwakes, and ivory gulls congregate in winter at the edge of *polynia*, where they can obtain food in the open leads. They also feed on polar bear kills, but maintain their spotless plumage by assiduous preening to remove the bloodstains that are the inevitable consequence of scavenging.

Throughout the forested areas of the Northwest Territories and Yukon about forty species of birds are year-round residents. The trapper's confiding friend, the grey jay, is one of the most common as it flits among trees chattering about its numerous food caches. Woodpeckers and boreal chickadees search the trees for overwintering insects while great horned owls, hawk owls, and boreal owls look for unwary mice.

Fall comes early in the North. A few warm days may linger toward the end of August but there is a chill in the air at night. The skies are clear blue, frost-tipped leaves touch the tundra with scarlet and gold, and blueberries and red cranberries cover the bushes. The clouds of biting insects are gone, the birds have finished their frenzy of raising families, and for a short time the North seems to rest.

Fall is a benevolent time of year for the barren-ground caribou. The bands, which have been widely scattered throughout the summer, gradually come together and drift southward. At first they wander slowly in small groups, grazing peacefully and putting on fat for the coming winter. The caribou forage on aquatic sedges and horsetails, which are still green and nutritious, and they actively seek out mushrooms that sprout in early fall.

The caribou are in their prime in the fall with sleek, dark brown coats and layers of fat. The bulls are magnificent with flowing white manes accentuating their dark coats and the shedding velvet of their antlers flashing red in the sun's rays as they start to thrash bushes to polish their antlers in anticipation of the coming rut. Like other northern ungulates, caribou put on weight before winter. A bull caribou may gain 100 kilograms or more of solid fat stored in layers seven or eight centimetres thick across its back. Much of it, however, will be used up during the frenzied activities of the rut.

Between mid-October and early November the caribou rut as they travel through open country in the boreal forest of the Yukon or across the frozen lakes of the Northwest Territories. By the time the rut is over, winter has settled on the North and the migration continues deeper into the forest, where the caribou will remain until spring, feeding on lichens, grasses, and shrubs in the forests and resting out on the open lakes.

Meanwhile, other northern animals are also preparing for winter — their longest season. Below the treeline, winter is not as dark and cold as in the Far North, but it is still severe. Stands of black spruce, jack pine, and tamarack break the force of the wind and the snow lies as a thick blanket rather than in wind-packed drifts as it does on the barrens. Temperatures still dip to the −40s and crack the trees with sounds like rifle-shots echoing through the forests. The largest forest-dwellers, the caribou, moose, bison, and wolves, remain active in their relentless search for food, while smaller animals rely on food cached during the bountiful days of summer and fall. Black bears and grizzly bears are like large ungulates in that they accumulate thick layers of body fat. Instead of remaining active during the winter, however, they enter dens dug into dry banks or under trees. They are not in a true state of hibernation because their body temperature remains only a few degrees below normal and they can arouse themselves.

During the summer black and grizzly bears feed on plants, mice, squirrels, and carrion. The barren-ground grizzly is an opportunistic hunter and will kill moose or caribou calves during the calving season. It is also capable of bringing down an adult muskoxen or caribou if an opportunity, such as an ambush or wet deep snow, presents itself. In fall, bears switch to intensive gorging on sugar-rich berries to accumulate the rolls of fat necessary to sustain them for the winter.

Other animals also store energy for winter, but in the form of food caches. Red squirrels occupy networks of tunnels connecting the mounds of spruce cones that they cached in the fall. On warmer days they emerge from their tunnels and scamper across the top of the snow carrying food from their stores. Muskrat and beaver spend most of the winter underwater in intricately constructed lodges with food caches located nearby.

Arctic ground squirrels also cache food in underground burrows, but their food is for poor weather days rather than winter rations, because these squirrels are inactive throughout the winter. They are the only true hibernating mammals in the Arctic. Unlike bears, ground squirrels enter a deep torpor with a body temperature only a degree or two above freezing.

The smallest Arctic animals — the lemmings, mice, and voles — do not hibernate but spend the winter under a blanket of snow where they feed on grasses, mosses, and woody shrubs such as purple saxifrage and mountain avens. The mice and lemmings in their snow tunnels are safe from owls and hawks but the sinuously elegant ermine can follow them down their tunnels. Ermine change colour in fall to an all-white pelage with a prominently black-tipped tail, which may serve as an eye-catching distraction to any swooping hawk or owl. The ermine is unusual among the Arctic carnivores in that its winter pelage does not become luxuriantly long and thick. Instead, the ermine copes with winter by sheltering in snow burrows and emerging frequently to make kills that fuel its high metabolic rate.

Other medium-sized Arctic mammals grow thick and luxuriant fur, which makes their pelts still some of the most sought-after fur in the world. The aquatic fur bearers, such as muskrat and beaver, and the larger relatives of the ermine — the fisher, marten, and mink — are all denizens of the treed areas. They are active throughout the winter hunting mice, snowshoe hares, squirrels, and even muskrats. The wolverine, weighing up to fifteen kilograms, is the largest relative of the ermine. Wolverines are found along the treeline and out on the barrens to the Arctic coast. Wolverines are primarily scavengers, cleaning up the prey of other animals, but they are also determined predators in deep, soft snow, for example, when their short powerful legs and large, thickly furred feet give them an advantage.

The lynx is another winter predator whose large, thickly furred feet are useful when hunting in the snow. The principal prey of the lynx is the snowshoe hare, and the lynx population cycle is tied to the ten-year cycle of declines and recoveries of the hare populations. The snowshoe hare is similar to the Arctic hare of the barrens and Arctic islands in that both species change in the fall to white pelage with black-tipped ears and thickly furred hind feet. Like snowshoe hares, Arctic hares experience population cycles. In the northern part of their range, which extends to northern Ellesmere Island, the high point of a cycle is extremely obvious, as the hares herd together in groups of 100 or more animals.

The great herds of hares are typical of the Arctic ecology, which is characterized by pockets of productivity dispersed in time and space. Sometimes the abundance is overwhelming. The "endless flowing rivers of caribou" astounded the early explorers; masses of lemmings lend themselves to erroneous portrayals in popular fiction as being moving carpets of animals pushing each other over cliffs into the sea; clouds of hatching blackflies seem like a "scourge from the devil"; walruses hauled out in the hundreds on rocky beaches shifting and writhing together are almost obscene in their mass. But these excesses of productivity are ephemeral. They are seasonal, like the nesting of migratory birds in the spring, or they may be cyclic, like the four-five-year cycles of small rodents, the ten-year cycles of hares, and the 50- to 100-year cycle of the caribou.

The survival of each species in the Arctic is intricately entwined and all follow the others through the peaks and crashes. In the past, the balance of the Arctic has been maintained and great losses have recovered either naturally or, as in the case of muskoxen, through imposed legislation. Today the Arctic faces far larger problems. Only a few years ago it was said that a blowout from an oil well or a massive spill was the single greatest threat to the well-being of the Arctic environment. But even those are issues which may, to a limited degree, be controllable. There are now grave dangers over which there may be no control.

The Arctic is no longer the last frontier isolated from the rest of the world. Global changes in atmosphere and temperature as a result of the "greenhouse effect" may begin in the industrialized world and, since recent time, in oil-producing countries of the Middle East, but their effects will be felt in the Arctic and a warming trend of even a few degrees would have major and possibly devastating implications for the wildlife and habitat. Will this just be the beginning of another long-term cycle? It is too soon to tell.

Valerie Alia
Native Art and Craft

Introduction

Native people today are reclaiming their art; nowhere is the process more evident or more active than in Canada's North. In 1989, Northwest Territories Minister of Culture and Communications Titus Allooloo acknowledged the transfer of 1,653 of the 3,600 Inuit works formerly in government collections. Canada's Inuit organizations have designated the Inuit Cultural Institute in Arviat (formerly Eskimo Point) to house the collection of sculpture, prints, drawings, wall hangings, and other works purchased by Canada's Department of Indian Affairs and Northern Development over the past forty years. Also in 1989, Northwest Territories land claims organizations and government representatives set up a co-ordinated archeological resource management program to be jointly administered by the Dene Nation, the Dene/Métis Negotiating Secretariat, the Inuvialuit Regional Corporation (representing Western Inuit), and the Tungavik Federation of Nunavut (which represents Inuit in all other Arctic regions).

These are major policy changes. Until 1951, the Royal Canadian Mounted Police had federal orders to seize Native peoples' ceremonial art and other important artifacts. Some items were hidden and survived intact. Others, many of great spiritual significance, went into non-Native public and private museum collections.

Despite much progress in returning control of northern art to northern peoples, enormous gaps remain in the literature on Canadian Native art. This is not because of ill-informed historians or scarce information, but because elitism and ethnocentrism are imbedded in art history and criticism. Myths abound, among them the myth that "serious" artists must receive formal training in professional institutions. The treatment of Native artists as "naive" or "primitive" remains a major offence.

Mainstream Canadian art history texts relegate Native art and artists to margins, footnotes, or appendices. The North appears as location or inspiration for "mainstream" artists. Galleries devote special exhibitions, floors, wings, or catalogues to Native art, which is thus segregated from the "Canadian" art in their collections. Vocal opposition notwithstanding, much of Canadian Native art remains in museums of natural history, including the nation's major collection. Two new national museums opened in 1989, the new National Gallery of Canada and the Canadian Museum of Civilization, which houses much of the enormous collection of Native art. Even the McMichael Canadian Collection, which treats Native artists with great respect, presents the Group of Seven painters as *the* country's artistic core. Its front galleries show Group of Seven landscapes without reference to aboriginal Canadian art, while the permanent collection of Indian and Inuit works resides in the upper wing.

Critics have addressed the influence of European and North American art on Native artists, concerned about loss of Native "innocence." Too little has been said of how Native artists have influenced others. The paintings of Pablo Picasso and the sculptures of Henry Moore are said to have been influenced by the work of aboriginal artists. Among the artists of today, Toronto painter Shulamit is one of those influenced by Native art (mainly, the prints and drawings of Kenojuak, Pitseolak, and Davidialuk). The Group of Seven (most notably, A.Y. Jackson and Lawren Harris) and their successors used Dene, Métis, and Inuit figures and the Arctic land but paid scant attention to the images produced by Native artists. Shulamit's work is affected by these images rather than by the romance with Arctic scenery that infuses so many non-Native works. This is no coincidence since she studied art history with George Swinton, whose seminal writing on Inuit sculpture continues to dominate the field.

Northern aboriginal peoples developed distinct cultures. But within each region they endured common conditions and intermarried — socially, culturally, and politically. Thus, while we can generalize about cultural specifics, northern cross-cultural interaction and influence are too considerable to ignore. I have taken this into account in structuring the following chapter.

The Relationship between Art and Craft

The distinction between "art" and "craft" has often turned on the association of objects and skills with women's and men's social roles. Men are most often designated artists and women craftspeople. Women have been in the front ranks of Native art all along. The depiction by outsiders of women's roles in traditional societies is often distorted. In the European tradition, women artists receive secondary treatment, if they appear at all. Although at the most basic level, utilitarian craft and aesthetically motivated art can be separated, I would challenge the conventional definitions and distinctions. Art/craft crossovers are numerous and complex, especially where historical evidence is concerned. I do not, therefore, separate "art" and "craft" but instead explore the development of northern Native artistic expression.

In subsistence societies, art is tied to livelihood and work roles. Practical first and beautiful second, it is usually called craft. Utility-free, or utility-secondary, art appears when there is surplus production, however scant. But art in some form is there all along, no matter how scarce the resources or how basic the economy. While early Native art emerged in the form of homes, tools, utensils, and clothing, it was never strictly utilitarian. Spiritual objects might be kept separate from daily use, but daily-use objects often had spiritual as well as aesthetic attributes. It is not *necessary* to add elaborate beadwork or fringe to a pair of moccasins or a caribou jacket, or intricate figures to the handle of a knife or spear. There is art to be found in form itself — the gracefully curved *ulu* (Inuit woman's knife) whose curve works a thousand practical wonders; the beautiful and practical kayak or canoe. That no people produces utilitarian objects without considering form and colour testifies to the universality of art.

Art in Daily Life
Clothing
In the Arctic climate, clothing obviously originated with need. But even under the harshest conditions, clothing was art as well as protection. Like everything else, it was imbued with spiritual qualities. The Inuit *amauti*, in some dialects *amautik* (woman's parka), for example, is both practical and a powerful symbol of a child-centred society. Infant death threatens everyone; infant survival is a triumph for all. One Netsilik child's parka collected in the early 1920s had over eighty protective amulets attached. Where infant mortality was high, protection of children was a cross-cultural constant and a dominant theme. Curator Bernadette Driscoll's 1980 Winnipeg Art Gallery "Inuit Amautik" exhibition was subtitled "I like my hood to be full." All women wore the *amauti*. The baby rode naked inside the *amaut* (pouch/hood), except for a fox or birdskin cap; the pouch was lined with a re-usable "diaper" of caribou skin or moss. The *amauti* figures importantly throughout the development of Inuit art and continues as a major theme in sculpture, painting, tapestry, and print by contemporary male and female artists.

Both artistic and political statements have originated with this woman's parka (and with clothing more generally). I have heard of stones thrown at women wearing the western "Mother Hubbard" (a dress-like calico parka with "sunburst" fur hood trim and no child-carrier) into eastern communities. Also called *kaliku* (from calico), the Mother Hubbard arrived in the early 1800s with trade between Hawaii and China and Alaska's Inupiat Eskimos. Inupiat brought it to the Mackenzie Delta a century later. Native people of the Arctic's west seem to be generally more acculturated than those in the East, but many view the Mother Hubbard as a symbol of cultural sell-out. In the late 1970s, an Arviat woman refused to make one for a young female teacher, saying that it suited only young girls and old women and was bad luck for a woman in her childbearing years.

Baffin Inuit parkas were apparently influenced by Viking caftan-style garments (as evidenced by 900-year-old drawings of Viking priests' robes) and by later European garments. Men's parka hemlines changed from a back tail and short-waisted front to the straight line seen today, sometimes with a front or side split. The design has remained relatively constant since the mid-1800s, but Hudson's Bay Company influence still shows up in the materials — caribou and sealskin remain in use, but the underlayers of *kamiks* (boots) and parkas (and sometimes, outer layers) are often of duffle cloth, embroidered or appliquéd in pattern derived from Native, European, and individual designs.

Amauti sashes — required to secure both the garment and the hood-riding baby — are woven of brightly coloured woollen yarn. The Pangnirtung Weave Shop sells them world-wide to both women and men. Pangnirtung crocheted men's hats (similar to those in northern Quebec and elsewhere) also cross gender barriers when they enter the non-Native market.

Footgear is especially beautiful, meticulously cut and sewn for warmth, dryness, and stability, and usually highly decorated. Indian moccasins once were distinctive from tribe to tribe, community to community. Today's Indian, Métis, and Inuit moccasins often look similar in cut and (usually floral, beaded) decoration. Traditional differences remain in some work; for example, differences in the cut and style of Inuit *kamiks* and Dene moccasins; pointed-toe South Slavey moccasins which contrast with the rounded toes of Dogrib moccasins; a mix of sealskin and beading, often seen in Inuvialuit moccasins. Intricate quillwork and moosehair tufting are restricted to Dene and Métis footgear and other clothing. Quillwork originates in the porcupine-inhabited Subarctic. Although the use of quillwork has declined over the years (often in favour of more beadwork), there are indications that some artists are returning to quillwork, and there is a modest resurgence of its use in northern and southern aboriginal work. Sealskin *kamiks* are almost exclusively Inuit. Snowshoes of gutstrung bone or wood appear in many regions.

The *amauti* is not the only gender-specific garment. In the Rankin Inlet area, for example, Inuit women's and men's mitts are designed according to social and work roles. Women's mitts are made from the skin of a caribou's front leg, with its elegant white stripe, and men's from the hind leg, less elegant but warmer, cut short on top to ease igloo-building and hunting. Mitts for younger children are fashioned from the fluffy, white leg of fawn caribou.

Skins are dyed or used in their naturally differing colours, often inlaid in elaborate patterns. Face-framing furs are warm, water-resistant, and beautiful. Some garments, such as *kamiks* and leggings, are made of sealskin; seal intestine makes excellent waterproof clothing for kayakers. Birdskins and down are used widely. Birdskin caps were worn in the Quebec-Labrador peninsula, where Inuit and Innu (Naskapi and Montagnais Indians) co-reside. Quillwork adorns garments and baskets in Labrador and other subarctic locations.

Subarctic eastern peoples produced clothing of caribou skin, trade woollens, and furs. In winter, Naskapi men wore fur-in, covered by layers of fur-out, garments, and elbow-length gloves and gauntlets. Seventeenth-century European writers reported active trade by the Naskapi's Iroquoian neighbours for esteemed Naskapi cloaks. Summer coats had flared skirts painted in intricate patterns, which grew increasingly elaborate as trade increased. One eighteenth-century specimen has red, gold, and black geometric figures that resemble Oriental carpets. Northern Plains Indian designs and materials found their way north, adapting to colder climates. Indians of the North used beaver, caribou, hare, moose, muskox, muskrat, mountain goats, Dall's sheep and porcupine, fish and waterfowl. Dene and Yukon Indian clothing was mostly of large-mammal hide decorated in red and black paint and beading. A Slavey baby bag from the late 1800s is of caribou with red, white, and black wool duffle and beadwork trim. Indian people used fringe extensively; fringe also appears in Inuit parkas, especially in the central Arctic. It has spiritual significance in some Indian and Inuit cultures. In the mid-1800s some Indian peoples made clothes of traditional materials (with decorative trade items) but often experimented with European styles, for example, European-cut men's jackets.

Northern Métis descended from mixed Dene, French, and Scottish parentage. Some were already in the region, others moved into the new Territory from the Red River area of Manitoba, following the conflicts of 1870 and 1885. Starting in the early nineteenth century, Métis were the first to decorate sled dogs with *tapis* — embroidered blankets later called "tuppies." Métis artists influenced others throughout the northern plains and southern Arctic. In the southern regions, they specialized in horse gear and clothing featuring finely tanned hides, loom-woven quillwork in geometric patterns, and silk and bead embroidery inspired by French Catholic missionary teachers. Métis women became known to Indians as "Flower Beadwork People."

Inuit parka forms fall into three main areas: Mackenzie in the west; the central Copper, Netsilik, Iglulik, and Caribou regions; and southern Baffin Island, Labrador, and northern Quebec in the east. In some places, the skin of the animal being hunted was used both as camouflage and for its mystical connection with the animal. Copper Inuit were especially good tailors, known for fine sewing and inlaid details that made use of the natural differences in the colouration of skins. Copper Inuit women's parkas had sharply extended shoulders, for beauty and ease of child-carrying and nursing. Here, unlike the more widely curved front apron seen in eastern parkas, the front flap or *kiniq* was v-shaped or long and narrow. Caribou Inuit used fringe to border their parkas. A 1916 photograph shows two Labrador women in dark parkas trimmed in lighter fur, their front aprons inlaid with a large white oval design that seems to circumscribe the uterus and birth canal.

Garment-making has long been the province of women. Certain tools — women's knives, needles, thimbles, and such — were specifically for women (and sometimes, created by them). These skills, which persist in today's clothing, sculpture, design, drawing, and tapestry, were developed long ago.

Within a garment's requirements — for amulets, shape, fringing, and other characteristics — an artist had considerable freedom to explore the limits of her/his community's (or region's) style. But although individuals might gain distinction for their art, co-operation was central. Shared work often meant that more than one artist created an object — a principle important for the understanding of contemporary co-operative practice. Some critics and entrepreneurs speak of "artists" and "their assistants," especially where drawing and printmaking are concerned. But the Western model is not entirely appropriate to northern art. Two artists who work together are just that — two artists working together.

Hair

The dressing of hair is an art with or without the beads, feathers, grease, bone, ochre, wood, and other decorations so often added by Inuit and Indians. The configuration of hair can define gender, social status, regional or cultural affiliation, or other distinguishing characteristics. Hair decoration is practical — ornaments hold unruly hair in place — but their primary use is decorative.

Body Decoration

Inuit tattooing was usually monochromatic and geometric — dots or lines fanning out, curving, or paralleling on forehead, cheek, or chin. Like the Inuit, Indians tattooed women more than men; Kutchin (Gwich'in) and Carrier Indians tattooed for spiritual and protective purposes. Others used tattoos and body paint to designate locale, clan affiliation, marital or other social status. Beothuk were called "red Indians" for their extensive use of red ochre for face and body decoration. Chipewyan men wore blue or black tattooed bars, plus temporary face paint in red (ochre) and black (charcoal), spiritual colours associated with death ritual and life cycle. Missionaries probably influenced the decline of tattooing. Jewellery of bone, beading, leather, and other materials was often spiritual and protective. Those who emphasize marketing sometimes treat jewellery as something entirely new, invented by teacher-entrepreneurs; they forget that northern peoples have always worn jewellery, and have traded it throughout the history of Native/non-Native trade relations.

Tools, Vessels, Utensils

Availability of both indigenous and trade materials meant a wide range of materials, including bone, ivory, quills, wood, bark, metals, tanned and untanned skins, grasses, reeds, and rushes. Some objects are specified for men's or women's use and/or manufacture. While objects may be distinctively regional or local, the continuities are striking. The Okvik Eskimos (Old Bering Sea, A.D. 300) decorated tools, such as the walrus ivory gut scraper, with elegant incised-line drawings; similar tools are found in Siberia and the eastern Arctic. Birnirk and Thule cultures (A.D. 500–1500) produced harpoon heads and other tools decorated with rows of dots and small curved figures from Siberia to Alaska, Canada, and Greenland. Early Inuit implements were usually of chipped stone and later ones of rubbed slate. Scholars have used artifacts as a guide to tracing Inuit movement eastward, from Siberia to Greenland.

The tools of art are themselves art. A walrus ivory Thule engraving pen is embellished with a flawlessly carved ball suspended in a basket-like case carved from the middle of the stem, which ends in an iron point. Ivory fish-line sinkers were incised with complex abstract or realistic figures. Oil lamps, seen across the Arctic, range from dug-out stone ovals to elaborate objects carved with human, animal, and other images.

Baskets appear in many cultures and locations. Wild rye, beach grass, birch bark, wool yarn, bird down, feathers, walrus and seal intestine, porcupine quills, and other materials are found in Dene and Inuit basketry. Inuit of the western Arctic lands wove exceptionally fine, tight baskets with geometric decorations (often of woollen yarn or beadwork) and knobbed, woven handles. In one example, a rattle is woven into the handle: opening the basket makes music. Inuit of the eastern Arctic added stone-carved handles, highly prized in baskets sold today.

The Dene of Great Slave Lake-Mackenzie River fashioned leather gun cases, and game bags of netted babiche and smoked skin decorated with wool or hair and quillwork. Spruce-root basketry was produced until the mid-1800s. Especially inventive were Dene drinking tubes of bird bone and incised geometic patterns, with a thong for extra portability. Spoons and scrapers of horn, and containers of birch-bark, were decorated with geometric motifs of possible spiritual significance. Representational art appears occasionally — animals on southern Yukon skin scrapers and a late prehistoric Mackenzie Delta "snowshoe needle" decorated with muskrat, beaver, and caribou incised figures.

Transportation

Indian canoes were painted for protection. Before an Inuit kayak goes to sea, it must receive spiritual decoration. This includes painting or carving the bow and stern, and sometimes the reshaping of the boat itself and/or adding amulets and human faces on the sides. Among the Kuskokwagamuit Eskimos in Alaska, spirit helpers (commonly depicted with sexual imagery) connect and protect the boat, the hunter,

and his wife. Kayak paddles, boat hooks, and other practical accessories are also decorated. The Inuit *umiak* accommodates several people, usually women, as well as freight. In earlier times, inflated sealskins were also used for transport. Central Arctic kayak design was unusual. One end was high and beak-like — loon-like, according to some observers who see in its design echoes of the powerful waterspirit bird. The sharp prow is not only graceful; it serves as a lethal anti-walrus weapon.

Musical Instruments

Some musical instruments serve primarily decorative functions and are only secondarily musical. Métis sleds made music when they travelled, because of the large jingle bells incorporated into the highly coloured sled dog traces and harnesses. Drum dancing is a more conventional expression of music (and dance), and is seen across the Arctic in Indian and Inuit cultures. Tambourine-thin Naskapi drums, with a carrying thong at one end, were painted (one example in a sunburst-like pattern). Dene also made huge, communal drums like those seen in the American Southwest (home of their Navajo — Dinee — cousins). Drumming is done by several people (usually men) seated around the common instrument. Inuit drum dancing is very different. Dancers and drummers (men and women) perform short pieces, while Indian drum dances are generally extended improvisations. Inuit drums are tambourine-like discs with a stick-handle that allows the fluid wrist action and quick turns that characterize Inuit drumming. The Copper Inuit wear special dance hats at drum dances.

Art in Spiritual Life

People, animals, land, and spirit ("religion") are united. In times of famine, Inuit carved small likenesses of animals as offerings to the spirits of animals whose concrete forms meant food. Many materials were used — whalebone, animal teeth, muskox horn, walrus and narwhal ivory, stone, wood. Designs, whether incised "drawings" or three-dimensional, were always spiritual in origin. Avoidance of offending the spirit world was a central Indian theme. Elaborate rituals, taboos, and myths were constructed around spirit-human relationships and numerous objects supported daily and special-occasion ritual use.

Medicine pouches, containing personally valued and sacred objects, are made of various materials and designs. These appear in all cultures, and the objects within are usually deemed to be of protective value to the wearer. The pouches can be moosehair, animal fur, basket, or other materials and are inlaid, embroidered, woven, or otherwise adorned with abstract or representational designs. They are further embellished with threads, yarns, beads, wood, bone (including amulets of various kinds), fringes, quills, and other materials.

Woven mats of rush and other materials serve both daily and ritual use. Ritual mats are adorned with animal and other spiritually significant forms. A Netsilik Inuit shaman's belt had small mock-knives of carved antler. The Inuit man's knife, or *pana*, is powerful on many levels; its practical uses include snow house-building, meat-cutting, and self-defence.

Masks

Athapaskan-speaking Indian tribes in Alaska adopted or adapted ceremonial masks, and were influenced in many other ways by their trade relationships with Eskimo neighbours from the lower Yukon River and Norton Sound. The Ingalik wore three kinds of masks: small forehead masks for messengers out to invite guests from a nearby village; large whole-face men's masks; and finger masks held by women when they danced with men. The legacy of these finger masks echoes in a recent painting by Iqaluit-Ottawa Inuit artist Alootook Ipellie. In his black-and-white painting titled "Inverse Ten Commandments," tiny finger-face homunculi tip the fingers of hands splayed palms-up in front of the self-portrait face.

Masks represent people, spirits, birds, or animals, and are always spiritual. Indians and Inuit of the eastern Subarctic and Arctic use bone and ivory for both religious and practical purposes, as in the mask-like snow goggles seen throughout the North. Masks were used for social events and religious ritual. Some, like the snow goggles, were part of daily life during long, white winters. Iglulik Inuit wore sealskin masks with and without fur in the autumn festival of Nuliajuk (or Sedna) seen frequently in contemporary sculpture. The pre-winter hunt festival was held in the eastern and central Arctic. Two masked figures of either gender led the festivities, one dressed as a man and the other as a woman.

Pictographs and Paintings

Pictographic art — realistic engraving — has been discovered at prehistoric Thule sites in Alaska, Canada, and Greenland and is said to be the Thule period's major contribution. The Naskapi and Montagnais Indian painting on garments was highly sophisticated. Indian peoples were skilled painters, using berries, flowers, fungi, minerals, and roots to produce a broad spectrum of colours, but preferring ochre (hematite) red and (charcoal) black. The pigments themselves were imbued with spiritual meaning. Kutchin artists were obligated to return something of value in exchange for taking sacred ochre pigment from the earth. Slavey men painted "the manifestation of . . . 'medicine'" on canoes, toboggans, and drums, for protective purposes.

Painting was not just a peacetime activity. Warfare required special protection. Chipewyan men painted red and black designs, representing power and protection, on wooden shields worn in battles with their Inuit neighbours. This unfortunate side of contact among northern peoples is part of a long and difficult history of co-existing amidst scarce resources, harsh conditions, and competition from outsiders.

Miscellaneous Sculptures

Not all three-dimensional objects found at archeological sites have uses understood today. Regardless of use, they can be appreciated purely as sculpture. From West to East, they include works in bone, ivory, and wood, many in animal or human form, and probably used ritually. They are beautiful both in form and in the designs often incised on the surface. Multiple images abound — animals engraved on other animals; animals transformed into other animals; humans transformed to animals (and vice versa).

No discussion of northern art is complete without mention of *inukshuks*, the humanlike stone "sculptures" seen wherever Inuit live, travel, or hunt. They are usually quite large and are seen at great distances, especially on land, where the absence of trees reveals every shape on the horizon. They are formed of large stones, laid on each other so that they remain in place for many years despite the perils of wind, snow, and water.

It is uncertain whether they once served primarily spiritual purposes. Over the years, they have had many uses. In a country that until mid-century had no significant communities, they were — and still are — landmarks for nomadic peoples seeking shelter, safety, or good hunting. They add a human dimension to what can look like an unpeopled land. They mark coastline or convey the special attributes of a place; they greet the traveller or point to danger — the arms may in fact point in a specific direction. Thus, *inukshuks* comprise a massive code for communicating details at great distances. Often, they were grouped in rows, so that huge hordes of people appeared to guard or threaten a place. *Inukshuk* rows were sometimes organized to lead caribou herds toward an ambush, by smaller-scale mortals.

The *inukshuk* is a major motif in Inuit art. It shows up in miniature — in jewellery and sculpture, in prints, and on clothing. In 1989, David Reuben Piqtoukun's contemporary *inukshuk* was installed in a Toronto office building, probably the most unnatural location yet found for this symbol of the link between endless land and continuing humanity.

The Development of Art for Exhibition and Sale

Art is the third most productive economic activity in the Canadian North. It employs 3,500 – 5,000 artists in the NWT and Yukon. Inuit are best known for sculpture and prints. Indian and Métis painting, clothing, and other art are reaching an increasingly wider audience after centuries of small-scale trade.

Native people have used their art for trade for centuries, but many objects remain private and sacred. Marketing was aided by whalers, missionaries, and others who came north. Today, Native people are working to re-separate their private from their public art, reclaiming their own spiritual objects and clarifying what is and is not available for outsiders to buy or view. The concept of ownership remains a major cultural division: non-Native buyers, be they institutions or individuals, buy to own; Native cultures retain a strong commitment to community ownership.

Native communities are taking control of the materials used for art, most notably stone. A network of artist co-operatives now extends across the North, linking the southern marketplaces with northern values. New efforts, such as the arts centre in Pangnirtung, the Dene Cultural Centre, and the Iqaluit Jewelry Shop, are fostering more exchange between northern and southern artists.

The annual Great Northern Arts Festival in Inuvik and Toonik Tyme in Iqualuit showcase aboriginal artists. Dene needlework — clothing, accessories, art and spiritual objects — is often sold privately, in small shops, at festivals or celebrations. Archie Beaulieu, Dolphus Cadieux and Sonny MacDonald are the best known of an array of Dene and Métis painters, printmakers and sculptors. Their work is shown in galleries and gift shows, shown privately, or sold by commission. The tradition of birch bark basketry continues in contemporary work, seen at its best in work from Fort Liard. Basket art, notably quill-decorated birch bark, culminates in works by contemporary artists such as those in the Kotchea family.

Contemporary sculpture is primarily identified with Inuit artists. Although there is no Dene or Métis "community" to parallel the community of Inuit sculptors, there are notable individual artists working in wood and stone. While there once was a certain snobbery about insisting on "primitive" sculpture, power tools are gaining acceptance. With their availability comes an infusion of new ideas, new materials (harder stone), new techniques.

Each of the Arctic cultures has produced an array of arts and artists, but the northern market has been dominated by Inuit art. The causes are complex. Inuit sculptors and printmakers had the advantage of concentrated, government subsidized production and marketing programs. The demand for Inuit art was possible only because a wide public became aware of its existence. All along, sophisticated dealers have manipulated the market for their own, and the artists', benefit.

Inuit artists were deliberately encouraged to develop their work along "fine art" lines. Despite the push for traditional subject matter, sculptors were asked to work on a larger scale (to meet non-Inuit standards that tend to equate greater size with greater value). A nomadic society required portability of all its goods; sculptures were tiny. The one development that does use the small scale and delicacy of earlier carvings is that of jewellery, most fully developed at the Iqaluit Jewelry Shop. Here, artists work in silver, ivory, stone, and other materials to produce wearable art. Their previous work in silver was found too costly to continue; when I was in Iqaluit in 1989, the last silver pieces were being sold off. More recently, artists studying at Arctic College have been encouraged to work in silver.

We can only guess what would have developed had Dene and Métis artists received comparable training and marketing assistance. Certainly, they and other Indian peoples of the North have produced fine artists and imagery exciting to those of us who come from other cultures. Arguments that Inuit art has more "universally" appealing images are flawed. Much of art — everywhere — is based on private imagery, sometimes so private that only the artist grasps its meaning. To sell, however, a work must have some meaning to the buyer — it must evoke emotional and/or aesthetic response, or be seen as an appropriate investment.

It is a truism that publics can be taught to want or "need" objects they have never noticed before. Inuit were producing art for centuries, for themselves and for visitors — whalers, explorers, traders. The creation of a desire to acquire Inuit art is a reality, whether we see it as mere business tactic or elevate it to the level of "aesthetic education." The main Inuit printmaking communities are: Holman on Victoria Island in the West; Baker Lake in the central Keewatin region; Cape Dorset and Pangnirtung on Baffin Island in the East. Inuit printmaking in the eastern NWT has had the greatest artistic and commercial success. Northern Quebec has also produced several important printmaking communities, including Ivujivik, Sugluk, Maricourt (Wakeham Bay), Bellin (Payne Bay), Povungnituk, Port Nouveau-Québec (George River), Inukjuaq (Port Harrison), and Poste-de-la-Baleine (Great Whale River).

There is no question that marketing programs have provided new opportunities for a transitional Inuit economy. But dealer profit has too often prevailed over artist profit, just as it does in the non-Arctic art world.

To be fair, marketing Arctic art costs. Dealers sometimes provide materials. And most dealers do not function individually but work through marketing organizations, such as Northern Art Marketing, Canadian Arctic Producers, the co-operatives, or the Hudson's Bay Company. Marketing requires costly travel to communities thousands of miles apart. Air transport of heavy sculptures is more difficult than of prints, tapestries, and other more portable works, and the markup must reflect such conditions. Artists north and south are taking more responsibility for showing and marketing their own work. Co-operative galleries are on the rise. The unique northern co-operative system was itself developed co-operatively, by Native and non-Native northern and southern artists and entrepreneurs.

These are exciting times for northern art. Since they first encountered strangers, Native artists have mixed old and new ideas and materials across cultural boundaries. The insistence on "primitive" expression came from a public schooled in noble-savage perspectives. Today, Pudlo's helicopters make sense to viewers of his prints, and David Reuben Piqtoukun thinks nothing of sculpting in Italian crystal alabaster or Arizona pipestone, in addition to the more traditional softer northern stone.

It is said that the marketing of contemporary Inuit art began when James and Alma Houston went north in 1948. The National Gallery of Canada introduced Inuit art in a 1951 exhibition, followed in 1958 by a Hudson's Bay Store sale in Winnipeg and a modest but historic show at the Stratford, Ontario, Shakespeare Festival. In the 1960s came printmaking at Povungnituk and Holman (distinguished for the work of Helen Kalvak, Peter Aliknak, Agnes Nanogak, and many others), sculpture at Baker Lake, the Canadian Eskimo Arts Committee, and the West Baffin Eskimo Co-operative at Cape Dorset. Following the precedent set by the co-operative marketing of Cape Dorset art, Canadian Arctic Producers, based in Ottawa, became the first Inuit-owned co-operative to wholesale art from the communities across the Arctic. Also in this period came a film on the life and work of Kenojuak, one of the first Native artists to achieve international prominence.

The 1970s brought prints from Baker Lake, Pangnirtung's fine tapestries, Spence Bay parkas and "packing dolls," Cape Dorset and Frobisher Bay (now Iqaluit) jewellery, and new attention for Cape Dorset printmaker Pitseolak Ashoona through a National Film Board production and her illustrated autobiography. With the emergence of Native self-government, government management is declining. The 1980s saw efforts to catalogue and organize collections and information, now being gradually sent north. The government-sponsored, comprehensive Inuit Artist File Index is a remarkable document, updated regularly to include Inuit artists both living and deceased; at last count, the Index included about 3,000 artists.

Major exhibitions by Native artists have continued to increase throughout Canada. New training programs, such as a 1989 hard stone mask-carving workshop in Iqaluit, are providing artists with opportunities to learn new materials, tools, and skills and to interact with artists from other places.

Jean Blodgett, the pre-eminent curator of Inuit art, has organized important exhibitions across Canada. Her 1986 Kenojuak retrospective at the McMichael and Jessie Oonark retrospective for the Winnipeg Art Gallery kicked off a new era. More recently, she organized a showing of lesser-known sculptors from Arviat, whose work is blockier and less polished but in many ways more exciting than better-known and more representational work from other regions. Major shows have been on the rise since 1985, particularly in the bigger cities. The Winnipeg Art Gallery has long been a leader in the field and in treating Native artists as *artists*, but the prairie city's remoteness from the rest of Canada means that its exhibitions remain localized. Vancouver, Montreal, Toronto, Ottawa are joined by smaller cities such as London, Ontario, which occasionally feature aboriginal and/or northern art. Like the history books, the galleries tend to specialize, and it is rare to see a Native artist featured in a gallery showing non-Native artists.

Perhaps because of the skilful marketing, Inuit artists have been more fully segregated and more typecast. Indian and Métis artists have been more generally mobile and have had more European-style training; thus, many of their works are in Western "fine art" materials or mix Native and non-Native materials and themes. Others, such as Yukon Tlingit artist Keith Wolf Smarch, use traditional themes and materials to create vivid new works.

Cape Dorset was the landmark experiment, with artists like Pitseolak Ashoona dominating the important first generation. In 1951, James Houston obtained a federal grant. There were only three families living in the community; most were still in permanent coastal hunting camps. Wage labour, social services, and schools encouraged the move into the community. In 1953 the Department of Indian Affairs and Northern Development asked Houston to develop arts/crafts in the North, and he decided to focus on Cape Dorset. He went to Japan to learn woodcut techniques and printmaking skills, sharing them with the Dorset artists.

Dorset artists used stonecut and stencil techniques. The original drawing was traced onto a flat stone surface, then details were cut into the stone. Stonecutting requires soft rice paper, such as mulberry paper, which is rubbed over the inked surface — a linear technique featuring sharp contours. In 1961, a year before he left Dorset, Houston introduced copperplate engraving as well, so that artists could work directly on the printing plate. Among those who excelled in the new medium were Iyola, Kananginak (known as the "Arctic Audubon"), and Ottochie.

Toronto artist Terrence Ryan joined Dorset's West Baffin Eskimo Co-operative at the end of the Houstons' stay. He served as principal artist adviser and in 1974 started the lithography studio. Hand lithography is a widely used technique that originated in Europe in the early nineteenth century. Pudlo Pudlat uses it especially well, pioneering his unique fusion of old and new imagery, working helicopters, modern ships, and Christian symbols into his prints and drawings. Johnniebo, who died tragically in 1972, worked in close co-operation with his wife Kenojuak, one of the best-known Canadian artists. Kingmeata is known for her realistic sculpture and spirit-inundated graphics, Peter Pitseolak for his sculpture, drawings, and photography. Lucy's drawings have been her major distinction, while Pauta is known for both sculpture and graphics. Pitaloosie works her sewing and drawing together, a theme repeated in the magnificent hangings and paintings of Baker Lake's Jessie Oonark. Kananginak, who specializes in birds and mammals, says he hated hunting as a child and started to draw animals instead.

Among other centres of art production in the North, Baker Lake produces prints that are more collaborative than those from Dorset and Holman. George Swinton reports that in Povungnituk, whose co-operative was started by Sheila and Jack Butler, a drawing by one artist is interpreted and often changed in the printmaking process (with extensive dialogue and collaboration). Pangnirtung graphics are usually stencilled, a technique that produces their characteristic soft look with its gradations of colour and shading. The sculptures of Karoo Ashevak, probably Spence Bay's best known artist, are infused with powerful spirits; his preferred medium is bone. His work has been compared with that of recent and contemporary European sculptors, but his vision is entirely northern and his own. Povungnituk artists experimented early with stencilling and now use stencil/ stonecut combinations. Povungnituk sculptures often link humans, animals, and the spirit world.

Encouraged and motivated by southern markets, northern Native artists are exploring new directions. At the same time, the northern artist now straddles two cultures, two very different worlds — that of a subsistence hunting-gathering society that, for the Inuit, was largely nomadic within living memory; and that of southern Canada, a highly technologized Western civilization that is beamed by multi-channel satellite to television sets in even the most remote Arctic settlements. Today, the cultural tensions inherent in the northern Native experience are reflected in some of the finest art that northern artists produce.

Central Arctic

Hannah and Adami greet tourists and visitors to Native Point on Southampton Island in the region's traditional garments and caribou *kamiks* by demonstrating the old ways of living and hunting. *Wolfgang Weber*

An elderly lady in Arviat dressed in her artistically embroidered and beaded *amauti* in front of the traditional caribou tent, demonstrating Keewatin craftwork to visitors. *Wolfgang Weber*

Inuit drummers at Arviat bring the past alive. This southern Keewatin community is home of the Inuit Cultural Institute and is well known for its artists' fine sculptures. The settlement took root in the 1920s when the Hudson's Bay Company established a trading post here, followed by a Catholic mission to make contact with the Padlirmiut-Inuit. *Wolfgang Weber*

Inuapik and his brother prepare their boat for a fishing trip at Coral Harbour, the only community on Southampton Island. This large island at the northern end of Hudson Bay also offers an abundance of wildlife with great herds of walrus, polar bears, and an extensive range of sea birds. *Wolfgang Weber*

Arctic char being air-dried on racks in the traditional way. *Wolfgang Weber*

The HBC established a post at Coral Harbour in the mid-1920s, bringing with it Inuit from the Baffin region, from northern Quebec, and from mainland Keewatin to repopulate this island, whose original inhabitants died in an epidemic during the winter of 1902–03. *Mike Beedell*

Catholic mission school at
Chesterfield Inlet.
William Belsey

The mission's greenhouse.
William Belsey

The Catholic Church concentrated its mission efforts toward the Inuit early in this century by building a huge mission school and a hospital at Chesterfield Inlet on the shore of Hudson Bay. *Danny Gasparik*

The Kaminuriak caribou herd on the barrens near Henik Lake. During the 1940s and 1950s, a dramatic shortage of caribou caused by a change in migration patterns of this herd resulted in starvation and great hardship for the Padlirmiut-Inuit at Ennadai Lake, 360 kilometres west of Arviat. *Roddy MacInnes*

Anguhalluk, Baker Lake elder, and granddaughter. Baker Lake is today the Arctic's only inland community. *Peter Thomas*

Newborn caribou calf, as seen south of Baker Lake. *Douglas Heard*

Small muskoxen herd in the
Melville Hills between
Coppermine and Paulatuk.
Wolfgang Weber

Umingmak, the Inuit's word for muskox, lowers his head into position to be able to gore his enemy. *Wolfgang Weber*

Inuit printmaker Mary Okheena, living and working in Holman, a community of 300 on the west coast of Victoria Island, famous for its lithographic stencil, stonecut, and linocut prints. *Tessa Macintosh*

The *Martha L. Black*, a modern Coast Guard icebreaker, at anchor at Cambridge Bay on Victoria Island, the regional administrative and service centre. During the 1990 sail of the Northwest Passage by Clark Stede, the ship and its crew under the command of Captain Mellis took the yacht *ASMA* on board in Franklin Strait for fifty hours to cut through a 150-kilometre icefield that blocked passage to open water further south.
Wolfgang Weber

Baling Arctic fox fur in
Spence Bay, a scene now of
almost bygone days.
Richard Harrington

Plane day in Coppermine.
When the plane from
Yellowknife arrives, almost
the whole village comes to
the airport. It is a
community with an
interesting blend of the new
and the old. The area from
here to Umingmaktok at

Bathurst Inlet and to
Cambridge Bay may have
once been the homegrounds
of the early Denbeigh and
Thule, and present-day
Copper-Inuit may have
evolved from these cultures
through the centuries.
Wolfgang Weber

Rankin Inlet is the Keewatin's transportation and service centre, a modern Arctic community of 1,500 people on the western coast of Hudson Bay founded by industry. A 1929 discovery of nickel resulted in the establishment of a mine in 1955, which was discontinued only seven years later but might be revived one day if world market prices rise.
William Belsey

Wives and children waiting
for their loved ones at
Rankin Inlet airport.
Wolfgang Weber

John and Simeonee Tatty
build their own new home in
Rankin Inlet.
Tessa Macintosh

The modern Rankin Inlet
school centre during a
blizzard in June!
William Belsey

Teacher Bill Belsey and his grade 5 class at the Maani Ulujuk School. *Elke Emshoff*

Dental therapist Janet Onalik teaches dental hygiene to pre-schoolers at the Katauyak daycare centre in Rankin Inlet. *William Belsey*

Archeology student
investigating fifteenth-cen-
tury Thule homesites on the
barrenlands at Meliadine
River near Rankin Inlet.
Danny Gasparik

Arctic ground squirrel,
named *sik sik* by the Inuit.
Roddy MacInnes

(Upper):
Female snowy owl is landing
near the site of her nest on
the tundra. *Brian Hawkes*

Ermine in summer stretching
high to look for prey.
Jim Brandenburg

3 a.m. midsummer rainbow at the base camp and fuel depot of an exploration crew, test drilling for gold in the Ferguson River greenstone belt southwest of Rankin Inlet. *Roddy MacInnes*

The summer is over! Exploration crew members with luggage and samplings of gold ore, leaving Rankin Inlet for Churchill and Winnipeg. *Elke Emshoff*

Helicopter bringing in new supplies of food and equipment to exploration camp on the barrens. *Roddy MacInnes*

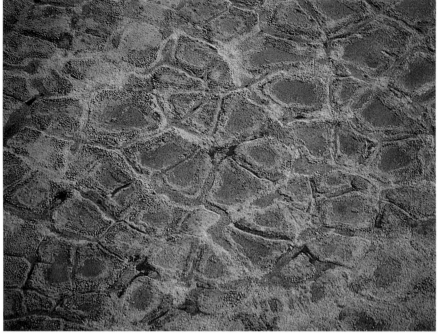

Polygon tundra: throughout the Arctic, the phenomenon of patterned ground occurs mainly in the moist coastal areas, resulting from the endless cycle of thawing and freezing. *Wolfgang Weber*

The spectacular Wilberforce Falls of Hood River, thundering down forty-nine metres, are the highest falls north of the Arctic Circle. *Wolfgang Weber*

Fall tundra of the barrens
between Mara and Burnside
rivers just south of Bathurst
Inlet on the Arctic mainland.
Wolfgang Weber

Two young gyrfalcons, Hope Bay area. *Kim Poole*

Peregrine falcon chicks in nest east of Bathurst Inlet, waiting for food. *Kim Poole*

Adult gyrfalcon in the Hope
Bay area off Melville Sound.
The gyrfalcon is now the
"official bird" of the NWT.
Kim Poole

Young polar bears at play on the sea ice near Wager Bay. *Donna Barnett*

Bearded seal sunning itself on an ice pan in Repulse Bay. *Danny Gasparik*

Native Bay, Southampton Island. In the summer, "freighter canoes" with strong outboard motors overtake the role of snowmobiles as a means of transport to the hunting grounds. *Wolfgang Weber*

In this isolated hunting camp
on the tundra of the
mainland barrens every
visitor is a welcomed guest.
Wolfgang Weber

Caribou bulls on the
fall-coloured tundra in
September near Jolly Lake,
just beyond the treeline.
Douglas Heard

Tourists — hunters, anglers,
and photographers — arrive
at Bathurst Inlet on Twin
Otter with floats.
Richard Harrington

Jeff MacInnis and Mike Beedell struggle to drag their catamaran *Perception* across the treacherous ice of the Northwest Passage during their 100-day journey between 1986–88.
Mike Beedell

German sailor Clark Stede and Australian Michelle Poncini navigated the Northwest Passage with their forty-two-foot aluminum yacht *ASMA* in 1990. *Clark Stede*

Inukshuk ("stone in likeness of man") along the Northwest Passage. *Wolfgang Weber*

Jeff MacInnis
The Northwest Passage

Over the sound of the grinding, boat crushing ice, I shout: "One, two, three, heave! One, two, three, heave!" Inching our fully provisioned 700-pound Hobie 18 forward requires every ounce of our combined strength. Driven by a strong current, this rubble pile of ice is in constant motion. Pausing to rest is impossible — our Hobie would be crushed within minutes. This is literally a "land that devours ships."

Mike and I struggled for two hours to drag the *Perception* across 400 yards of ice. It was a nightmarish conglomeration of pieces of all sizes, shapes, and ages, some rising ten feet out of the water, all of it shifting, creaking, and grinding away in the current, threatening to pin our legs if we took a false step. At times the boat's bows would be over our heads as we hauled it along on its runners, hoping it could withstand the stresses and strains it was undergoing.

Across the roof of North America, the Northwest Passage weaves 2,500 miles through the Arctic archipelago of islands. Beginning in the mid-1500s, early explorers searched for a faster route to the Orient and the riches that lay there. The names of Davis, Hudson, Baffin, Franklin, and many early explorers crowd the maps of the Arctic, where these heroic men tried, failed, and often died in their attempts to sail this labyrinth of ice. Roald Amundsen needed three years between 1903 and 1906 to complete the Passage in his motorized sailing vessel, the *Gjoa*. I hoped we could be the first to sail the Northwest Passage in a solely windpowered boat, a dream that is now four centuries old.

The Inuit have inhabited the High Arctic for thousands of years. They lived near and hunted on the waters of the Northwest Passage. These resourceful people survived and thrived in one of the most unforgiving environments on earth.

Non-Native exploration of the Arctic began with the Vikings. Archeological discoveries in the eastern Canadian Arctic give evidence to these early travels in the thirteenth century. Not long after the discovery of America by Christopher Columbus, a northern passage was considered as a route to the riches of the Orient. This new continent acted as a frustrating barrier to a direct route to the markets in the Orient.

John Cabot was the first to search for a northern passage, starting in 1497. In 1576, Martin Frobisher mistakenly believed he had discovered large quantities of gold on Baffin Island, near present-day Frobisher Bay. His pursuit for a passage was interrupted by a greed for gold.

Despite many expeditions by brave explorers, a route through the labyrinth of Arctic islands eluded them. The merchant companies who backed these voyages lost interest in finding a viable route and withdrew their support.

After the Napoleonic Wars, the British Navy ruled the seas. In need of challenges for the men and for national prestige, the British renewed their interest in the Northwest Passage. In 1845 Sir John Franklin with his two ships *Erebus* and *Terror* set out to conquer the Passage. Franklin was the leader of two previous overland journeys to the Arctic. On the first of these treks the brutal conditions nearly destroyed the entire group. At one point the men were so desperately hungry that they ate their leather boots to stay alive. The second journey was better prepared and succeeded in adding a few more miles to the map of the Canadian Arctic. Now on his third and final journey, Franklin was outfitted with two ships, 128 men, and enough food for five years. Into the maze of islands and ice they crept. Entering Lancaster Sound and sailing around Cornwallis Island, they spent their first winter near Beechey Island where several men died. The following summer the two ships edged down Peel Sound. All of the men on board must have felt extremely excited; they were close to achieving the Passage.

In mid-September, ice slammed hard against the hulls, trapping them off King William Island. For nearly two years the ice threatened to destroy the ships. Slowly, scurvy — and food poisoning, caused by lead-soldered tin cans — set in. Many sailors met their death here and also Franklin died, on June 11, 1847.

The following April the surviving men abandoned the ships to begin a futile march south. Along the frozen coast of King William Island the men trudged. Weakened severely by hunger and illness they began to die one by one, some of them falling in their footsteps. The final camp was on a bleak rocky shore called Starvation Cove. The last few members of the expedition perished at this spot.

Back in Britain the Navy became concerned after two years of silence from the Franklin expedition. Search expeditions were dispatched to find the lost expedition. Over an eighteen-year period, more than fifty ships ventured into the Arctic in search of Franklin. Unfortunately, they were not able to arrive in time to save the men or even solve the Franklin mystery.

One of the ships involved in the search was a three-masted barque named *Breadalbane*. She was crushed by the ice and sank in fifteen minutes on August 21, 1853. My father, Dr. Joe MacInnis, became fascinated by the possibility of finding her on the ocean floor. He has led more than twenty diving expeditions to the High Arctic, which focused on science and human performance. During one of these research projects he became the first person to dive under the North Pole.

His search for the *Breadalbane* began in 1978, with a small expedition using inflatable boats to tow an underwater side-scan sonar device. I was able to join him on this project, but the ice conspired against us and the ship was not found. Two more years of effort using a Canadian Coast Guard icebreaker were needed before discovering the *Breadalbane* resting majestically on the ocean floor, 100 metres below the surface.

Delayed by ice until 1983, we established an ice camp over the ship. During a series of thrilling dives using a one-atmosphere diving suit, we put a man back on the deck of the *Breadalbane* 140 years after she sank. This fascinating encounter with the world of the early explorers inspired my dream of sailing the Passage.

It would not be until 1903 that a man splendidly prepared for finding the Passage set off on his quest. Roald Amundsen was a great explorer and a meticulous planner. He cycled, jogged, skied, and even slept with his window open on cold Norwegian nights to prepare himself for his three-year journey through the Passage. His relations with the Inuit were rewarding and educational, and the wealth of knowledge he gleaned from these highly skilled people paved the way for his attainment of the South Pole by dog team.

Consumed by this age-old challenge, we began the fascinating process of devising an expedition to see if, with today's technology, we could sail the Passage. Our greatest asset was the people who shaped the equipment and tactics for this dangerous endeavour. Without their enormous assistance the journey would never have begun.

Why a Hobie Cat? This was the most-asked question. In my mind, the two-man Hobie represents with its specially strengthend structure all of the outstanding qualities necessary for success in one of the harshest environments of the earth. Fast under sail and with the ability to be hauled over the ice, it allowed us to adapt to the constantly changing conditions. Knowing that the boat was a proven design in more southern latitudes told us that it should be able to handle other difficult situations.

By combining today's technology and Inuit ways of working with the environment, it seemed possible that the Passage could be sailed. Two years of planning, testing, and preparation saw our team of advisers grow to more than 100 people, who helped solve the multidimensional problems the Passage presented. Borrowing proven equipment and systems from diverse areas such as diving, mountaineering, aeronautics, and sailing, we designed our expedition to respond to the conditions in the Arctic, which demand adaptability in order to survive.

All of our survival equipment, camping gear and food had to be carefully chosen and placed within the small confines of the boat. Our food consisted of 1.5 pounds per person a day of dried and freeze-dried food. We used specially designed neoprene waterproof bags on the tramp to store some of our equipment and the rest went carefully into the hulls.

Our suits were one-piece Gore-tex DUI diving drysuits with latex neck and wrist seals.

We were fortunate enough to interest almost thirty corporate sponsors; two of our largest were Hobie Cat and the Labatt's beer company. Without the support of all these companies, the journey would never have been possible.

One of the most important aspects was choosing the person to crew with me on this voyage. Four months before departure I teamed up with Mike Beedell, who has spent the last ten years exploring and photographing the Arctic.

A 4,000-mile drive — from Toronto, pulling the boat — carried us west then north to Inuvik on the Northwest Territories, the farthest north you can go by road in Canada. Like most Hobie sailors we drove to the end of the road to launch our cat — ours just happened to be a very long road.

On July 21, 1986, Mike and I set out from Inuvik, which sits on the edge of the silt-brown Mackenzie River. Following the Mackenzie ninety miles down to the Beaufort Sea, we headed east through the ice-infested waters. Much to our dismay, there was less than 100 miles of open water before a wall of ice blocked the route ahead. Slowly we progressed against head winds into the maze of ice.

Mike and I settled into the routine we tried to follow throughout our voyage. Rising at seven, we would eat, then break camp and set sail for at least twelve hours. The distance covered each day ranged from a low of ten miles, mostly paddling or hauling the boat along the shore when there was no wind, to 100 miles of exciting downwind sailing. Generally, the travel was agonizingly slow. Two-thirds of the time was spent tacking into the wind, which nearly doubled the sailing distance. Months later I learned that the headwinds I had cursed all summer had been pushing the ice out of the gulfs and straits into which we sailed.

For safety reasons we always sailed with land in sight. This meant we had to sail deep into three large bays before they could be crossed. Franklin Bay, the largest, was named for Sir John Franklin in 1826 during his second Arctic expedition. We read some vivid journals of these voyages during our journey, and this heightened our respect for and wariness of the Arctic environment.

Where we slept at night depended on the terrain and the availability of fresh water. Cliffs and rocky ground complicated site selection. We also had to haul the cat far enough up on the beach to avoid high tides and big waves. Making camp took time and it was often close to midnight before we hungrily ate our freeze-dried dinner. There is plenty of daylight at that latitude, so the time between eating and when exhaustion sent us to our sleeping bags was spent exploring, photographing, or writing in our journals. Always, though, we kept a wary eye peeled for bears.

Snow began to fall in late August, signalling the fast-approaching winter. We spent our last night of the first year pinned down by an easterly storm in a place also called Starvation Cove. Appropriately, this was where we broke open the last of our food rations. Stuck in the cove, cold and hungry, we could almost understand how the early explorers would occasionally be driven to eat their leather boots.

During the first year we sailed more than 1,000 miles and then left the boat at Cambridge Bay for the winter. In the summer of 1987 we returned to Cambridge Bay and surveyed the horizon. There were no trees, no open water, only an endless ocean of ice. It looked hopeless. The ice forecasters appeared to have been right — there would be no sailing this year. It was a problem that plagued us all summer. The first ten miles were spent half-sailing, half-dragging our Hobie across the uneven ice. Hauling the boat was so strenuous that sweat dripped off our bodies despite the sub-zero temperatures.

A northwest wind moved the ice just far enough off Victoria Island to allow a narrow opening. The euphoria of making progress kept us travelling for twenty hours that first day.

Our good fortune halted abruptly when we tried to cross Icebreaker Channel, which took twelve days of fear and frustration. From a deck-level perspective, the ice stretched on infinitely. This maze of ice was constantly in motion, creating a crushing confusion of pack ice. Multi-year ice that thrust skyward over twenty-five feet in places created an undulating frozen landscape. We picked what looked like a promising lead and sailed into it, only to reach a dead end. Time and time again our efforts proved futile. There was open water ahead but it was rapidly being filled in, and we suddenly realized that the wind and current were conspiring to imprison us in the grinding, moaning ice. With desperate effort, we dragged the boat across the drifting pans to where the water remained free and sailed down a fast-closing lead.

Stranded at last amidst the pack ice, we could only haul our Hobie up onto the ice and wait for conditions to improve. With the ice constantly shifting, our only safe place to sleep was on the trampoline of our cat. The bows of *Perception* were pointed into the wind to present the smallest profile and the tent was securely erected on the tramp. Inside the tent, burrowed deep within our sleeping bags was the only place of relative comfort. Even as we drifted off to sleep our constant thoughts were of the ice breaking beneath the hulls or of a polar bear encounter.

Waking often during the nights adrift on the ice, we would look outside to assess our situation. This icy world made our insides burn from uncertainty. Morning brought an endless ocean of ice in all directions, reaffirming that helpless feeling we went to sleep with.

Ten days of sailing, drifting, and hauling our cat around and across the ice brought us to the point of utter dismay. Mike swept the horizon with his 500-mm telephoto lens, seeing nothing to the east. Finally, he spotted land, but it was off to the west. Our hearts sank: the ice had forced us far off course into a huge semi-circular arc, leaving us further behind than when we started. We were numb with frustration, and our summer seemed over almost before it had begun.

While Mike started off to scout for other options, I ducked into the tent to retrieve a small stuff sack I'd packed in Toronto in anticipation of a time when our morale would need a boost. In it were a red top, red pants, red tuque, black belt, and white beard. I quickly slipped them over my drysuit and presto — Santa Claus! Mike stood in speechless surprise as I ran across the ice toward him. The event brought us both to laughter and reminded us that humour is an important part of a survival kit.

The ice trapped us again on the east side of the Royal Geographical Society Islands. At this point our best option was to haul the boat across a 100-yard isthmus of land. With great reluctance, we unloaded our gear and grunted our Hobie across the tundra. Further up on the island we spent two hours hauling our boat through jumbled house-sized pieces of ice before reaching open water.

An ice-free ocean permitted us an easy passage to King William Island. As I scanned this land for the first time, my mind drifted back to the days of Sir John Franklin's last expedition when his two ships became imprisoned near our present position. Our two expeditions crossed paths almost 150 years apart, but I could still see these brave sailors. Scurvy, hunger, food poisoning, and the ice besieged the Franklin expedition until the remaining men abandoned their ships and began a death march south.

Our progress was rapid until we reached the east side of King William Island, where last winter's ice still engulfed most of Rasmussen Basin. Two days and ten miles of soft, rotting ice later we arrived in Gjoa Haven. Most of one day was spent hauling our Hobie along the narrow gap between the ice and the shore. Our feet felt like lifeless stumps as we waded through frigid water hour after agonizing hour.

North of Gjoa Haven the weather became worse. Approaching the Tasmania Islands in heavy winds and a violent sea, we sailed past three polar bears, a mother and her cubs, hunting on a larger iceflow. We sighted two more polar bears within an hour before being forced ashore due to extreme winds. Onshore we spotted a seal carcass stripped to the bone. Sharing the same terrain with these polar carnivores made sleep elusive many nights.

We progressed rapidly due north, running with an approaching storm. Two days later, near the top of Peel Sound on August 31, winds howled at sixty miles per hour, creating waves two stories high. Mike and I were in the middle of a gale on a piece of ice barely large enough to hold our eighteen-foot Hobie. We were riding, it seemed, an endless roller coaster into destruction. Each swell lifted our tiny island of ice up and over the frothy, wind-lashed crest, only to drop us down the other side. Fog obscured our horizon; we were landless on an ocean of boat-crushing ice.

We were ready for the worst, dressed with every piece of survival equipment: our weatherproof Gore-tex suits covering five pounds of insulative clothing, our emergency location devices strapped to our bodies, our one-man survival seats tied to our waists, and our stomachs stuffed with as much food as time would allow. Fully equipped, our defences were nothing in comparison to the white nightmare that engulfed us.

Using all our combined strength plus two mountaineering ice screws driven into the ice, we rode the storm ten miles across Aston Bay. Finally, we crashed into the main pack of ice. After pushing our boat two miles over the moving pack we kissed the ground, thrilled to be alive.

Veteran Arctic pilot Willie Laserich described the summer of 1987 as the worst he had experienced in twenty-five years of flying.

For the second year our journey came to a halt. The last day was spent sailing in temperatures of −5°Celsius with the lines and deck covered in ice and our bodies numbed by the windchill factor of −20°. That night and for the next day a snowstorm with winds of forty-five miles per hour lashed the sky and the low ground where we were huddled. To keep the tent from being destroyed, we built a snow wall. Winter conditions forced us to abandon our Hobie on the tundra just 500 miles from our goal.

Even though it took months before I could fully feel my toes, we were determined to complete the Passage. Eleven months later we scanned the distant tundra high up in the aircraft that was returning us to Cape Anne. I wasn't sure if our Hobie would still be where we had left her. During the long winter she had to withstand two months with temperatures down to almost −60° Celsius, a few 100-mph wind storms, and the threat of polar bears who eat anything in this harsh land.

Much to our delight our Cat was still in excellent shape. After a day of minor repairs we were off on the ocean again. Sneaking into Cunningham Inlet we were able to sail among pods of beluga whales in their natural setting. In this unique shallow inlet there is an annual pilgrimage of some 1,500 belugas who come to rub away the yellowing outer layer of their skin and emerge a beautiful sparkling white. These whales, also called "sea canaries," entertained us with chirps and whistles.

Deep in their inlet, two of the whales had accidentally beached themselves on the delta of a small river near a scientific research station. The scientists estimated the small one's age at three months, and it was whining and trembling be-

tween bouts of desperate thrashing movements, clearly traumatized by beaching. We could all feel her distress with poignant clarity, and decided to try and get her back into the water. With great effort, the four of us managed to spin her around and began towing her backward into deeper water. Slowly, we were able to inch the enormous creature back into deeper water until, with one final thrashing movement, she was afloat and quickly swam off. The other whale was simply too big for us to budge.

As we sailed eastward, huge swells rolling in from Greenland forced us to share a rocky beach with the world's largest carnivores, a fascinating and frightening experience. Often when the ice breaks up during the summer months, the bears are forced ashore, away from their staple diet of ringed seals. As they scavenged for food, living predominantly on their fat layers, Mike and I observed two bears return to the same beach, four days in a row, to eat long strands of seaweed thrown ashore by severe winds.

One morning, trapped in our mummy sleeping bags in our tent, we were startled out of a deep sleep by the hissing and pawing of a polar bear, just two feet from our heads, that weighed more than our boat. It felt like our hearts were going to explode as seconds of terror passed while the bear decided our fate. Our "third tent mate" was a 12-gauge shotgun that was our means of last resort against bear attacks. Fortunately, the bear decided we weren't going to be his breakfast.

Sailing past glacier-capped mountains, we approached the end of our 2,500-mile journey. Memories and experiences of the last 100 days flowed through our minds. We have been exposed to great hardships, at times terrifying natural forces that made us adapt quickly or perish. From our deck-level perspective we could intimately glimpse a land with incredible beauty and deadly harshness.

At 5:08 a.m. in the morning of our 100th day, speeding into Baffin Bay, the spray from our twin hulls made rainbows in the sun as we completed the first sail-powered voyage through the Northwest Passage. We journeyed through these waters on its terms and only tried to respond to its challenges. We were fortunate to have survived those treacherous waters.

In my journal I wrote: "August 17th, 1988, 6:50 a.m.: I sit here at Button Point snug in the ruins of a Thule Inuit hut that is at least 400 years old: as old, in fact, as the dream of sailing the Northwest Passage. A four-foot-high wall of rock and whalebone protects me from the howling wind. The wall next to me is supported by a 100-pound bowhead whale skull, its powder-white surface is cracked and crevassed by time. Orange lichen, which takes more than a century to grow, is creeping over its surface.

"The now open room is about twelve square feet, and I am sitting on the sleeping platform that runs around the perimeter, writing with bare hands, a luxury not often permitted on this voyage. I've been up for nearly twenty-three hours but I cannot sleep. The joy and excitement are too great.

"Our Hobie Cat rests on the rocky beach, the wind whistling in her rigging, her bright yellow hulls radiant in the morning sunlight. . ."

Lynn Maslen
Vegetation of the North: Perennial Phyto-Patterns

From a distance, northern landscapes are a mosaic of plant communities and land forms, the two inextricably connected. On closer investigation, individual species and the more detailed patterns they create become distinguishable. Whether photographed from a remote-sensing satellite, observed from an airplane, or discovered first-hand, vegetation patterns of varying scales and types are everywhere, patterns created by history, topography, soils, and climate.

Floristics

Canada's northern flora is characterized by two main features: relatively few species and a low degree of endemism. Compared to temperate or tropical regions, northern lands have a species-poor (simple) flora. In the Northwest Territories, for example, there are 1,113 vascular plant species, in the Yukon Territory approximately 1,250. By contrast, the island of Jamaica, covering an area less than a hundredth that of the NWT, hosts almost three times as many vascular species.

Nor are most of the resident species endemic to Canada's North. Many are circumpolar or circumboreal in distribution; that is, their range is more or less continuous across the Northern Hemisphere. A good example is fireweed, the territorial flower of the Yukon. Widespread throughout both territories, it is also found in Alaska and Eurasia. Tree species found in the North are, however, confined to North America, although most have closely related species that occupy similar ecological roles on other continents.

Furthermore, some "northern" species are not even restricted to northern climes. With respect to latitudinal distribution, four categories of plant species occur in the territories. These are (from north to south): *Arctic species*, those confined to the Arctic region, though often found further south in high altitude environments; *subarctic species*, those whose range is centred on the northern limit of forests; *boreal species*, those whose range is centred further south in the coniferous forest belt; and *temperate species*, those whose range extends into the North, but which are mainly confined to regions of grassland and broad-leaved forests. Roughly one-half of Canada's northern flora is composed of Arctic or subarctic species.

The depauperate nature and low endemism of Canada's northern flora is partly a result of the region's harsh growing conditions, but also partly a function of time. From a geological perspective, Canada's North is a very young landscape. Approximately 20,000 years ago, during the Pleis-tocene epoch, northern Canada, with the exception of a few ice-free refugia, was completely ice-covered. Maximum ice coverage during this glacial period occurred about 18,000 years ago and the ensuing deglaciation proceeded slowly, over millennia.

As a result, Canada's northern regions have been free of ice and glacial lakes for as little as a few thousand to a few hundred years. As climatic conditions ameliorated, species that had retreated south before the advancing ice now moved north again and those that had survived in refugia gradually expanded their ranges. It is generally agreed that of all species present in the North today, the Arctic species survived glaciation in northern refugia. The presence of the other three species types is thought to be a consequence of post-glacial northward migration. Both of these processes, range expansion and migration, are ongoing, resulting in increasingly wider distributions for some species.

Although the majority of species found in Canada's North are not unique, they are uniquely distributed, on both a large and small scale, since the vegetation patterns and plant communities here are products of the relationship between flora and environment. Canada's North is characterized by two distinct climatic zones, the Subarctic and the Arctic; each zone has a corresponding prevailing type of vegetation. The Subarctic is characterized by boreal forest, which is dominated by coniferous tree species. The Arctic is dominated by tundra, characterized by the absence of trees. In the NWT, these two climate-vegetation categories (*formations*) meet at the latitudinal treeline, which runs southeastward from the Mackenzie Delta in the northwest to the western shore of Hudson Bay at approximately latitude 60° North. The treeline, then, effectively dissects the NWT into a large, western, wooded region and an even larger, eastern, treeless region. These same two formations are present in the Yukon but there, Arctic tundra is restricted to a 50- to 100-kilometre-wide northern coastal strip.

Subarctic Zone
Boreal Forest

The transcontinental boreal forest, or taiga, is Canada's most widespread landscape. Covering large parts of most of the provinces and encompassing much of the territories, this coniferous forest is relatively homogeneous and simple in structure. The forest canopy comprises only a few needle-leaved tree species and is dominated by either spruce, pine, fir, larch, or combinations thereof. In some areas, depending on local conditions, broad-leaved trees such as birch, aspen, and alder may also be abundant. The understorey is typically quite open. Large shrubs are widely scattered, although low-growing shrubs may attain a greater density. Herbs are usually few in species and sparsely distributed, and the forest floor is covered with a thick layer of mosses or lichens. The soil is highly organic, often peaty. Bogs are a common local feature.

The presence of numerous berry-bearing shrubs, such as blueberry, crowberry, bearberry, and cranberry, is a distinctive feature of the boreal forest. In the fall the scarlet bearberries and bright red bog cranberries add singular highlights to the spectrum of autumnal colours. The berries provide abundant food for numerous species of birds and mammals, including humans. Harvesting these autumn fruits is a popular pursuit for northern residents.

In the boreal forest, often referred to as a "fire forest," naturally occurring forest fires have always been widespread and frequent; today fires sparked by humans are not uncommon. Natural selection therefore has favoured the perpetuation of species that are adapted to fire — species able to withstand a fire without serious damage, establish quickly on burned over areas, or both. Jack pine and black spruce are noteworthy examples of such pyric species. Both these coniferous species possess serotinous cones (that is, their cones remain on the trees, tightly closed, for indefinite periods), which open only in response to intense heat, such as that experienced during a fire. After a fire, the exposed seeds drop from the cones, ready to germinate, ensuring that the species present before the fire is also one of the first species to establish after the fire. Furthermore, seedlings of these conifers are well adapted to the exposed, warm, nutrient-rich soil that results from fire. Communities dominated by white spruce, which does not have serotinous cones, are often replaced by stands of either jack pine or black spruce following a fire. A mosaic of abruptly defined communities within one region can often be explained, at least in part, by examining the fire history of the region.

The wooded portions of the Yukon and Northwest Territories are also part of the boreal forest, but with a twist. They lie within the Canada's Subarctic zone. Plants growing in the Subarctic are subject to long, cold winters, and short, relatively warm summers, with long days and litte precipitation. Extreme temperature fluctuations are common in all seasons. Perhaps most importantly, the entire Subarctic is underlain by *permafrost*, a significant ecological factor. Permafrost is defined as any substrate (rock or soil) that remains at or below 0 °C for two or more consecutive years. Except for land in proximity to large rivers and lakes (which warm the surrounding substrate), all of the Northwest Territories and Yukon are underlain by permafrost. (In the most southern regions it is generally described as discontinuous, that is, absent in small pockets due to microclimate or soil conditions.) This permanently frozen substrate is overlain by an *active layer*, a layer of soil that thaws and refreezes on an annual basis in response to seasonal temperature variation. This layer, where all biological activity occurs, varies greatly in depth from a few centimetres to several metres, depending on a variety of factors such as soil texture and moisture, microtopography, aspect, vegetation cover, and

the amount of sunlight received at the soil surface.

The presence of permafrost greatly influences northern vegetation. The frozen ground prevents deep root penetration, therefore shallow rooting species, like black spruce, do best here. The contact between the active layer and the permafrost table acts as an impermeable barrier to soil moisture, often resulting in cold, water-logged soils. Permafrost also restricts the cycling of soil minerals, creating a relatively infertile growth medium. The annual freezing and thawing of the active layer leads to unstable soils that churn and heave, and can, in turn, uproot plants, particularly the vulnerable seedlings, snap ice-encased plant roots, and twist or otherwise deform long-lived plants such as trees.

Northwest Territories

In the NWT, boreal forest plant communities exhibit a distinct, zonal, distribution pattern corresponding roughly to latitude. From south to north the vegetation gradually changes from closed-canopied coniferous forest to open-canopied forest, which in turn gives way to a forest-tundra vegetation before grading into true arctic tundra. From the borders of Alberta and British Columbia to the south shore of Great Slave Lake, relatively dense closed-canopied forest prevails. Here boreal species are abundant and the flora is similar to that found in northern Alberta and Saskatchewan. Trees, particularly white spruce, attain a fairly large size, suitable in places for commercial purposes. The protected environment of the river valley and the ameliorating effect of the relatively warm, southern river water on permafrost allow this forest type to extend up the Mackenzie River Valley as far north as Great Bear River. Due to the closed nature of this forest, it is not universally considered to be true subarctic vegetation.

Northward, the forest changes considerably and becomes subarctic woodland. Trees become smaller and more sparsely scattered, the canopy more and more open. In the low Subarctic, white spruce and black spruce are the dominant species. White spruce favours drier upland sites, black spruce, wetter, lower-lying areas. Ericaceous (heath) shrubs, particularly Labrador tea, are common. Whereas in closed taiga the ground cover is primarily composed of feather mosses, in open taiga lichens are a more important feature of the forest floor; almost everywhere there is a patchy lichen cover so abundant that these forests are called subarctic lichen-woodlands. Further north, in the high Subarctic, drier upland sites are covered by thinner stands of spruce with a nearly continuous carpet of lichens featuring such species as *Cladonia mitis* and *Cladina rangiferina*.

Although a conspicuous component of most subarctic plant communities, lichens are often neglected in descriptions, perhaps because they are not well understood. They are frequently confused with mosses because of their similar growth forms but are in fact quite different from mosses and not even related. Members of the fungus kingdom, lichens are a unique entity, the result of a symbiotic association between algae and fungi. They thrive in northern regions because they are well adapted to the adverse, fluctuating conditions that characterize the North. In the event of drought or extreme low or high temperatures, lichens are able to lose their tissue water quickly, stop all metabolic processes, and pass through unfavourable periods in a quiescent state. Lichens are also well adapted to the long, dry subarctic summer days; they can absorb their meagre daily water requirements directly from the morning dew or from moisture in the air.

Furthermore, lichens are ecologically important to subarctic communities. Unlike most plants, many lichen species are able to transform, or fix, elemental nitrogen gas into a usable form. Fixed nitrogen, essential for plant growth, is typically in scare supply in northern soils. When lichens decompose, their fixed nitrogen returns to the soil and becomes available to other plant species. Lichen-woodlands are, moreover, vital winter habitat for barren-ground caribou with certain lichen species, such as *Cladonia stellaris*, comprising a high percentage of their winter diet. The common name for these species, "reindeer lichens," reflects their importance to caribou.

North and east of Great Slave Lake, these subarctic woodlands take on a new appearance, influenced by the underlying Precambrian Shield bedrock. The gently rolling terrain is sparsely covered with open-canopied spruce-lichen woodland; interrupted frequently by exposed rocky outcrops and dotted with innumerable, variably sized lakes. In the Yellowknife vicinity, on the north shore of Great Slave Lake, Precambrian rock outcrops dominate the landscape, and vegetation distribution patterns are strongly influenced by the availability, texture, and moisture-holding capacity of the soil. Shrubs, herbs, and mosses grow wherever soil depths permit, often in surprisingly shallow deposits, frequently at the bases of outcrops or in rocky crevices where organic material has accumulated. Scattered among the rocks, in the wetter depressions, *Sphagnum* mosses are commonly found in association with saxifrage, grasses, moisture-loving sedges, and horsetails. In the spring, the more uniform, open, boggy areas are dotted with flowering herbs, some with large, showy flowers, such as cloudberry and the delicate *Parnassius*.

One visually striking component of this landscape is the epilithic lichens. Most of the exposed rock surfaces have been colonized by several species of lichens. Once smooth, barren surfaces have, over time, become encrusted with a patchwork of lichen species, each uniquely shaped, shaded, and textured. Distribution of species is influenced by the parent material (whether or not the rock is acidic or basic), moisture and light availability, and time elapsed since the rock was exposed. These patterned rocks are undoubtedly a distinguishing feature of the area. During the midnight twilight of midsummer, the highly reflective light-green and yellow lichens endow the rocky landscape with an eerie crepuscular glow.

Also in this region, jack pine, though nearing the northern limit of its range, is commonly found in stands on glacial deposits of sandy or coarse soils. These almost pure stands of pine have little understorey vegetation but often support scattered bilberry or bearberry shrubs and a patchy mat of lichens. Jack pine was recently adopted as the official tree of the Northwest Territories, and although not as ubiquitous as some other species, its adaptability and tenacity render it a fitting territorial symbol.

Forest-Tundra Ecotone

In the high Subarctic, woodland communities become increasingly more open and are frequently interspersed with patches of tundra. Further north still, the tundra patches become larger and more frequent, until finally trees can no longer be found. This zone of transition from woodland to tundra is referred to as the forest-tundra ecotone. Viewed from the air the transition can appear quite abrupt, but in some areas the ecotone encompasses a band as wide as 100 kilometres. In places, forest communities will extrude quite far into the tundra, their distribution dictated by the location of protected habitats such as river valleys. The actual treeline, which lies somewhere within this band, is therefore not really as clearly demarcated as its descriptor suggests. The exact point where trees cease to occur is often difficult to determine, and at these high latitudes, even the definition of a tree may at times be problematic. Species routinely classified elsewhere as trees may occur here (in a favoured locality) but may be dwarfed or decumbent, no longer resembling what we generally recognize as a tree. Should a spruce or birch individual that is less than one metre tall with a trunk diameter of six centimetres really be considered a tree?

While species composition in this mosaic of forest and tundra is fairly consistent, species dominance changes considerably — an expression of several interrelated factors: past and present micro-climate, topography, edaphic (soil) conditions, fire, and glacial history. In general, willows and birches are conspicuous components of the ecotone, usually in the form of tall shrubs. The tree species found at the edge of this zone vary locally; each species of tree has its own treeline, reflecting different growth requirements. On a macro-scale, white spruce is usually the most northerly tree species. However, in the east, north of Manitoba, the treeline commonly consists of larch and black spruce. Once again, lichens carpet the forest floor. Epiphytic lichens are also common, black spruce trunks and branches their favoured habitat.

The position of the forest border, and the factors governing it, have been the subject of much scientific research and debate. It is now generally accepted that its position is in some way a consequence of climate; exactly how is not really understood. On a macro-scale, the treeline is coincident with a number of climatic factors, such as the summer position of the frontal zone that separates Arctic air masses, and the 10 °C July isotherm (a line joining points where the mean July temperature is 10 °C). Low summer precipitation has also been postulated as a major factor limiting tree growth. Whatever the case, fossil records indicate that the treeline is a dynamic phenomenon. Despite the impression of timelessness that expansive northern landscapes leave, vegetation patterns are not static; the position of the treeline has shifted repeatedly over millennia, probably in response to changing climates. Fire may also have played an important role by removing trees that may never re-establish.

Yukon Territory

In the Yukon, plant distribution is strongly influenced by the mountainous topography that dominates the territory. Most of the Yukon Territory is characterized by fairly open white spruce/paper birch forests. Dry upland areas and all but the north-facing slopes are dominated by these two species. Numerous shrubs, such as alder, wild rose, shrubby cinqfoil, and cranberries, are frequently present. Forests on the colder, north-facing slopes are dominated by black spruce, commonly associated with willows, alders, Labrador tea, and numerous other shrubs. Relative to the NWT, a few notable differences occur in Yukon boreal forest. Larch is quite rare, and jack pine is absent — its niche filled by lodgepole pine, which occurs in the southern interior. Alpine fir, absent from the NWT, is also locally common in southern mountain ranges.

At higher elevations, forested slopes generally give way to alpine tundra. A trip along the Dempster Highway, Canada's northernmost major road, reveals this altitudinal pattern and offers awe-inspiring vistas of open, diverse country. The highway begins in the forested region near Dawson City and cuts through the Ogilvie Mountains, Eagle Plain, and the Richardson Mountains before crossing the continental divide into the NWT. At these high elevations a multitude of plant communities exist, rich in shrubs, herbaceous species, mosses, and lichens. The distribution of species is strongly influenced by the texture, temperature, and moisture of soil and by wind and slope aspect. Micro-conditions dictate species distribution and communities often change abruptly with topographical features. At very high altitudes, vegetation cover may be patchy, reflecting, among other factors, the harsh edaphic conditions. On the eastern slopes of the Richardson Mountains, trees are once again present and the remainder of the highway traverses various woodland communities until the road terminates in the town of Inuvik, NWT, just north of latitude 68° N. Most first-time visitors to this town are surprised to discover that it lies a few miles within the northern edge of the forest border. The moderating effect of the Mackenzie River allows trees and many other boreal species to extend this far north, almost to the Arctic Ocean. Many of the islands of the nearby Mackenzie River delta support dense, species-rich shrub communities.

The northern Yukon (that region beyond the Yukon's treeline at latitude 68° N.) exhibits yet a different phyto-pattern, again owing largely to climate and topography. Here, alpine, Arctic, and subarctic communities meet. The interior basin, Old Crow Flats, is separated from the coastal plain by several mountain chains, and there is a corresponding vegetation zonation. The relatively warm, wet interior basin is occupied by a variety of sedge and shrub communities. In the rugged mountains to the north, growing conditions are harsher and high elevations support only sparsely scattered communities of hardy species such as saxifrage and alpine bearberry. The coastal plain, or north slope, has a more continuous vegetative cover and is classified as Low-Arctic tundra. Sedge tussocks, primarily cottongrass, and low shrubs figure prominently in these communities. In this region, a refugium during Pleistocene glaciation, true arctic species are common, such as Saxifraga foliosa and the grass Alopecurus alpina. Wetlands, with distinctive communities of sedges and mosses, are widespread on the coastal plain. The western portion of the Yukon coastal plain is an important calving area for the Porcupine caribou herd.

Arctic Zone

Most of the eastern, mainland NWT and all of the northern archipelago lie within the Arctic tundra formation although, strictly speaking, not all of this area supports tundra vegetation. The terms arctic and tundra are often used incorrectly. In the broadest sense, tundra is a treeless but vegetated level to undulating plain. The Arctic is that region lying north of the northernmost extension of trees; not all of the Arctic is vegetated. The prevailing phyto-pattern in this climatic zone is one of generally declining plant cover and a reducing number of species as one moves northward, a pattern reflecting the harsh growing conditions in the Far North.

The Arctic is characterized by long, very cold winters with little sunlight, short, cool summers with nearly continuous daylight, and year-round strong winds that dry the soil and carry abrasive material such as soil particles and snow crystals. The entire zone is underlain with permafrost, usually very close to the soil surface. In spring, rapid snowmelt releases short-lived flushes of water, the most important annual source of moisture available to plants. Very low precipitation during the rest of the summer ensures an extremely dry growing season. However, even in wetter localities, conditions are still severe. High moisture content in the active layer can retard soil warming, often causing summer soil temperatures to hover just above freezing.

Such unfavourable conditions have, nevertheless, been exploited by a wide variety of plants with an astonishing array of strategies that enables them to survive and, in most cases, thrive. Many Arctic species have thick waxy cuticles that reduce the amount of water that would otherwise be lost due to constant, dessicating winds and twenty-four-hour sunlight. Stems and leaves of many species are covered with "hairs" that afford protection against extremely cold temperatures. Many species achieve additional protection from the wind by not shedding dead stems and leaves but retaining them to form a dense insulating layer that envelopes the living parts of the plant.

Most shrubs grow very low to the ground and have either short, erect branches, or long, creeping stems. This minimizes damage from the fierce winds and increases the likelihood of securing the protection of the thin snow cover during the winter months. The arctic willow, unlike its more southern sister species, has prostrate, never erect, stems, and seldom exceeds a height of a few centimetres. Caespitose plants, those that grow in dense tufts, and cushion plants (low-growing, compact plants with thick overlapping leaves) are also common. Both growth forms help reduce wind velocities near the ground and decrease the amount of leaf surface exposed to evaporative winds.

Polar adaptations also include special reproductive strategies. Most Arctic species are perennials and many of these circumvent the short growing season by producing next year's flower buds during the autumn or by initiating growth in early spring when temperatures are still below freezing. Some even begin growing while still buried beneath the snow. Though many Arctic species reproduce through seed, most perennials are also capable of vegetative reproduction that requires less energy and can be achieved under less favourable environmental conditions, thus increasing the chance of successful reproduction. Most species have extensive networks of creeping stems, underground shoots, or rhizomes, from which new plants can sprout. Some species may only reproduce through seed occasionally, in very exceptional years.

Nevertheless, many Arctic forbs also invest much energy in sexual reproduction and have flowers specially adapted to capitalize on the short season. Arctic poppies and mountain avens (the territorial flower of the NWT) both have large, parabolic-shaped flowers that act as a radiation trap. The flowers maintain their orientation toward the sun throughout the course of the long day, maximizing received radiation. The parabolic shape reflects solar rays toward the centre of the flower, raising the temperature of the reproductive organs and increasing the chance of producing viable seeds in such a short summer. Arctic heather has much smaller, bell-shaped flowers that hang down toward the soil and trap heat as it rises from the ground.

Plants growing in such harsh conditions respond readily to any factor that can ameliorate local growing conditions. Available moisture is of crucial importance, particularly in the High Arctic, where only a few centimetres of rain may fall during the summer. The interplay between topography and soil moisture is largely responsible for the mosaic pattern of Arctic vegetation. A well-drained, warm hillside may be carpeted with species that thrive on dry soil, such as lapland rhododendron or purple saxifrage, with the base of the hill supporting a community that flourishes in moist conditions: a dense mat of mosses interspersed with sedges and willows, for instance.

Other favourable habitats include protected river valleys, crevices of rocks, bases of cliffs where temperatures are higher due to reflected sunlight, and the periphery of late-melting snow patches that provide a more continuous moisture supply. The paucity of suitable plant habitat results in dense clustering of many individuals and species around favourable sites. The brevity of arctic growing seasons, the short-lived moisture supply, and this clustered plant distribution culminate in a widely synchronous spring blooming. Summer in the Arctic is heralded by a profusion of colourful wildflowers, which, in some localities, completely cloak the earth, belying the severity of conditions.

It is widely accepted that the Canadian Arctic has three distinct vegetation types or zones, although the names given to them by botanists vary. One very descriptive classification, based largely on plant cover, is that of tundra, polar semi-desert, and polar desert. Tundra is the collective name given to a mosaic of treeless, low-growing (usually less than fifty centimetres tall) plant communities that provide a more or less continuous plant cover. Such communities are typically found in the Low Arctic (mainland Arctic and parts of the southern Arctic islands). In the early exploration days, Europeans labelled this seemingly inhospitable region the Barren Grounds, a misleading name that does not do the landscape justice.

The Low Arctic is far from barren as tundra communities can, in places, form a very dense plant cover, capable of supporting vast numbers of caribou and other wildlife species. Many plant species, particularly the lichens and mosses, which also occur in other vegetation types, are able in the extreme conditions of the Arctic to dominate plant communities. On the mainland, dense dwarf-shrub tundra is widespread, dominated by shrubby birch and willows. Further north, shrubs become less common, eventually giving way to communities of grasses, sedges, and flowering forbs such as moss-campion, mountain avens, and saxifrage.

Polar semi-desert, which dominates the southern part of the Arctic archipelago (the Mid-Arctic), is also a mosaic of similar but less productive communities, providing a less continuous vegetative cover. Here, as much as 50 per cent of the land may be barren, depending on local conditions. Cushion plants, grasses, lichens, and some forbs are particularly common in polar semi-desert communities.

In the High Arctic, where annual rainfall is often less than fifteen centimetres, the polar desert is the true barren ground, with only a very thin, patchy plant cover. Where present at all, the vegetation is typically a single layer of lichens, mosses, and liverworts that closely hug the ground. The more protected sites may support a scattering of cushion plants, grasses, and sedges.

Elements of all three vegetation types may occur anywhere in the Arctic, but as a general rule, they follow this latitudinal zonation. As in the Subarctic, the zones are most often joined by transitional gradients rather than separated by distinct boundaries. The position of the zones generally conforms to climatic parameters.

Thermal Oases

Scattered throughout the High Arctic polar desert are a number of small thermal oases, anomalously warm areas that support relatively lush vegetation. Very simply put, the influence of prominent topographical features on several climatic variables produces a very local but significant increase in summer temperatures, resulting in a warmer, longer growing season. If sufficient moisture is present, as is the case in low-lying areas, this warming allows the formation of communities more similar to those found in the Low Arctic than those in the surrounding jejune landscape. Though rare (accounting for less than 5 per cent of land area in the High Arctic), oases are exceedingly important biologically and therefore worthy of attention and protection. Wherever they occur, these exceptionally productive areas form the bases of food chains and so support a multitude of species that otherwise could not survive at these high latitudes. The oases also provide important nesting habitat for a range of birds as diverse as snowy owls and red-throated loons.

One such oasis is Polar Bear Pass, a National Wildlife Area on Bathurst Island that supports more than 350 plant species and is home to lemmings, Arctic hares, Arctic foxes, caribou, and muskoxen. Lake Hazen, on northern Ellesmere Island, is Canada's most northerly thermal oasis, at approximately latitude 82° N. Here, daily maximum summer temperatures often exceed 10°C, far higher than temperatures in other localities of similar latitude.

Patterned Ground

Throughout the Arctic, and less so the Subarctic, in certain localities the spectacular phenomenon of patterned ground occurs. Bare or thinly covered soils often display geometrical, repetitive patterns in the earth: mounds, stripes, circles, rectangles, or polygons. The specific pattern shape and structure vary between sites, usually according to the soil moisture content of the area. These almost perfectly geometrical, consistent patterns are formed by a network of trenches or ridges, or marked out by stones. They are common in wet, coastal areas but rare in very dry ground. The genesis of each pattern type differs, and although it has been heavily researched much remains unclear. However, as a general rule they result from differential freezing and thawing of soils, differential movement of soil particles, or a combination of both. The scale of these patterns ranges from less than a metre to as large as thirty metres.

The formation of patterned ground produces a variety of environmental conditions available for exploitation by plants. Those spots where most soil movement occurs remain uncolonized due to the continuous disturbance, but the more stable areas provide a range of microhabitats that plants selectively colonize. As a result, the ground pattern is often accentuated by a corresponding vegetation pattern. One common Arctic feature, sorted polygons, has unstable barren centres but the ridges support a thick cover of mosses, sedges, grasses, or even shrubs, depending on the precise conditions or the size of the ridges. In more stable areas, plant cover may be more continuous, but differential moisture conditions still produce an observable pattern. Wetter areas, such as the low centres of polygons, support an assemblage of species that is entirely different from that found on the drier, ridged perimeter. In the alpine tundra of the Richardson Mountains, the underlying patterned ground is beautifully manifested by distinct, coterminous, circular groupings of shrubs, herbs, and mosses.

Botanic Gardens

In Whitehorse, the Yukon Gardens offers an opportunity to learn more about local flora. These privately owned botanical gardens are designed to display examples of both indigenous flora and introduced species. Numerous northern species, temperate garden flowers, and a vegetable garden with typical, more southern produce all flourish under the same conditions, illustrating that the long summer days can compensate for a short growing season. However, most of the introduced species are annuals that must be replanted every spring, as, unlike the native species, they cannot cope with the rigours of a northern winter.

In Yellowknife, a local charitable organization, Ecology North, is hoping to establish more traditional botanic gardens that would serve not only as a tourist attraction, exhibiting local flora, but also as an herbarium, with preserved and catalogued specimens of northern indigenous species. Long-term plans include species from other northern countries, interpretive displays highlighting the various adaptations that plants employ for survival under boreal conditions, and a seed bank for the preservation of endangered tropical plant species. (Seeds could be carefully stored in capsules and buried underground where permafrost would maintain them in a dormant but viable state.) This is still in the proposal stage, and if formalized, these ideas would take many years to implement. Hopefully, however, the initial phases will be operating soon.

First-time visitors to Canada's North are often struck by the vastness and apparent uniformity of the landscape. However, familiarity breeds a keen appreciation for the diversity of the terrain and its vegetation. The magnitude and variety of this region renders description, in anything but broad generalities, a formidable task. More detailed investigation will, however, yield fascinating discoveries. Be they trees, shrubs, or lichens, in communities or in isolation, plants interact with their environment to form subtle and striking vegetation patterns — those integral and unique elements of northern landscapes.

Ethel Blondin
The Dene and Métis

> Our Dene nation is like this great river. It has been flowing before any of us can remember. We take our strength, our wisdom and our ways from the flow and direction which has been established for us by ancestors we never knew, ancestors of a thousand years ago. This wisdom flows through us to our children and our grandchildren, to generations we will never know. We will live out our lives as we must, and we will die in peace because we will know that our people and this river will flow on after us. *(Frank T'Seleie, Fort Good Hope chief, to Berger Inquiry)*

North America is often referred to as the New World. In comparison to the Old World of Europe, which gave birth to the modern nations of North America, the phrase is accurate. But for the aboriginal inhabitants of the western Arctic, the Dene and Métis, North America is not the new world. It is their only world.

The Dene do not measure their occupancy of the western Arctic in terms of centuries as the European cultures do, but in millennia. The arrival of the Dene in what is today the Northwest Territories predates recorded history. While Athens basked in its glory as the cradle of Western democracy and the Roman Empire rose and fell, the Dene had already been living in the western Arctic for thousands of years. By the time Christopher Columbus arrived in North America in 1492 and mistakenly labelled its inhabitants Indians, the "New World" of the Dene was nearly 10,000 years old.

The Dene are believed to have migrated to North America from Siberia across the former Bering Sea land bridge. The exact dates of the migration are unknown but the Dene and Métis of today are direct descendants of these original inhabitants of the land of the western Arctic. The world they came upon was one of extremes. The winters are long, cold, and dark. The summers are brief but intense, with the sun rarely setting during the height of the season. The Mackenzie River flows through the heart of Dene and Métis land, which is bordered by the barren grounds to the east and the Mackenzie Mountains to the west. Animals such as caribou and moose provided the base of their lives as a source of food and clothing. The Chipewyan, South Slavey, North Slavey, Dogribs, and Gwich'in, along with the Métis, are the direct descendants of the original inhabitants of this land. Together, the five former groups form what is known as the Dene Nation.

To understand the Dene and Métis one must understand the importance they invest in the land. After thousands of years living intimately with the land, the Dene have maintained a tie that has been lost by the vast majority of humanity. There is no feeling for a Dene or Métis like living in the bush. Everything in the Dene's environment is imbued with life, including the air they breathe and the water they drink. Land, water, air, animals, and people are one organic unit in the Dene world. Land is seen as a gift from the creator that should never be abused. If part of this unit is harmed the entire system begins to fail. This gift is becoming harder to hold onto because of the abuse heaped upon it by pollution. This abuse is akin to assault for the Dene, both to the land and to themselves.

Every human in the Dene and Métis view of life is to be valued and respected. Human life is sacred. The spirituality of the Dene forbids people from prejudging others — people have no history upon first meeting, they must be seen for what they are.

The Dene's unity with their environment and their traditional lifestyle were unalterably changed by a very simple act — the signing of the organizing charter for the Hudson's Bay Company. In 1670, Charles II of England gave the "Company of Adventurers" a charter granting them title to the land encompassed by the rivers flowing into Hudson Bay, a total of 1.5 million square miles. The charter didn't touch the Mackenzie Valley, the heart of Dene territory, but it set in motion the drive into the interior of the continent for fur-bearing animals.

The granting of this charter cannot be overestimated in the history of the Dene. A foreign king, with no right to grant title to the land of North America other than a misguided belief in his divine right, set in motion the fur trade in northern Canada. No longer would the Dene be hunters alone, following the migration of the caribou to satisfy their needs. The Dene would become intimately linked to the search for fur to satisfy European clothing tastes. In the wake of the fur trade would come missionaries, gold seekers, and government officials.

Several explorers made their way into Dene territory but the man whose legacy is still most prominent is Sir Alexander Mackenzie. In 1789 he canoed down the Deh Cho (which now bears his name as the Mackenzie River) in search of the west coast of Canada. His journey established the path for travel into Dene lands and the establishment of fur-trading posts.

> In the old days we lived in tents made of twelve moosehides with room for three families. We made it smokey at night to keep the mosquitos out. There were so many mosquitos that when we moved camp, we had to hold up a burning branch. It was a hard life. We didn't even have a decent blanket. In winter we wore rabbit skin hats, pants and jacket and hide mitts. Even when it was very cold we still went out

to check our snares . . . . It was a hard life but a good life. *(Philip Simba, Dene elder)*

It is no longer fashionable in Europe to make a living from the trapping of furs. To many Europeans there is no difference between trapping fur and working in a bank for a living, and in their view the former is morally indefensible. But trapping is more than a way to make a living for the Dene and Métis. Even before Alexander Mackenzie introduced trapping as an economic pursuit it was a way of life. Animals provided clothing. One group of Dene, the Hare (North Slavey), even took their name from the rabbits that were the source of most of their clothing. Trapping is a seasonal, cultural, and social pursuit. It is something the Dene and Métis feel will be there for them as long as they treat the animals with respect.

In a world of high unemployment there are people who have known nothing but life on the land. Through a combination of hunting, fishing, gathering, and trapping the Dene were able to live. Even when the price of furs dropped they could still clothe themselves and their families. Trapping ordered the cycles of Dene life until the 1960s and still exerts a large influence on many today. In the fall the women prepared for the upcoming hunt by weaving snowshoes and *mukluks* while men prepared and loaded the sleds and tended to the dogs. People only came out of the bush to bring back furs and re-equip themselves in December. January to March was the best season for fur because this was the coldest time of year, and the families of the community returned to the bush. They came back in April or May to hunt for beaver or muskrat. In the summer the families returned to the land once again to set up fish camps, which provided food for the summer.

> My husband's family taught me how to work and I learned how to make drymeat and dryfish and how to tan hides and set snares, I also learned how to sew and do quill work and embroidery. I love to sew, especially with quills. Once I was able to do all these traditional tasks . . .. I was much more confident. *(Helen Canadien, Dene elder)*

Life on the land influenced the organization of Dene culture. Traditional leaders were semi-hereditary chiefs. They were always chosen by consensus, usually because they were good hunters and trappers who could support their communities and speak on their behalf to outsiders. It was no small responsibility to be a leader, and the chiefs of Dene bands were always respected for their abilities. The Canadian government has done away with that system and substituted elections, but a sense of consensus still exists among Dene and Métis communities when they choose their leaders.

No written code of laws existed to rule Dene communities, but if there was an affront to the community there was a gathering of the chief and an unofficial council of advisers. Major issues were discussed openly and directly, unfettered by legality and bureaucracy.

The unofficial council of advisers was usually made up of elders. The role of elders in modern Dene communities is in flux, but elders traditionally were teachers who helped to raise children and passed on the knowledge of the Dene. They also oversaw the rites of passage for children.

> I was brought up the traditional way. When a girl reached puberty in those days, she had to leave the camp and live alone, sometimes for as long as two months. Then if a man spoke to you your mother would give you a good beating . . . . My mother would always say, don't look at that man, he's not providing for you . . . . Don't listen to them. That's how she tried to protect me. *(Liza Loutit, Dene elder)*

When girls reached puberty they were sent into the bush alone. People were not allowed to see them and they were to have no contact at all with men. During that time the young woman would go about her traditional activities of hauling water, chopping wood, gathering berries, and learning to sew. An elder brought her out of the bush and gave her an offering of blueberries and a cup of water.

Boys on the brink of manhood were required to kill a moose or caribou to cross the threshold into adulthood and earn his rifle and shell. Once he had killed his first big game a young man would serve it to an elder in the community out of a sense of honour.

The next step for young Dene was marriage. Traditional marriages were often arranged by elders, who were responsible for ensuring that blood lines didn't mingle. Once Christianity had arrived, the Church often only anointed those who had already been chosen by arrangement, thus giving special sanction to the traditional marriage. Today, the traditional marriage has all but disappeared and there are an alarming number of common-law arrangements. Elders still prefer to see marriages sanctified because it is the best contract for marriage and best for the family.

> Then my father suggested I marry and have children. He said he would look for a wife for me. He found a woman who was pitiful. She had no parents and was homeless. I married her and since then I have worked very hard. *(Baptiste Gargan, Dene elder)*

The traditional roles of Dene men and women could be viewed today as oppressive. But it was understood by a husband and wife that they shared a burden, a burden to survive. They were responsible for supplying the family with food, shelter, protection, and transportation. It was understood their conflicts were not about their roles but how they dealt with the outside world and its challenges. Both sexes worked equally hard. Husband and wife were part of an extended family with support from elders in the community. Children were very much loved and accepted by the community. Becoming a godparent was a special responsibility. In many ways the entire community was one large family. Customary adoption was viewed as a way to keep a child in the family and the child was always given to someone who was trusted. That type of family now faces extreme pressures. Extended families are disappearing and the role of the elder with traditional knowledge in a world where the wage economy is dominant is diminishing. There is a high incidence of single-parent families.

> After I was married I had fifteen children. I have only five boys and two girls left to me now. The worst time in my life was when I came close to death. I was pregnant and went out to check my snares. I became ill and my baby was born dead on the trail. I was taken to the mission and I stayed there for a week and I recovered. *(Adeline Constant, Dene elder)*

Certain people played special roles in the communities. Midwives represented the full cycle of Dene life. Children were born into their hands and the same midwives (usually elders) dressed people when they died. Spiritual leaders provided protection for people in many areas of their lives. They prayed over water to purify it for use or burned spruce boughs to purify the air before a storm.

Medicine people also played special roles. Medicine power was respected and coveted. It was believed that certain sorts of medicines were possessed by a small number of special people. It is rarely spoken of by the Dene because others often belittle its value. Indeed, to speak of medicine power is taboo because of its sacred nature.

The Métis emerged as part of the Native community with the fur trade. The offspring of white men and Native women, they developed their own distinct culture, which was nonetheless tied to the land. Today the Métis and Dene are intricately woven together, often being brother and sister, husband and wife, grandparents and grandchildren.

The introduction of the fur trade also brought Christianity. Although Catholicism today is the dominant religion of the Dene, there are mixed feelings about the effect of Christianity. The philosophy of cherishing one's fellow man is easily accepted by the Dene. But experiences with the Church have often marred these messages. The control exercised by priests and nuns is resented in many ways, yet the contributions of various missionaries, such as Petitot and Stringer, are recognized.

The ambivalence felt toward the Church's role in Dene cul-

ture can be directly traced to the establishment of missionary schools in the western Arctic. Children were separated from their families for ten months a year and often longer. The separation of the child from the family was very traumatic. There are adults today forever marked by that experience. People have had to rebuild their lives, and while many have endured, many others have not. It is hard to explain the effect residential schools can have on Dene and Métis children. Familiar with nothing other than the freedom of the bush, where there were no restrictions other than those set by nature, the children were thrust into an extremely disciplined and often harsh environment. It was a culture shock for the young Native students taken from the bush and sent to the mission schools of Inuvik, Fort Providence, Fort Simpson, or Fort Smith. Children often lost their language, the only way to communicate with their parents. While many came out of these schools better prepared to deal with the modern world than their parents, the often harsh and insensitive treatment of the schoolmasters was a poor substitute for the warm and loving experience children have with their parents. Only the strongest students were able to hold onto their culture.

> My happiest time of my life was raising my family in the bush. We had to move into town so the children could attend school. Since that time it has become harder and harder for us to return to our way of life. *(Joseph Sabourin, Dene elder)*

Today the outlook for Dene and Métis who haven't retained their ties with the land is bleak. Alcoholism, drug abuse, and domestic violence are common in most Native communities. Unemployment is often over 50 per cent in the communities where there are few jobs. Those who survive are the ones who have held onto their heritage with the land or who have adjusted to mainstream society despite all odds.

The current predicament of the Dene and Métis stems primarily from two treaties signed with Canadian government less than a century ago. The treaties — Treaty 8 and Treaty 11 — are just two of more than 400 the British and Canadian governments signed with Native people. Treaty 8 was signed in 1899 and covered the area inhabited by the Chipewyan south of Great Slave Lake. Treaty 11 was signed in 1921 to cover the remaining land used by the Dene and Métis in the Mackenzie Valley.

The treaties are held up, paradoxically, both as examples of broken promises and as the basis of a better future for northern Natives. The chiefs who negotiated the treaties considered them to be covenants of friendship between separate and sovereign nations. The treaties were meant to guarantee the Dene's right to the land "as long as this land shall last," in the words of one government agent. But the federal government has used the treaties to strip the Dene of the right to govern their own lives. In the eyes of the government, Dene became wards of the state who are granted privileges instead of people with inherent rights. The treaties and later legislation also drove wedges within the Dene community, setting up artificial divisions based on who has "status" as an Indian and who, as a result, would receive government largesse. Until 1960 an act as simple but as fundamental as casting a ballot in a national election stripped a Dene of Indian status. The Métis were not even recognized by the treaties. They were derisively known as half-breeds.

> And the Indian agent said, "As long as the sun shines and the river flows this is your land to hunt on forever . . . .. This land is yours. As long as we pay the treaty, nothing is going to change." "If this is so, we will take the treaty," the chiefs said. *(Johnny Jean Marie Beaulieu, witness to Treaty 8)*

The term "treaty" is actually misleading because treaties imply an agreement between equal parties. Dene leaders viewed them as such, but the federal government used the treaties to serve its own aim of pushing its control farther north in Canada. The treaties do renounce the Dene's aboriginal right to the land, but the treaties are written in very legalistic English, which few white laymen, let alone unschooled Dene, would have understood. Dene chiefs accepted government assurances, through interpreters, that the treaties were simply friendship agreements allowing whites the right to use their land.

Both treaties were negotiated by the government for economic reasons. The frenzied search for gold in the Yukon Territory in the late 1890s led many white prospectors through the lower Mackenzie district. With the possibility of large gold finds looming, the government sought a treaty giving it control over the development of the land. This led to Treaty 8 in 1899. Economic concerns prompted the government to sign Treaty 11 in 1921 for the remainder of the Dene lands. The Northwest Territories had long been known to contain oil deposits but the discovery of major fields at Norman Wells gave the government the impetus it needed to negotiate another treaty.

Once the Dene discovered what they had signed it was too late. Rights to hunt and trap — the rights the government had promised to protect for eternity — were restricted. Game laws were soon enacted preventing the Dene from hunting, fishing, and trapping as they had for thousands of years. At the same time government legislation would prevent them from enjoying the basic rights of other citizens.

The condition of the Dene worsened terribly after the treaties. Smallpox, measles, Spanish flu, and particularly tuberculosis ravaged the population through the 1920s, culminating in a flu epidemic in 1928. By 1937 the Dene or-

ganized themselves to boycott the receipt of treaty payments at Fort Resolution. They received some minor concessions but it was too late to rebuke the treaties themselves.

> While all the afflicted whites finally recovered, the swift and savage scourge claimed a terrible rate of mortality amongst the poor natives. It gave little or no warning . . . .. Corporal Halliday and Constable Jack Emerson found a Yellowknife village deserted with thirty starving dogs left behind. When they made a patrol to Goulet's camp at the Gros Cap they discovered twenty-six Indians had died of the plague the seven survivors having fled in panic . . . . *(Jean Godsell, wife of a Hudson's Bay Company inspector in the 1920s)*

These treaties, however, have become the basis for the Dene's renewed claims to their land. In 1973, sixteen chiefs filed a caveat in the Supreme Court of the Northwest Territories laying claim to 450,000 square miles. The claim was judged valid by Justice William Morrow and now forms the basis of the Dene and Métis land claim negotiations with the federal government. The Indian agents who negotiated the treaties thought the chiefs were uneducated but their foresight was prophetic. The work of the original treaty chiefs stood up in court and has formed the basis of the modern land claim negotiations, which speaks well of people who were considered savages.

The modern political consciousness of the Dene/Métis began to emerge in the 1960s. Beginning with the Red Power movement traditional chiefs and young leaders such as James Wah-Shee, Georges Barnaby, and Georges Erasmus began to test the limits of government control over their lives. White advisers were very influential in the beginning but the Native leaders soon began to develop their own positions. The result was the creation of the Indian Brotherhood in the early 1970s. It was succeeded by the Dene Nation and the Dene Declaration of 1977. The declaration proclaimed to the government that the Dene were a nation of people distinct and unique to the western Arctic. Government officials ridiculed this concept of a nation but the Dene today are known by no other name than the Dene Nation.

A galvanizing force for these Dene and Métis leaders was an inquiry into a proposal to run a gas pipeline down the Mackenzie Valley in the mid-1970s. The federal government appointed Mr. Justice Thomas Berger in 1974 to review the proposal and, government officials hoped, give quick approval to the project, which would unalterably change the lives of Dene and Métis.

A consortium of twenty-seven Canadian and American companies planned to build a 3,860-kilometre gas pipeline from Prudhoe Bay in Alaska across the northern Yukon to the

Mackenzie Delta and down the Mackenzie Valley. To the government's surprise, Berger expanded the nature of his inquiry by travelling up and down the Mackenzie Valley and delta for three years, visiting the Dene and Métis in their own communities and soliciting their views on the effect the multi-billion-dollar project would have on their villages and traditional lives. Meetings were held informally in community halls and schools with elders given a chance, often for the first time, to express their views on the actions of the government directly to its representative. Berger saw the project as yet another attempt by the government to absorb and assimilate the Dene and Métis into mainstream white culture. To the surprise of many, he recommended a moratorium on a pipeline through the Mackenzie Valley for ten years until the Dene and Métis had a chance to settle their land claims.

> For us in the [Mackenzie] valley here, it's a decision: do we want to continue on as Dene people? Or do we want to forget that and become like everybody else? The decision before us, I think, has been made already, and people are acting on it. Clearly we want to remain as Dene people. We do not want to assimilate. *(Georges Erasmus, to the Berger Inquiry)*

The Berger Inquiry was a bombshell for the government and a major victory for the Dene and Métis. It allowed people to uncover their feelings about who they are, what they represent, and what the land means to them. Many people in the Northwest Territories have forgiven the Dene and Métis for their opposition to this massive economic development project. Now, the Dene and Métis recognize that they have equal rights to the economic fortunes of the land they live on. Their participation in the Berger Inquiry helped them lay the basis for the land claim — if it doesn't serve the interest of the majority of the people, what good is it? If a development doesn't improve lives the people won't be prepared to accept it.

The past two decades have been devoted to negotiating a land claim agreement that will give the Dene and Métis control of their destiny again. Aboriginal title remains to be defined by the courts but it has been recognized as a concept by the British and Canadian governments since 1763. The federal government, however, is trying to give the Dene and Métis what amounts to little more than trinkets and beads once again instead of recognizing their special rights to land. The original claim of 450,000 square miles has been whittled down to 70,000, and the $500 million offered by the federal government is meant to compensate for 200 years of occupancy of Dene lands.

The land claim will also give the Dene and Métis a say in the management of wildlife and the economic development of the land. But the land claim still presents problems to the Dene and Métis. It is being negotiated as an exchange of real estate and money. This is antithetical to the traditional view of land. The Dene believe they are the land. They often can't understand that, once the claim is signed, most of the western Arctic will belong to someone else.

But a land claim is only the beginning of the solution for the Dene and Métis, who are afflicted by many social problems. Gaining title to the land will help the Dene and Métis restore and strengthen their ties to the land. The final words on the world of the Dene and Métis come from Richard Nerysoo during his testimony before the Berger Inquiry:

> It is very clear to me that it is an important and special thing to be Indian. Being an Indian means being able to understand and live with this world in a very special way. It means living with the land, with the animals, with the birds and fish, as though they were your sisters and brothers. It means saying the land is an old friend and an old friend your father knew, your grandfather knew, indeed your people always have known . . . we see our land as much, much more than the white man sees it. To the Indian people our land really is our life. Without our land we cannot — we could no longer exist as people. If our land is destroyed, we too are destroyed. If your people ever take our land you will be taking our life.

(Researched by Craig Harper)

Northern Frontier

To commemorate the 200th anniversary of Sir Alexander Mackenzie's pioneer trip up the Deh Cho, the Mackenzie River, to the Arctic Ocean, a 1,700-kilometre international race organized by Dene leaders using voyageur canoes took place in July, 1989. *Hälle Flygare*

An old riverboat in Jean Marie River, located at the confluence with the Mackenzie. For thousands of years, Dene have lived on these lands. Today, the people of this tiny community still hunt and trap for their living. The people of this settlement have become well known for their fine porcupine quillwork. *Hälle Flygare*

Reliance, with a fur trade history dating back hundreds of years, is located at the far eastern end of McLeod Bay of Great Slave Lake. It is now an outpost camp and a staging point for barrenlands travellers. *Hälle Flygare*

Although Dene have lived and hunted in the Yellowknife area for thousands of years, a permanent settlement wasn't started until gold-bearing rocks in the Precambrian Shield were discovered here in 1934. Now a bustling capital city of 15,000, Yellowknife is a unique combination of the old and the new, of tradition and innovation. *Wolfgang Weber*

The Giant Yellowknife mine is one of two large gold-mining operations near Yellowknife. *Wolfgang Weber*

Pouring gold bullion at Giant; this mine mills over 300,000 tonnes of gold-bearing ore per year. *Gerhard Reimann*

The Legislative Assembly of
the Northwest Territories in
session. *Tessa Macintosh*

Dene interpreter Margaret
Mackenzie of Yellowknife.
Tessa Macintosh

Young Natives are learning
to administer their lands and
their lives. Dene surveyor
Henry Lockhart is working
at Snowdrift on the eastern
shores of Great Slave Lake.
Tessa Macintosh

The docks and channels of Hay River, a lively and modern community of 3,000 at the southern shore of Great Slave Lake, are a beehive of activity for the five months' shipping season here, servicing tugs and barges that provide transportation up the Mackenzie River and along the Arctic coast. Hay River is also the centre of the lake's commercial fishing industry, which supplies much of North America with lake whitefish. *Wolfgang Weber*

The church at Fort Providence, a scenic Dene community located high atop the banks of the Mackenzie. Here, Dene culture thrives, with an active Slavey language centre and with the traditional skill of Dene women who craft moosehair tufting and quillwork. *Wolfgang Weber*

Picnic in settlers' dresses on Canada Day on the banks of Slave River in Fort Smith, a community of 2,500 on the 60th parallel. It was once a crucial link in the chain of fur-trading posts along the Mackenzie route to the Arctic Ocean. *Wolfgang Weber*

(Upper):
Fort Resolution's forest fire crew. This small community is one of the oldest settlements of the area, with a history dating back to the building of a North West Company post in 1786. *Fran Hurcomb*

163

NWT Forestry Service helicopter scouts a bad forest fire. Bush fires in summer are frequently caused by lightning. *DIAND / Erik Watt*

Pulpit Rock marks The Gate, a break-through of the South Nahanni in a narrow hairpin turn in Third Canyon. *Wolfgang Weber*

The Cadillac Mine in the Mackenzie Mountains west of Fort Simpson was opened during the last silver boom. When the mine was ready to operate, world market prices dropped dramatically and the mining company had to close down. *Wolfgang Weber*

Alexandra Falls on the Hay
River plunges down
thirty-three metres. Many
highway travellers stop and
picnic here. *Wolfgang Weber*

Early fur traders had to portage twenty-five kilometres around the Slave River Rapids from Fort Fitzgerald to what is now Fort Smith. *Richard Harrington*

The fifteen-metre Louise Falls on the Hay, with a campground at riverside, is only nine kilometres from the tiny community of Enterprise. *Wolfgang Weber*

(Upper left):
Bison in Wood Buffalo
National Park.
Wolfgang Weber

(Upper right):
Wood bison are protected in
the Mackenzie Bison
Sanctuary, seen here at Caen
Lake. *Kim Poole*

(Lower left):
Lynx kitten in Mackenzie
Bison Sanctuary. *Kim Poole*

(Lower right):
The porcupine is found
everywhere in the Subarctic,
observed here with quills in
defensive position. *Kim Poole*

Bison herd in Wood Buffalo National Park. This park, at 44,800 square kilometres larger than Switzerland, is a subarctic wilderness of large rivers, bogs, forests, lakes, and meadows. Home to the bison, the park contains as well the last nesting grounds for the endangered whooping crane, is a breeding area for white pelicans, and further provides a habitat for 200 other species of birds and for large populations of beaver and muskrat.
Wolfgang Weber

Many Dene of Fort Liard, a lovely small community near the British Columbia border, prefer to spend the summer out in the bush hunting and fishing, as well as pursuing the ancient art of quillworking on birchbark baskets. Archeological work has shown the area to be one of the oldest continuously occupied aboriginal sites in the NWT, dating as far back as 9,000 years.
Wolfgang Weber

Dene hunter Charlie
Football of the upper Snare
River carrying caribou
home. *Wendy Stephenson*

Trapper's cabin at Snare
Lakes with beautifully
prepared furs of beaver,
marten, wolverine, Arctic
fox, wolf, and red fox.
Fran Hurcomb

"And the Indian agent said, 'As long as the sun shines and the river flows, this is your land to hunt on forever. . . .'" (Johnny Jean Marie Beaulieu, witness to Treaty 8, 1899). *Tessa Macintosh*

Trapper Philip Goulet repairs canoe on spring hunt, while grandsons are watching to learn.
Fran Hurcomb

(Upper):
Kevin Kodzin and Elvis Lafferty on wooden float in spring breakup on Snare Lake. *Wendy Stephenson*

Johnny Neyelle of Fort Franklin making snowshoes.
Tessa Macintosh

The fall-coloured treeline
(forest-tundra ecotone)
at Humpy Lake,
230 kilometres north of
Yellowknife. *Douglas Heard*

Osprey young on nest close
to one of the many lakes
northwest of Yellowknife.
Kim Poole

Common loon breeding at
Pontoon Lake in July.
Douglas Heard

Lunch break at the shores of Great Slave Lake: Jochen Rothmann and Alan Kaylo enjoy preparing the freshly caught fish, with onions, for a relaxing meal.
Wolfgang Weber

Trophy lake trout such as
these are found in many of
the large and small lakes of
the NWT. *Wolfgang Weber*

Bush pilot Ted Grant is
flying with his Twin Otter
tourists and hikers into the
mountains of Nahanni
country and taking freight
into the isolated settlements
of the Northwest.
Wolfgang Weber

177

The lively Dene community of Fort Simpson is set on a low island at the confluence of the Liard and Mackenzie rivers. It was built in 1804 as "Fort of the Forks" and later renamed for George Simpson, who amalgamated the North West and Hudson's Bay companies. Around 1828, the York boats began freighting on the Mackenzie and the settlement became the hub of fur trade activity for the Mackenzie Valley. Later, paddlewheelers stopped here, too. *Wolfgang Weber*

The ferry across the Liard connects Fort Simpson with the highways to the south. Ferry service between May and October is replaced by an ice bridge in winter. *Wolfgang Weber*

The captain of the Fort Simpson ferry. *Wolfgang Weber*

The Grotte Valerie, largest known cave of First Canyon, has become a graveyard for many Dall's sheep over the past 2,000 years. The sheep sometimes slip down the icefall or lose direction in the dark. *Wolfgang Weber*

Entrance to Grotte Valerie. *Wolfgang Weber*

Igloo Cave, one of hundreds of caves in the karst lands of Nahanni and Ram plateaus, is filled with stalagmites and stalactites of ice.
Wolfgang Weber

Dall's rams on the steep ridges of Ram Plateau. *Wolfgang Weber*

Sand blowouts: concentrated air currents of the Flat River Valley in Nahanni park have carved the soft sandstone rocks into picturesque pillars. *Wolfgang Weber*

The table mountains of Ram Plateau, northeast of Nahanni National Park, are a preferred habitat of Dall's sheep. Far below, the Ram River is winding its way around forest-covered hills.
Wolfgang Weber

Grizzly mother and her two
cubs walk along the upper
Thelon River.
Wendy Stephenson

Moose feed in summer on
aquatic plants.
Wolfgang Weber

Grizzly bear on the
Yellowknife River.
Wendy Stephenson

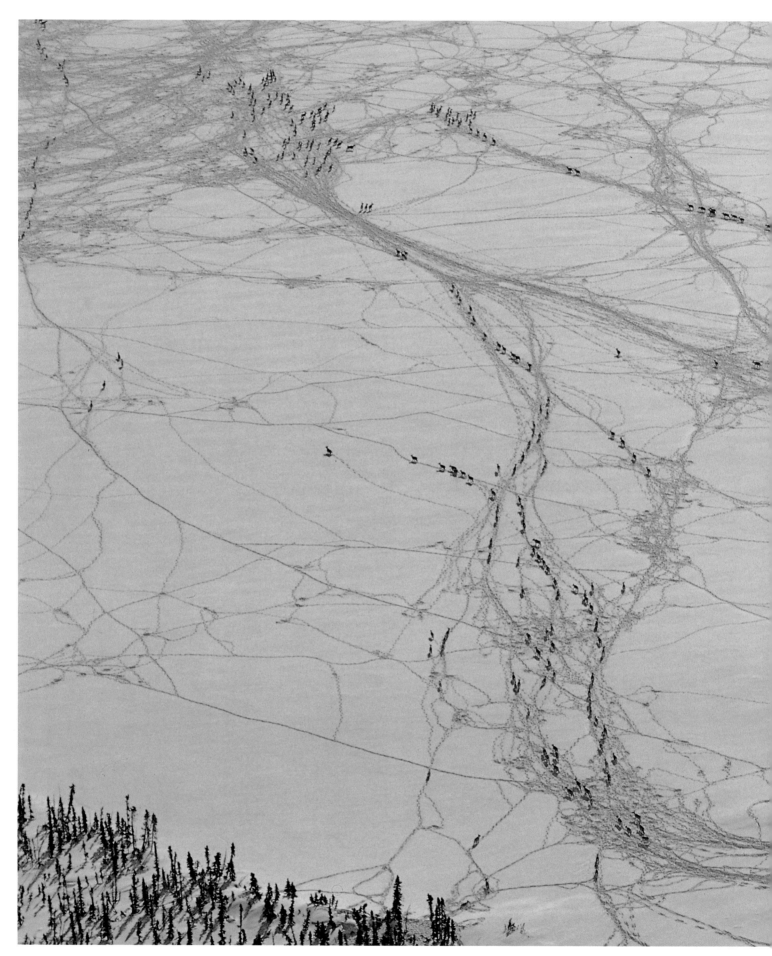

Trails on Gordon Lake,
north of Yellowknife:
caribou migrating north in
April. *Douglas Heard*

Even in the long, cold winter months, Yellowknife is a hospitable place with many activities. The city remains a small clearing in a vast wilderness, content in its role as a frontier town.
Fran Hurcomb

Alaskan Tommy Desjarkeis, contestant in the annual Arctic Winter Games, held in 1990 in Yellowknife.
Fran Hurcomb

The one-foot (or two-foot) "high kick" is a special contest dominated by Inuit youngsters at the Arctic Winter Games.
Tessa Macintosh

(Upper):
The Firth sisters, international cross-country skiers from Inuvik, and companions enjoy sports at the Yellowknife Ski Club.
Tessa Macintosh

This is the way a beaver trap
is set in the ponds and lakes
in winter. *Fran Hurcomb*

Along the Mackenzie, Dene
are drying (and freezing)
their freshly caught fish on
hanging stages.
Fran Hurcomb

Fall fishing on Great Slave
Lake. *Fran Hurcomb*

Tundra wolf on Gordon
Lake in April, 120 kilometres
north of Great Slave Lake.
Douglas Heard

Aurora borealis with Big Dipper (to the right), as seen from barrenlands Ptarmigan Lake northeast of Reliance. As the Inuit say: rubbing one's hands brings the Northern Lights closer, clapping the hands pushes them away. *Natalie Abel*

Homesteading at Snare Lakes, 200 kilometres north of Yellowknife: Wendy Stephenson carrying home firewood on *toboggan* (Indian sled) with small dogteam. *John Stephenson*

The mountains of the Ragged Range northwest of Nahanni park form a natural border between the two territories. *Wolfgang Weber*

Meltwater ponds lend summer colour to a glacier in a spur of the Ragged Range.
Matt Bradley

Slowly awakening to spring, the South Nahanni River winds more than 1,000 metres below limestone bluffs and banded dolomite walls of its First Canyon.
Matt Bradley

Sunset on Rabbitkettle Lake
at the northwestern edge of
Nahanni National Park,
close to which are the

thirty-metre-high mounds of
the Rabbitkettle Hotsprings.
Wolfgang Weber

Early summer angling in
Great Slave Lake.
Wendy Stephenson

Just outside of Nahanni park's northwestern border and part of the Ragged Range, the Cirque of the Unclimbables rises to 2,700 metres and challenges mountaineers from around the world. *Wolfgang Weber*

Climbing to 2,276 metres, Mount Wilson is close to the source of South Nahanni River and is on the border between the NWT and Yukon. *Matt Bradley*

One of the many steep granite walls in the Cirque. *Wolfgang Weber*

A roaring cataract at the heart of Nahanni National Park with almost twice the height of Niagara, Virginia Falls on the South Nahanni smashes against a huge rock pillar and thunders down ninety-six metres.
Wolfgang Weber

Two American wilderness tourists are fighting their way through the dangerous rapids — modestly named George's Riffle — of the South Nahanni's First Canyon. *Matt Bradley*

The South Nahanni has dug itself deep into the Mackenzie Mountains. *Wolfgang Weber*

Erik Watt
A Very Special Breed

It began, as most northern adventures do, innocuously enough: two float-equipped Cessna 195 lightplanes setting out from Coppermine, on the Arctic coast, for Norman Wells, some 600 kilometres to the southwest on the Mackenzie River. It should have been a routine flight in dependable aircraft over terrain relatively easy to follow, tracking the north shore of Great Bear Lake — the world's eighth largest — half the way. The Norman Wells airport had a radio beacon on which to home, and with full tanks and only one passenger in each plane, flying range was no problem.

Other factors were involved, though. Pilots George Gonzales and Dick Warner of Aklavik Flying Service were both comparatively new to the North (many northern pilots usually are, since the Yukon and Northwest Territories are two of the few places in Canada where fledgling commercial pilots have a good chance of finding work). And the North's almost always unpredictable weather is usually even less predictable in September, with freeze-up imminent.

September 29, 1956, was a typical fall day in the North. The weather was fine in Coppermine when government biologist George Hunter and his wife, who'd been doing fisheries research in the Barren Lands all summer, climbed aboard and the planes took off, and the Norman Wells forecast was excellent. Nearing Great Bear, however, Gonzales and Warner ran into light snow, which soon became heavier.

At that point, more experienced pilots might well have turned back or sat down on the nearest lake to let the storm blow over. But, like their passengers, both pilots were anxious to get home. There'd been no indication of major weather disturbances in the forecast, they reasoned. They'd likely be out of the snow in no time . . .

Four hours later, tanks almost empty, they were safely down on Sherman Lake, cradled amid the heavily treed, rocky hills of the Precambrian Shield, 200 kilometres northwest of Yellowknife . . . and almost 90 degrees off course. The pilots were more embarrassed than concerned. Warner had siphoned Gonzales's remaining gas into his own plane to climb up for a quick look around. They knew, now, they were only seventy-five kilometres or so from the Rayrock uranium mine.

Both planes carried adequate survival gear and emergency rations for a couple of weeks. Each had a battery-powered SARAH (Search and Rescue and Homing) transmitter for broadcasting their position. There were plenty of trout in Sherman Lake, and while there was a sprinkling of snow on the ground they had both tents and down-filled sleeping bags.

Relax, they told the Hunters. A search would have begun an hour after their planned arrival time at Norman Wells. As soon as a search plane came within range of the SARAH transmitters, they'd have some gas flown in and complete the trip.

Twelve days later they knew they were in trouble.

There was a search, all right (Royal Canadian Air Force and civilian aircraft would log 540 hours of flying time and cover 35,700 square kilometres of territory in that hunt). But they were concentrating on the area north of Great Bear, along the planes' supposed route, not between Coppermine and Yellowknife, almost due south.

They were well west of the Coppermine-Yellowknife air route, and the hills, plus the North's notorious atmospheric conditions, had apparently blanked out their distress transmissions. And Hunter had cut his hand while cleaning a fish. What had first seemed a minor injury had developed into a serious case of blood poisoning. He needed medical help, in a hurry.

Warner volunteered to walk out to Rayrock.

Rayrock was "just over the hill," half an hour by air. On foot, over snow-slippery rock, through tangled undergrowth, threading a maze of now half-frozen lakes, thick forest, and still-soggy muskeg in temperatures that hovered just below freezing, an exhausted, shivering Warner was still several miles from Rayrock when, eight days later, on October 18, he stumbled across a party of Dene hunters who took him by canoe to the minesite.

The air search was winding down by then, but the searchmaster and an RCAF Flying Boxcar were still at the Sawmill Bay airstrip on the south shore of Great Bear. The Boxcar was airborne within minutes of Warner's arrival at Rayrock and, an hour later, circling the two stranded planes, dropping supplies and a radio.

A lot had changed in the eight days since Warner's departure. Sherman Lake was frozen over now, but the ice was only a couple of inches thick; too thin to support an aircraft on skis but thick enough to puncture the floats of a seaplane. It would take several days to bring in a helicopter from southern Canada, and they didn't have several days. Over the radio, Mrs. Hunter told them she'd been preparing to amputate her husband's hand, in a desperate final effort to save his life.

The Boxcar flew on to Yellowknife for a quick council-of-war. A ground expedition would take as long to get in as a helicopter . . .

Bush pilot Jim McAvoy wasn't invited to that hastily organized meeting though he and his brother, Chuck, were two of the most experienced pilots in the NWT. Jim McAvoy's flying career was a running battle with officialdom and he was then grounded for some infraction of air regulations. But word of the dilemma got to him quickly enough.

McAvoy never did like meetings. He just jumped into his float-equipped Cessna 180 and took off from still-open Back Bay.

An hour later, with little daylight left, MacAvoy was studying frozen Sherman Lake. Then, his course of action decided, he headed down, leveling off bare inches above the ice.

He made one long pass down the lake, bouncing the rear of his floats on the ice to smash it. Then he swung around and landed in the narrow, ice-choked channel he'd created, bundled the Hunters and Gonzales aboard, and took off again, miraculously without smashing his floats.

Hunter was in hospital in Yellowknife, getting emergency treatment before his flight south for successful surgery, while the official rescue party was still trying to decide what to do.

Jim McAvoy's rescue mission — only one of many he would fly — occurred more than three-and-a-half decades ago, but it's still the perfect example of what northern flying can be, and of the men who do the flying. (McAvoy "retired" several years ago, but still flies in the North in the summers. His brother vanished without a trace on a flight north of Yellowknife in the 1960s.)

ELTs (Emergency Location Transmitters) have replaced the SARAH equipment, and in both the Yukon and NWT high-tech aids to navigation have taken over from the uncertain radio beacons, the hard-earned knowledge, and the raw guts by which the North's early pilots flew. There are few settlements without airstrips, complete with glide-path visual aids. Many bush planes today are equipped with satellite-served navigation systems with which a pilot, in theory anyway, can simply punch in his course and then settle back to enjoy the scenery.

But the North hasn't changed. You can still take off from Fort Providence, 220 kilometres southwest of Yellowknife, in perfect weather and find yourself skimming the trees in the midst of a fall blizzard an hour later, desperately searching for Yellowknife airport, your retreat cut off by a storm that blew in from nowhere. Or in the midst of a white-out, a condition caused by ice crystals suspended in the air, undetectable until you're in it and, once you are, with your only visibility straight down. (Over snow, which looks the same as the air around you, you have no visibility at all.)

Nor do those fancy electronics, subject as they are to human and computer glitches, substitute for skill and instinct and knowledge.

That was brought forcibly home in the fall of 1988 to the pilots of a Boeing 737 jetliner that took off from Yellowknife for Resolute Bay via Cambridge Bay, 1,500 kilometres southwest, with a full load of passengers. They broke out of the overcast near Churchill, Manitoba, 1,150 kilometres southeast . . . and they were just plain lucky. Churchill was the only airport within their remaining range that could safely accommodate a 737.

In the modern Yukon, only Old Crow, a tiny community 180 kilometres from the Arctic coast, is not served by year-round road, or connected by scheduled air service. But across the rugged Mackenzie Mountains in the Northwest Territories, the aircraft still is the prime mode of transport in a land whose communities are usually at least 200 kilometres apart and where highways are few.

Yukoners are as proud of their pilots as the NWT is of its fliers, but in the NWT there's a constant — if usually unconscious — awareness that at any moment your life may be in the hands of a pilot of whom you may never have heard. And you *know* that pilot will put his life on the line if there's any chance of saving yours. This has created an instant bond between the pilot and the non-flying resident of the NWT. A fatal crash in the Yukon will cause sadness and sympathy for the victims and next-of-kin. But in the NWT, the death of a pilot is a death in the family, a real blow to people who never knew him. And the good pilots are as well known in the NWT today as the Wop Mays, Grant McConachies, Punch Dickinses, and Ernie Boffas of the pioneer days were.

The difference is that May, McConachie, Dickins, and Boffa were national heroes, known to every schoolchild, in their heyday. In today's North, Duncan Grant, Hoobie Hoobanoff, Mike Zubko, Fred Carmichael, Willie Lazarich, and Ivan Rand, legendary figures on their own turf, are all but unknown south of the 60th parallel.

From Edmonton, Canadian Airlines or NWT Air whisk you to Yellowknife in an hour and forty-five minutes today, in comfortable, wide-bodied Boeing 737 jets. An hour later, well-fed and relaxed, you're taxiing into the terminal at "The Wells," as Norman Wells is known across the North, ready for a day's business.

It wasn't always that easy.

Site of the North's first producing oilfield, Norman Wells was the destination of the first commercial flight into the North, in 1921. One of the two German-built, single-engined Junkers monoplanes that started that historic flight never did reach its destination. The other took two and a half months!

That wasn't the first flight north of the 60th parallel, which separates the two territories from the southern provinces. Four U.S. Army Air Corps aircraft claimed the honour a year earlier with a then-incredible 13,500 kilometre flight from Long Island, New York, to Nome, Alaska, and back, on which the four De Havilland 4B biplanes touched down at Whitehorse and Dawson City.

Epic though that flight was, however, it pales in comparison to the adventure of the two Junkers.

Captain St. Clair Streett, who led the American flight, survived his full share of accidents and heart-stopping moments in the First Alaska Air Expedition of 1920. But though they flew over miles of uncharted wilderness, they were preceded at each leg by ground parties that picked out landing areas and arranged for fuel, repairs, and spare parts. And their journey was made in the summer.

Pilots Elmer Fullerton and George Gorman and their two mechanics, Pete Derbyshire and Bill Hill, flew into an Arctic winter in their open-cockpit, ski-equipped Junkers for Imperial Oil Limited. Imperial had made its first important oil find late in 1920 and hoped to fly in its own prospectors ahead of the rush of prospectors it knew would arrive once navigation opened on the Mackenzie River in June.

Fullerton and Gorman blazed their own trail most of the way, relying on Derbyshire and Hill and their own ingenuity if anything went wrong. There was no aviation gas north of Great Slave Lake; they'd have to use the same low-octane fuel trappers used in their outboard motors. There was no weather forecasting, and not even a telegraph line for communications. Leather helmets and fur-lined leather facepieces, plus all the clothing into which they could bundle, were poor protection in temperatures that could, and did, dip to −40° Celsius, and the agonies their mechanics endured on the ground, often working bare-handed with superchilled metal, defy the imagination.

Few of the people they met had ever seen an aeroplane. One group of terrified Dene trappers riddled the tail of Fullerton's aircraft with rifle fire when they landed at Lower Hay River, first stop on their 1,250-kilometre flight from Peace River in northern Alberta.

Fullerton's Junkers was christened *Vic*; Gorman flew the *René*. A federal land surveyor named William Waddell flew with Gorman and Hill in the *René*, and Fullerton and Derbyshire carried Royal Canadian Mounted Police Sgt. Hubert Thorn, returning to his post at Fort Good Hope on the Mackenzie in the *Vic's* enclosed, but unheated, cabin.

They left Peace River March 22, 1921, lost two days sitting out a blizzard in which they'd landed at Fort Vermilion, not far south of the NWT border, and finally reached Fort Simpson on the Mackenzie on March 24 after refuelling at Port Providence, near the confluence of the Mackenzie.

Gorman found an open area that looked large enough for a landing and set down. One ski struck a frozen rut left by a sled, and the impact was too much for the cold-brittle metal undercarriage. It collapsed and the Junkers skidded to a stop, tail high in the air, one ski and its propeller smashed.

Fullerton, in the *Vic*, was luckier. He touched down safely, if bumpily, to find Gorman and his passengers unhurt.

The *René*, for all the violence of its landing, was relatively undamaged, but the *Vic's* engine had been running rough. So the pilots decided to instal the *Vic's* propeller and one of

her skis on the *René* to finish the journey. The *Vic* would have to wait for a replacement prop until one could be brought in by riverboat.

The repairs took precious time, because breakup was getting closer. But early in April the *René* was ready. She rose fifty feet into the air . . . and her engine died.

Again, the people aboard were lucky. But the *René* was beyond immediate repair, and the one remaining propeller had been destroyed.

Lesser men would have quit, right there, but lesser men wouldn't have undertaken that flight in the first place. Maybe, said Hill, we could *make* a propeller.

And they did. Two of them.

Hudson's Bay Company clerk Walter Johnson, they discovered, was a cabinetmaker. The Bay had some oak and birch boards, seven inches wide, that trappers used in building their carioles, or toboggans. Laminated together with glue made from moosehides and hooves, seven of the planks formed a block from which a new prop could be carved with hand tools. Then, using the most-intact prop as a template, Hill and Johnson painstakingly fashioned a delicately balanced replacement that, tested on the *Vic* on April 22, performed perfectly!

Just before daybreak next day, Fullerton was roused by an excited native. The *Vic* was parked on a frozen snye — a backwater — and breakup had arrived. The snye's ice was already crumbling and when Fullerton (and Derbyshire), with Gorman as a passenger, took off an hour later from what remained of his "runway" — perhaps 100 metres of rough ice — his skis left a wake across open water before he gained full flying speed.

There was no hope, now, of reaching The Wells and returning, on skis; floats would be needed. Not sure if he'd find snow or ice to land on when he got there, and hoping he could with the fuel he had aboard, Fullerton flew directly to Peace River, a 750-kilometre journey over unmapped, heavily treed, and partly hill country (which they already had flown — on a slightly different route — on their way north a good month ago), and arrived there with twenty minutes' gas remaining, and a still-frozen lake below.

Gorman continued on south, to get a new propeller and other spares. Fullerton stayed to help switch the Junkers onto floats. And near the end of May the float-equipped *Vic* soared aloft from Peace River once more, Gorman and the spares and Fullerton's new passenger Dr. Theo Link, Imperial's chief geologist, in the cabin.

Most of the lower Mackenzie was clear of ice by then, which made the refuelling stops easier. Nor did Derbyshire, as he and Hill had done on the first venture, have to drain the oil from the engine every night to prevent its freezing solid, then reheat both engine and oil in the morning with plumber's blowpots to thaw them out before pouring the oil back in.

Gorman and the spares were dropped off at Fort Simpson, where they discovered Hill and Johnson had produced a second perfect propeller in their absence and had fitted it to the nearly repaired *René*. Then Fullerton and his passengers carried on to Fort Norman, only sixty kilometres south of Norman Wells by air. They landed on the river on June 2, and smashed one float on a chunk of drifting spring debris.

The *Vic* just made it to shore. There, a small scow was hastily jury-rigged to replace the shattered pontoon, and Fullerton floated ingloriously down the river to finish his epic journey.

It was August 21, five months after their initial departure, when the *Vic* and *René* dropped down out of a drizzly sky over Peace River to land on the river. And, true to form, to one final disaster.

The ill-fated *René* hit a sandbar and flipped over on her back, Gorman, Hill, and an accompanying newsman barely escaping with their lives. Rescuers in boats plucked the three from the water. The shattered *René*, carried downstream by the swift current, wound up on another sandbar, never to fly again.

The *Vic*, still using her homemade propeller, carried on, her place in history secure. But the *René* lives on, too. Her handmade propeller — painted red because there was no shellac in Fort Simpson with which to finish it properly — sits today in the Prince of Wales Northern Heritage Centre in Yellowknife as a proud reminder of four men who wouldn't give up.

Fullerton signed on with Norwegian explorer Roald Amundsen that next year, in an attempt to fly over the North Pole. He and the Junkers he planned to use got as far as Kotzebue, Alaska, just north of the Arctic Circle, by ship, but Amundsen's expedition never got off the ground. Fullerton's co-pilot took the reassembled Junkers up on its first test flight and crashed while landing, wrecking the plane and cancelling the expedition.

There were no aircraft in the skies of the territories for the next three years. Canada's infant aviation companies concentrated their efforts on developing air services within the provinces, finding aircraft better suited to Canadian winter operations and learning, though bitter trial and error, how to keep their planes aloft in sub-zero temperatures.

Then, in the summer of 1925, the first amphibian appeared in western Canada, a Vickers Viking flown by J. Scott Williams and Jack Caldwell for Laurentide Air Services, a Quebec company. It was a flying birdcage of struts and rigging, but it could land on water as well as the forest clearings or farmers' fields that then served as airstrips, and an American exploration company hired the Viking, christened the *Bouncing Bruno*, to fly claimstakers into the wilderness of northern British Columbia in search of gold.

On one of their last trips of the season, the stakers flew into Frances Lake, 150 kilometres inside the Yukon boundary. The manager of the isolated Hudson's Bay post on the lake had the thrill of a lifetime as the first plane he'd seen taxied up to his dock. But the stakers had no luck, and the Viking headed back south.

That fall, as Caldwell and the *Bouncing Bruno* headed back east, a close-mouthed old prospector with a glass jar full of rich gold samples made his appearance in the bars of Calgary. There was lots more where the samples came from, he said, right on the surface.

A group of Calgary businessmen heard of the prospector, quickly organized a mining syndicate, and, after checking the samples, bought the man's unregistered claims and hired him to lead them to the find the next year. The *Bouncing Bruno* sounded like the best way to reach the strike, north of the Saskatchewan border. They purchased her and hired Caldwell to fly her.

The Viking was shipped by rail to northern Alberta in the spring of 1926. Then, just as preparations for the summer exploration program were nearly complete, the old prospector, busy spending the money he'd made, got into a barroom brawl. His skull was fractured and he never regained consciousness.

He'd given the syndicate a vague location, some 300 kilometres north of the provincial boundary on a height of land. He'd marked his discovery with a cross made of boulders, he said, and he'd left his Dene wife camped there to await his return.

That was all the syndicate had to go on, but they were already committed. Caldwell spent that entire summer searching for that cross and campsite, in vain. When the lakes began freezing up in September, he and the exploration party had no choice but to abandon their search.

Whether there really was a property rich in gold, or what happened to the prospector's wife — if, indeed, she or the rich discovery ever existed — is a mystery to this day. But the gold in those samples was real enough.

Then, in October, 1927, a young Edmonton pilot named A.D. "Andy" Cruickshank established the North's first air service at Whitehorse, Yukon's capital.

Cruickshank had an all-metal Ryan monoplane on wheels, the same type of aircraft with which Charles Lindbergh, in May of that year, had made the first solo crossing of the Atlantic. He christened her the *Queen of the Yukon* and shipped the plane to Skagway, Alaska, by steamer.

His wife, Esmee, was one of his three passengers as he roared down a makeshift runway of planks, borrowed from a nearby sawmill, on October 25, 1927, bound for Whitehorse.

That was a hair-raising flight. Cruickshank was barely airborne when he hit the end of the "runway" and just managed to skim the surface of the sea until he had enough flying speed to climb. It took him another twenty minutes of following twisting mountain valleys to gain enough altitude to clear the peaks that barred his path. But ninety minutes later he touched down in Whitehorse, to the cheers of its citizenry.

Yukon Airways and Exploration Co. Ltd. lost no time getting into business. Cruickshank inaugurated mail and passenger service between Whitehorse, Dawson, and Mayo, a 750-kilometre route over rugged terrain, on November 11 and flew that circuit, on wheels, all winter.

That was an exciting venture, but its lifetime was short. Cruickshank sold out in 1928 to fly for rapidly growing Western Canada Airways on the Prairies. His successor, a pilot named Cameron, didn't last long. The Ryan was wrecked when it broke through thin ice while landing at Mayo, and Cameron was killed.

Four years later, Andy Cruickshank vanished on a flight between Fort Rae and Great Bear Lake. Searchers found the wreck, and the bodies of Cruickshank and two passengers, on a heavily wooded slope south of the lake.

By 1928, aircraft were no longer a novelty south of Great Slave Lake, along much of the Mackenzie River, or even on Hudson Bay or the Arctic coast of the Northwest Territories. Yukoners, too, were growing familiar with the sound of aircraft engines. But the great, treeless Barren Lands had never been deeply penetrated.

Punch Dickins couldn't resist that challenge. He'd flown to Baker Lake, on 150-kilometre deep Chesterfield Inlet on the western shore of Hudson Bay, with a mineral exploration team headed by Col. C.H. McAlpine. Now, he turned his Fokker Universal southwest across the barrens for Lake Athabasca and the tiny settlement of Stony Rapids on its eastern arm.

It was a long and, fortunately, monotonous 800-kilometre flight over rock and muskeg, lakes and rolling hills, without a sign of life until Stony Rapids lay below. They stayed here for two days before setting out for Fort Smith, 360 kilometres west-northwest, on the Alberta-NWT border, their last stop before turning south.

Gas was in short supply at Stony Rapids, so Dickins took on just enough fuel there to get him to Fort Smith . . . almost. Following the Slave River, with just fifty kilometres to go, Dickins suddenly found himself gliding for the water, out of fuel. Condensation had frozen in his gas gauge the previous night, giving him an erroneous reading.

Dickins, McAlpine, and the two other passengers were trying to decide what to do when the Northern Transportation Company's steamer *Northland Echo* came into view. Dickins hailed her skipper, in hopes he might have some aviation gas aboard.

Yes, Dickins was told, there was avgas on the barges the *Echo* was towing. It was consigned to some fellow named

Dickins who planned to do some flying out of Fort Smith the following summer.

Northern aviation took off in 1929. Mining exploration was in high gear. The Royal Canadian Corps of Signals had established radio stations in the major settlements along the Mackenzie and weather forecasting would be available for that area now. And the federal government was planning an air mail service down the river to Aklavik in its delta. (Dickins became the first aviator to reach Aklavik, on a scouting trip in July that year.)

Col. McAlpine was back again, this time on the Arctic coast. The disappearance of the two planes carrying his party that fall sparked not only the greatest air search Canada had ever known but also filled in huge areas of the map previously shown as unexplored. McAlpine's party was rescued after a harrowing ordeal, but in the hunt for them search pilots — including Dickins, Wop May, and Andy Cruickshank — covered thousands of kilometres of previously unexplored territory.

On December 10, 1929, two red-painted Bellanca Air Cruisers and a Lockheed Vega left Edmonton's Blatchford Field airport for Waterways, the end of steel, 450 kilometres north. Western Canada Airways' general manager Cy Becker and Idris Glyn-Roberts flew the Bellancas and Capt. Maurice "Moss" Burbridge, the Vega.

Wop May was waiting with a third Bellanca and some five tons of mail at Waterways. Ahead lay thirteen stops, the last of them, Aklavik.

On December 27, after relaying their cargo downriver, May and Glyn-Roberts took off on the last lap of that landmark journey, landing in Aklavik in a forty-below mist with the Christmas mail.

The Canadian Arctic had just become part of the twentieth century.

Two world wars and the threat of a third have opened up Canada's Arctic.

The First World War left Canada with a pool of pilots like Wop May (whom Germany's famed Red Baron, Manfred von Richthofen, was pursuing when he was shot down), Dickins, Fullerton, and Cruickshank, eager to continue flying and willing to take just about any risk for the chance to do it.

The Second World War gave the North its major airports: Watson Lake and Whitehorse airports in Yukon were built as part of the Northwest Staging Route to Russia, via Alaska, over which thousands of warplanes were ferried to the Soviets. Hay River, Yellowknife, and Norman Wells airports in the NWT supported the wartime Canol project, a pipeline from the oilfield at Norman Wells to Whitehorse, rammed through the Mackenzie Mountains in an incredible eighteen months.

The Cold War and the missile threat produced the Distant Early Warning (DEW) Line and a string of airstrips roughly 75 kilometres apart along the entire Arctic coast of North America, as well as supporting Canadian airfields like Iqaluit (Frobisher Bay) on Baffin Island and Churchill in Manitoba. And DEW Line communications needs developed the first radio network capable of surmounting the Arctic's fearful atmospheric conditions.

There are reminders still of those grim wartime days all over the North. One of the best known is Million-Dollar Valley in Yukon, where three hopelessly lost B-25 Mitchell bombers, Russia-bound, landed in perfect formation and virtually undamaged in deep snow when they ran out of gas.

But it still takes tough, brave men to fly in the North . . . and stay.

Duncan Grant of Yellowknife is one. He's remembered for a lot of things, including the day at Shingle Point, near the Yukon-NWT border, when he set his lumbering Avro Anson light transport down like a helicopter in a 150-knot gale to pick up two critically injured DEW Line workers.

Grant had literally to fly the aircraft with his brakes on just to hold his position on the tarmac while men on the ground tried to get the injured pair aboard, and everything loose on the site — lumber, fuel drums, equipment — whizzed past the Anson. The ground party couldn't keep their footing in the wind. A DEWLiner who'd volunteered to fly with Grant finally flung a rope out the cabin door, tying his end to the pilot's seat. The other was tied to each of the two stretchers, in turn, and the DEWLiner hauled the victims into the cabin while the ground party held the stretchers aloft.

Miraculously, none of that lethal debris smashed into the plane before Grant hauled it off and flew to Aklavik, whose one doctor worked on the pair until noon the next day, and saved both.

Bill Spencer and Mike Halecki were captain and first officer, respectively, of a Winnipeg-based Transair Ltd. DC-4 that flew into Cambridge Bay, in the central Arctic, a few days before Christmas in 1960. They had half a dozen senior DEW Line officials aboard who "just had to be there," plus six forty-five-gallon drums of gas for the return flight, since Transair had no fuel cache at the site.

A forty-below blizzard was blowing when they reached Cambridge Bay, and the DEWLiners quickly vanished. Spencer and Halecki were left to refuel the plane themselves with a portable "wobble" pump. Its coiled hose shattered into little pieces when they tried to unwind it. Spencer and Halecki had to pour their fuel into fire buckets and carry them, two at a time, through the emergency doors and out onto the wings to fill the wing tanks. They were so badly frostbitten they could hardly restart the engines when they were finished, and as they fled south the aircraft itself began to freeze up.

Their radio went first, then the cabin heat, then their control cables and hydraulics. They had only the four engines to steer with: throttling back the port engines to swing left, the starboard to turn right; increasing or decreasing power to climb or descend. And they didn't know how long the engines would last.

Coral Harbour, 1,100 kilometres southeast of Cambridge Bay, was the nearest airport large enough to handle the DC-4. Halecki managed to crank the wheels down by hand and Spencer somehow set the big plane down on the Coral Harbour strip. With no brakes, all he could do was chop the throttles and pray.

The lone towerman on duty at Coral Harbour nearly fell off his chair when a DC-4 suddenly appeared out of the darkness, flashed past the tower, and finally rolled to a stop 400 feet past the end of the runway, in a fortunately level overshoot area. It just sat there, ignoring his radio queries. He finally bundled up and drove out to the plane on his snowmobile.

"Jump down and I'll give you a lift into the terminal!" he shouted as the pilot's window cracked open.

"We can't!" Spencer yelled. "We're frozen into our seats!"

A month later they were both back on the job.

Medivacs — evacuating sick or injured people by air — rarely make headlines in the North any more, even in northern newspapers. There were nearly 17,000 medivac flights in 1985 in the NWT (the latest figures available), and a good 10 per cent of those were emergencies.

Most settlements have only a nursing station with one or two trained nurses and few surgical facilities. Nurses — and Mounted Police, Hudson's Bay Company managers, clergymen, or anyone else who happened to be there in an emergency — have accomplished medical miracles, including complex surgery, but serious cases are flown out whenever possible. It's not unusual for a scheduled mainline jet to wait on a runway until some seriously injured victim can be flown in by bush plane from an outpost camp for hospital treatment in the south.

Courage and dedication aren't always enough, though. Like their seat-of-the-pants predecessors, modern bush pilots still need sharp wits. There was, for instance, the pilot of an NWT Air DC-3 with a touring Edmonton theatre company on board. When he let down his gear to land at Gjoa Haven, a small Inuit community on King William Island, the port wheel stuck, halfway down. One of the elastic cables that kept the ski of his ski-wheel undercarriage properly positioned had snagged on something. He couldn't lower the undercarriage any farther and he couldn't retract it, along with the other wheel-ski, to attempt a belly-landing in the snow. And he wasn't anxious to attempt a one-wheel landing on Gjoa Haven's rock-bordered airstrip with a full payload of passengers in the back.

He warned the passengers to tighten their seat belts and hang on. Then he put the DC-3 into a series of shallow dives, jerking the nose sharply up each time, hoping to shake the balky undercarriage loose.

All that did was scare the daylights out of his already white-knuckled thespian troupe.

Then . . . inspiration!

Northern aircraft all carry emergency gear; it's a long way between airports if you have to set down unexpectedly. Most emergency kits include a .22 calibre rifle, in case the rations run out before help arrives and ptarmigan or Arctic hares are needed for food.

The captain sent his first officer back to the emergency box in the tail to dig out the rifle. Then, while the first officer took over the controls, he cranked open his cabin side window, drew a bead on the tangled cable and fired.

He got it with his fourth shot. The wheel dropped into position with a satisfying clunk! and he made a perfect landing to a standing ovation from the cast.

Bush pilots still like to talk about good and bad luck, and recall legendary adventures. But hangar talk today is more likely to be about the last jump in fuel prices or insurance premiums, shrinking profit margins, the cost of obtaining badly needed new aircraft, or the problems of deregulation, which allows almost unlimited competition.

Almost every aspect of life in the NWT is still dependent, to some degree, on small single- or twin-engined aircraft and the pilots who fly them. Even Yellowknife, the territorial capital, is completely cut off from the outside, except by air, for as long as six weeks at spring break-up, since the Yellowknife Highway crosses the 1.5-kilometre-wide Mackenzie River by ferry in summer and by ice road in winter.

Some forty small charter and scheduled airlines and about 100 pilots still provide the only air service to forty-nine of the sixty-four widely scattered communities in the Northwest Territories. Indeed, they afford the only transportation services to many of those forty-nine communities, aside from annual sealift or winter road operations that bring in such bulk supplies as fuel, building materials, and heavy equipment.

Much northern flying is done on wheels today; most communities now have maintained airstrips. But beyond the settlements, floats and skis — or oversized, underinflated tundra tires, which make it possible to land on snow, soggy ground, or gravel beaches — and the "off-strip" pilot still rule.

Typical of the modern bush operation is Ted Grant's Simpson Air, based at Fort Simpson on the Mackenzie. Simpson Air flies everything from four-passenger Cessna 185s to a speedy, pressurized King Air and the workhorse Twin Otter; it carries everything from groceries, government officials, fuel, prospectors, geologists, mail, tourists,

and oil workers to sick or injured patients in urgent need of medical attention.

Like its competitors, Simpson Air runs a seasonal business. Its aircraft may fly fifty to sixty hours per week in summer, around the clock, taking advantage of the twenty-four-hour daylight. But in winter, with summer tourist and exploration traffic gone and few hours of daylight, Grant considers himself lucky to find southern operators to lease his Twin Otters for enough to cover his own leasing and insurance costs. His smaller planes, flying on combination ski/wheels, will barely earn enough to cover operating costs in winter.

Today's bush planes are expensive, too. A used Twin Otter can cost anywhere from $500,000 to $1.2 million (the last models, produced in 1986, were worth $2.2 million new). It will burn sixty to seventy-five gallons of fuel per hour — at $3.50 to $5 per gallon, or higher in remote locations.

It costs $20,000 to insure a Twin Otter, and major engine overhauls every 3,500 hours can cost up to $250,000 if engines must be replaced. Pilots (each plane needs two in summer, as pilots are allowed to fly only 120 hours a month) earn about $5,000 a month. Hangar and office heating and electricity can cost $6,000 per month in winter.

Given those costs and a Twin Otter charter rate of about $700 an hour, not many modern bush operators can aspire to the success of a Max Ward or Grant McConachie, who built their small bush operations into internationally operating Wardair and Canadian Pacific Air Lines (CPA).

Two major airlines — Canadian Airlines (Canadian North), CPA's and Wardair's successor, and Air Canada — dominate the major routes in the NWT and Yukon now, with their subsidiary or "connector" airlines handling most regional services. But the small bush plane, still, is the one link to the world outside for many tiny northern communities.

John U. Bayly
Wilderness Travel

North is a direction, a mere point of the compass needle, isn't it? Of course. But it is more than that. For example, the mere addition of a definite article transforms it into "The North." Thus transformed and capitalized, it evokes images of endless forests and windswept trackless barrens. The North in our collective imaginations is a desolate and lonely land. At the same time, it is cherished as a country where the rivers are teeming with fish and as the habitat of the last great herds of caribou and muskoxen.

Such images, over the centuries, have drawn men and women of adventure to the North. It is, perhaps, an artificial distinction to separate adventure travellers in Canada's North from other travellers. The North is, after all, a land where people are constantly on the move, a place where every journey can be an adventure. Even those who choose space-age technology and twentieth-century comfort in their modes of Arctic and subarctic travel are advised to be well shod, warmly clothed, and to have their sleeping bags along . . . just in case.

In any event, artificial though the distinction between adventure travel and other types may be, I will try to draw that distinction. By adventure travel, I mean travel without a dominant economic, scientific, military, or exploratory purpose. I seek to separate out by those exclusions that handful of people who come to the North "just because." This group of people (and I expect most members would dislike being considered part of any group) is well and amusingly described by the late Victorian adventure traveller Warburton Pike in *The Barren Ground of Northern Canada*, an 1892 account of his travels in Canada's Far North.

In many of the outlying districts of Canada an idea is prevalent, fostered by former travellers, that somewhere in London there exists a benevolent society whose object is to send men incapable of making any useful scientific observations to the uttermost parts of the earth, in order to indulge their taste for sport or travel.

Several times before I had fairly started for the North, and again on my return, I was asked if I had been sent out under the auspices of this society, and, I am afraid, rather fell in the estimation of the interviewers when I was obliged to confess that my journey was only an ordinary shooting expedition, such as one might make to the Rocky Mountains or the interior of Africa, and that no great political reformation depended upon my report as to what I had seen.

In earlier times, many adventure travellers were lured by the hopes of pitting their tracking and shooting skills against those of wild creatures. The muskoxen held a special fascination for such travellers. Those shaggy beasts provided Caspar Whitney, the nineteenth-century American adventurer and writer, with his geographic goal as well as part of the subtitle of his 1896 account of his adventures: *On Snowshoes to the Barren Grounds — Twenty-Eight Hundred Miles After Musk Oxen and Wood Bison*. But, hunter though he was, Whitney confessed at the opening of his book that it was more than hunting that drew him to the North.

And why had I turned my face towards a country which seemed to hold naught for the traveller but hardship? Well — certainly to hunt musk-ox, the most inaccessible game in the world, and to look upon his habitat at the period of its uttermost desolation; certainly also to study the several tribes of Indians through which I must pass on my way to the Barren Grounds; and *en route* to hunt woodbison, undoubtedly now become the rarest game in the world. Possibly, too, I went that I might for a time escape the hum and routine sordidness of the city, and breathe air which was not surcharged with convention and civilization.

To him who has scented the trackless wilds, and whose blood has gone the pace of its perils and freedom, there comes, every now and again, an irresistible impulse to fly from electric lights, railroads, and directories; to travel on his feet instead of being jerked along in a cable-car; to find his way with the aid of a compass and the North Star, instead of by belettered lamp-posts. At such a time and in such a mood the untamed spirit chafes under the pettiness of worldly strife, and turns to the home of the red man.

It was to the home of the "red man" or aboriginal peoples of the North that these sophisticated world travellers of an earlier era turned. Some who yearned for northern adventure initially appeared oblivious to the fact that this wild country was home to several tribes of Athapaskan Indians, who are now referred to as the Dene, and to the Eskimo, for whom the term Inuit is now all but universally used. Still other adventure travellers sought out the society of these aboriginal inhabitants of the country as purposefully as Whitney went to track down the muskoxen. David T. Hanbury, whose rich account of travel in the Keewatin region was published in 1904, was one of these. In the preface to his wonderful *Sport and Travel in the Northland of Canada* he describes far too modestly the narrative of his adventures.

In this narrative I have endeavoured to give a plain

and unvarnished account of twenty months' journeying through the Northland of Canada. The book deals with sport and travel, no attempt having been made to accomplish elaborate geographical or other scientific work. I have written of the Eskimo as I found them, having, with my two white companions, lived their life, sharing their habitations, clad in deerskins, and subsisting on caribou and musk-ox meat in winter, or on fish in summer. Of the Indians, with whom I have been much longer acquainted than with the Eskimo, I have also written without prejudice.

Of course, not all adventure travellers choose the North with the same clarity of purpose demonstrated by Whitney and Hanbury. Some have more romantic reasons for their choices. For Lady C.C. Vyvyan, an English Edwardian gentlewoman, one of Robert Service's poems and a letter from a travelling school friend planted the seed in her mind. The idea eventually led her and a female companion down the Mackenzie River to its Arctic delta and an arduous crossing of the continental divide by way of Rat Pass in the Richardson Mountains. In the opening chapter of her *Arctic Adventure* she describes the source of her inspiration.

> In 1913 a school-friend of mine went with her father to San Francisco and thence on a tourist steamer to Alaska. She sent me, from Skagway, a volume of Robert Service's poems and a letter describing vast and desolate tracts of muskeg country.
> That letter and those poems haunted my day-dreams for years. There were certain lines that filled me with a yearning restlessness. . . .
> As for my friend's letter, I lost it long ago but I never forgot her description of that wild and silent land.
> Some twelve years later Gwen Dorrien Smith and I were sitting down with an atlas between us discussing the wild places of the earth. I quoted some of those poems and we turned the pages of the atlas to North America.
> What about Alaska for our next journey? We had tried each other out in a rough trip through the Balkans in 1924 and we each considered the other to be adequately tough for a new, a longer and a more exacting adventure.
> In the event we did, both of us prove to be adequately tough, and the adventure did prove to be more exacting.

I do not mean by my examples to suggest that adventure travel in the North was a phenomenon of earlier times. Adventure travel is alive and well in the North in the latter part of the twentieth century. People continue to be drawn here like pilgrims to a vast cathedral. They come from all around the globe. Some, like the late Naomi Umera of Japan, take on Herculean quests, sending periodic dispatches back for those at home to read in their newspapers as the adventure continues. Umera travelled alone from Greenland to Alaska by dog team over two winters. Wherever he stopped he sent an account of his most recent adventures by Telex to his sponsor, a Tokyo newspaper.

I must tell you of a chance meeting I had with this Japanese hero. It was late winter in Tuktoyaktuk. Umera had just completed a difficult crossing of the Husky Lakes in a howling blizzard. A number of his dogs had perished and it was reported that he had harnessed himself to the sled and dragged the load in with them.

After a brief rest and enough time to prepare his dispatches, he had made his way to John Steen's snowmobile repair shop, where I happened to be. He was dressed in polar bear leggings and what looked like a First World War aviator's cap. In one hand he clutched a sheaf of papers; in the other he held an American Express card.

Our hero, it seems, was trying to arrange to have a 1,500-word story sent by Telex to his Japanese newspaper. With difficulty, he tried to explain in his limited English what he wanted and how he wanted to make payment. Mr. Steen was not impressed. The Telex had been painstakingly written out in Roman orthography. To John Steen it looked like gibberish. He refused to send it and didn't want to accept the credit card. In the end Naomi Umera had to resort to using the telephone. It seems that there are some things you just cannot buy with your American Express card! Such are the trials of an adventurer.

Unlike Naomi Umera, most adventure travellers shun publicity. These anonymous ones quietly slip their canoes into northern waters and paddle away without a word or a sound. If they write of their travels, it is for their own secret pleasures or for a circle of friends and travelling companions.

More than twenty years ago I came into Canada's North as an adventure traveller. I carried with me images of endless spruce forests and rugged barren lands. I had my share of the collective imagination that drew me into the North.

What kept me here was not the lonely land and the rivers teeming with fish, but the people. For the North is people. People on the move, people in a constant state of going somewhere or just having arrived from someplace, people on foot, people nosing their boats up river, people arriving home from the hunt, people travelling by air, on snowshoes, or on skis. On Great Slave Lake fifteen miles from town in early May I have encountered cyclists out for an evening ride on candling ice. Across the same lake after dark on an August night while motoring back from my fishnets, I have almost run down two kayak paddlers. I invited them to my camp for tea and a warm place to sleep. No, they said. They wanted to take advantage of the windless conditions and hoped to reach the Mackenzie River before the end of the next day. Who they were, or where they were going, I never learned. Again, I say the North is people travelling. The best-loved campfire tales are travel stories. And every one is an adventure.

During the Mackenzie Valley Pipeline Inquiry Mr. Justice Thomas Berger was once asked by the late Jim Wolkie of Tuktoyaktuk if he would like to hear a story. It was the account of three men who had been stranded on an ice floe for two months. Of course, the Judge said he would like to hear it. "Well," said Mr. Wolkie, "to tell the story properly takes four days." My wife tells me she thinks it took two days for the telling. No matter! You get the idea. The full account of the adventure must be told. And the story in all its details is as fresh and popular as a recent anecdote.

None of this should surprise you. The aboriginal people of the North were originally nomads. The early explorers, traders, and adventurers had to adapt to traditional ways of travel and take advice and guidance from the Natives they encountered. The distances are great, the difficulties of travel are sometimes insurmountable, and the experience is always humbling. A person's worth in the North has traditionally been measured by how competently he travels and how companionable a travel mate he is.

One way of learning the value of good travelling companions is to have bad ones. On a trip down the Nahanni some people I know got on so poorly with their fellow travellers that they split up the food and equipment and travelled separately. On another river trip — this one between the NWT and the Yukon — two men I knew stopped talking to one another. They communicated indirectly through their other travelling companions. Even without that burden, the trip was a difficult one. And the burden was borne not only by the two who could not get along, but by their companions as well. Such experiences are seldom forgotten.

And so, whatever draws adventure travellers to the North in the first place, frequently the impressions of and encounters with people enrich the experiences they take away with them.

Lady Vyvyan wrote of her travel adventures a quarter of a century after she and Miss Smith were guided through Rat Pass by Lazarus Sittichinli and Jim Koe. As guides, the two men were superb. But let us hear what Lady Vyvyan had to say about them as she looked back on their parting at Summit Lake.

> If ever two men had earned their wage by faithfulness and labour, these two men were Lazarus and Jimmy . . . Lazarus was a fine fellow. He had never failed us in any particular being gifted with muscles of iron, a cool head and a sure judgement. By comparison Jimmy was a pale shadow, but where Lazarus led he

would always follow, and it was with real regret that we said goodby to these two faithful companions.

It is a pity Lazarus was not a writer. It would have been interesting to have an account of the whole adventure from his point of view. Of course, as an incurable adventure traveller and latter-day wilderness guide, I have some stories of my own.

At the mouth of the Yellowknife River on the north shore of Great Slave Lake a road bridge crosses the water. There, twenty years ago, on a windy August afternoon two parties of adventurers met, their routes, by coincidence of time and geography, intersecting.

Parked in the campground was a streamlined mobile home, mudcaked, stone bruised, its Florida licence plate barely legible. On the side step of this twentieth-century covered wagon an elderly man sat, patting the head of a small white poodle.

Pulled up on the narrow beach were three aluminum canoes piled with packs. The canoes were dented and scratched. One was badly in need of body work. There were six of us — unshaved men in checkered shirts and windproof jackets. We sat around a campfire or leaned on paddles drinking tea.

We six piqued a curiosity in the voyageur from Florida and to satisfy it, he approached me. "Is this as far as you can go?" he began. I expect I looked puzzled. It was as though I were trying to understand someone speaking in a foreign language. "I mean," he explained, "I've been on the road three days from Peace River and I guess this is it. I've run out of road."

This man had run out of road. I compared his odyssey with our own. We had travelled more than 400 miles in the previous three weeks, paddling when we could, carrying when we had to, navigating without road signs and relying on maps on which four miles were compressed into an inch.

Resisting the temptation to lecture the old man about the wilderness at his doorstep, I mulled over his question once more. It came to me, suddenly, that we were at identical points in our northern journeys. He was as far along as the highway would carry him. We had been brought to the end of our journey by the river that emptied into Great Slave Lake. As varied as our separate northern adventures must have been, we were facing the same bittersweet realization — that this was as far as we could go.

We had, by different routes and means, arrived at the identical turning point in our respective journeys. We had to return to the world from which we came. What that meant for the man from Florida I do not know. For the six of us, it meant a two-mile paddle down Yellowknife Bay to the city docks, a civic reception (for our trip had been part of the Northwest Territories Centennial celebrations), and a flight home to eastern Canada. There we would pick up our six separate lives. Except for a jolly reunion to swap photos and drink to one another's health, we might never come together again. We braced ourselves for that in the solitude of our individual thoughts as we paddled ourselves in to Yellowknife. We had accomplished what we had set out to do. We had enjoyed one another's company. But the adventure was all too quickly over and, in turning our faces back to the world of men, we had gone as far as we could go.

The world of men. We planned the trip to escape that world. We sought three weeks of solitude. We wanted to go back to basics, to live on the land, to sleep on the ground, and to cook over an open fire. Float planes had dropped us at our starting point. In our modern lightweight, all-but-indestructible boats, we travelled on freeze-dried and dehydrated foods. We navigated using maps generated from sophisticated aerial photographs. We recorded our adventures on 35 mm. film.

However, in another way we found our solitude. Except for a small party of archeologists, we encountered no one until we were twenty miles from Yellowknife. The human companions we sought along the way were dead men. The accounts of explorers in whose footsteps we followed led us on. We carried selected photocopies of their journal entries in plastic bags in our packs. Sometimes at night as we relaxed by the fire, we took them out, unfolded them, and read excerpts to one another. We celebrated their exploits and thought of ourselves as their latter-day equivalents. Hearne, Franklin, Akaitcho, Matonabbee. To this day, their names stir and kindle into flame the campfire embers of my memory.

Strangely enough, it was not an explorer's campsite but one of more recent origin that made me reconsider my view that escape from the world of men is the rationale for northern wilderness travel. Late one afternoon we had beached our canoes at the west end of Winter Lake. As often happened when we landed, we began to explore. Somebody found a scroll of birch bark with a row of holes evenly spaced along its edge. Perhaps it was a fragment of canoe parchment which, in previous centuries, walking parties often carried so that boats could be made when the waters opened. On the crest of a sandy esker were two graves covered with logs and surrounded by hand-hewn pickets. They had been painted once but the seasons had silvered them.

Along the sunlit beach, I found an arrangement of stones. There was nothing dramatic about it. Another person might have overlooked the stones entirely. But, to me, there was something familiar about their arrangement. Three flat stones arranged in the shape of a "U" with an opening twelve inches across told me this had been a fireplace. It was the kind of fireplace may father had taught me to make. With a grate or a couple of metal bars, a pot or pan would have been no more than six inches off the ground. Here was evidence that the builder was used to travelling in the barren lands where an hour's gathering may yield no more wood than enough to boil tea and fry a pan of fish. Grasses grew where once a fire spat and crackled.

Something about this fireplace was so familiar that, scarcely knowing why, I turned over one stone and then another. There, under the second stone, was a spool from which film had been wound. It was an unusual film size and I knew at once from that evidence and the arrangement of stones who had left it there.

I sat on my haunches, the rusty spool in my hand, warmed not only by the sun but also by the realization that this was not the fireside of an explorer or Dene trapper but, unmistakably, the work of my father who had travelled the Snare River half a decade earlier and whose trail I had, that day, crossed. For me, that was the most wonderful discovery of the trip. It gave me comfort to know I had found a familiar trail.

My reaction to my "discovery" was probably a sign that I was not cut from the cloth from which explorers are made. To be the first to chart the uncharted wilderness is an experience every explorer yearns for. To take back maps, however crudely drawn, and tales of places hitherto unknown has sustained many an arctic and subarctic traveller who has found himself weatherbound or lost on a windswept shore. My friend and fellow traveller, the late Eric Morse, had the makings of an explorer. It was a pity he was not born a century earlier because by the mid-twentieth century there was too little northern country that had not been previously charted and described.

Eric Morse had to content himself with the role of a latter-day explorer. During his lifetime he and his various companions paddled virtually all of the fur trade and exploration routes in Canada that could be navigated by canoe. It was a rare privilege for me, as a young man, to be invited in 1972 to join Eric, who was then in his seventies. It was especially exciting to be asked to accompany him on the Taltson River, the upper reaches of which had never been the subject of an explorer's pen.

We flew in to Dymond Lake about 125 miles north of Uranium City, Saskatchewan. Though we were below the treeline, we could see from the size of the spruce trees that the edge of the barrens was not far away. Our first camp was a flat but spongy site behind a willow-lined shore. On the hill behind us were two spruce trees, their trunks bare to a height of eight feet. Branches were growing thickly above. Such trees are called "lob sticks" or "lop sticks." They are easy to make with an axe and stand out as camp or trail markers for decades. Somebody had been on this spot before us. Perhaps they were Chipewyan hunters or trappers, Eric had commented. When one is exploring, the rules seem to be that it does not count if aboriginal people have previously discovered and used the country. It is not part of their tradition to do accounts of their travel. Writing diaries appears to be a hallmark of exploration. So, in a way, and in spite of the lob sticks, the Morse party could still say it was the first through this area.

Imagine our surprise a few days later to beach our canoe where others had recently camped. There was not only a fire site but there were fresh tracks on the beach as well. It had rained and snowed enough a day earlier to have erased all previous tracks. We reckoned, therefore, that our fellow travellers were no more than a day ahead of us. No one spoke of it, but for the next two days we travelled longer and paddled farther than was our custom. Toward the end of the second day, we ran a short rapid and found the people we had been following. They were wind-bound on a lake shore and camped in the trees. The two men came down to the beach and introduced themselves. Dalen and Randy Bayes were from the United States. Dalen, the older one, had been on the river before, but not so far upstream. The younger one was there for the first time. If we got ahead of the Bayes party, there was still a chance for the Morse party to be "the first" in the sense the explorers use the term.

We camped with Dalen and Randy, shared their fireside, and swapped tales as wilderness travellers do. Dalen, a millwright from Washington state, had read widely about northern adventure and travel and seemed to know Eric Morse's published works as well as Eric did. I think perhaps he understood Eric's yearnings to be an explorer, too.

The day following our meeting we set off, the two canoe parties together. We in the Morse party paddled seventeen-foot Grummans. These canoes are aluminum, flat-bottomed, seaworthy, and almost indestructible, but they are not very fast. The Bayes brothers had a Chestnut cedar strip canvas canoe that moved like a trout through the water. We were incapable of overtaking them. And yet, at every bend, Dalen and Randy waited for us to catch up. Then, about mid-afternoon when we had stopped for a snack, Dalen said they were going to make an early camp and rest for a day or two as they were well ahead of schedule.

The Morse party paddled on another ten miles or more before making camp. We never saw the Bayes brothers again, and I believe to this day that Dalen sensed the Morse party's need to be first. His graciousness and silent understanding touched me. Over the years, it has stood as an example of the consideration people show to one another on the trail. It is not an isolated example.

Standing on top of a loaded komatiq on an April afternoon, I had picked out two black dots on the blinding white frozen surface of Great Slave Lake. Did I see them or did I imagine them? They were not my imagination. The black dots aroused the interest of my lead dog and he made straight for them. For several hours he had taken his direc-tions entirely from my voice commands. I could see that he was relieved to have something real on the horizon to head for.

"Fishermen," I said hopefully to my father. They could just as easily have been ravens. The spring sky was the colour of pearl and met the snow-covered lake somewhere ahead of us. I could not tell where the lake ended and the sky began. There was nothing to provide scale. Under such conditions, an object may sometimes appear to be on the horizon and, in reality, be no more than a few steps away.

As luck would have it, they were fishermen, and not far from the horizon. As we approached, we could see the light from a snowmobile as it bounced over a hard snowdrift. In half an hour we were upon them. We anchored the dogs and went to where the men were pulling up a fish net. It was Jonas Johanssen and his partner, Bunny. I had met them before in Yellowknife. Two burnished silver whitefish had already been set aside for us. I produced a thermos and we passed around a cup of sweet tea. Hot tea is the communion wine of the winter trail and the cup is always passed around with appropriate reverence.

"I figured you might want fish," said Jonas, the older of the two men. Bunny grinned. "Can we pay you for them, Jonas?" I asked. He looked amused. The idea of money changing hands between the four of us in that expanse of white was too absurd. "You don't have to," he said. I knew we did not have to. I also knew I had no money. I turned to my father. He dug around in his trouser pocket. Underneath his spotted handkerchief was a folded two-dollar bill. "How about that!" exclaimed Jonas as he took the money offered. Of course it was a most unusual setting for commerce and our exchange was quite unrelated to the value of fish or money. What we were really trading was wilderness courtesies in a tradition older than memory. The tea and a bit of gossip would also have been fair trade. But we had the money and it would be useful when Jonas went to town for supplies.

Before we resumed our journey, Jonas asked whether we had our map. We produced it and he showed us were his camp was located. On the return trip we were to stop there for a meal and, of course, with the news of our adventures.

News of the country is the northern traveller's most negotiable commodity. I have dined out on it often and received change in return. News of ice and weather conditions, the whereabouts of a portage, and the details of game sightings are among the valued items of exchange.

Without knowledge of the country travel can be dangerous. Early explorers, ignorant of the Arctic and Subarctic, fared best when they put themselves into the hands of seasoned travellers and the aboriginal people of the country. Samuel Hearne could not have travelled to the mouth of the Coppermine River and returned safely to Fort Prince of Wales without the aid of Matonabbee and his Chipewyan wives and followers. Earlier he had tried with less competent guides and had been forced to return in failure. Sir John Franklin would, in all likelihood, have perished before 1821 had it not been for the generosity, concern, and knowledge of Akaitcho and Keskarrah and the other Yellowknife Indians with whom he and his party travelled. Perhaps if he had asked about the country, John Hornby and his two companions would not have become the tragic heroes of the Thelon that their slow starvation in the spring of 1926 made them.

How do you find out about the country? You can read, of course. Explorers' journals and the accounts of the more recent adventure travellers are available. But, for my money, there is no substitute for sitting down and chatting with somebody who has been wherever you want to go.

In 1980 four of us agreed to travel by dog team around Great Slave Lake. None of us had made the journey before, though we had all handled dogs for years. All but one had done extensive winter camping. We knew we needed to find someone who knew firsthand what we were likely to encounter.

We sought the advice of seasoned traveller Charlie Saunders. Charlie had three times circumnavigated the lake by dog team without human companions. "The cabins change, the people change, but the lake stays the same," Charlie told us. Charlie's advice kept us from trying to travel in blizzard and white-out conditions unless we could see and navigate by the sun. Once Charlie himself had been storm-bound for three consecutive days while crossing the North Arm of Great Slave Lake. He just camped in his sled and waited it out.

One afternoon near the beginning of our expedition, in a world that looked like cotton wool, I thought about the quiet courage that Charlie's ordeal had required. With a companion I sat on a caribou skin for several hours. We had our backs to the wind, sipped our tea, and discussed how long three days alone under such conditions would seem. It was difficult to imagine.

Later in the same trip, while we were harnessing dogs in the sawmill yard at Fort Resolution, we were approached by Jim Balsillie. Jim told us he had taken the Christmas mail to Fort Providence by dog team in 1925. He had come out specially to tell us about Sulphur Point, where the Buffalo River empties into the lake. It seems that there is deep water off the Point and with the great sweep of open water, the ice freezes, breaks up, and freezes again many times. It is called, simply, rough ice. Jim said that there would be lots of it around Sulphur Point.

Rough ice means jumbled slabs as smooth as billiard balls set at odd angles. Between the slabs are cracks in which a man can break a leg. These cracks are often filled with snow.

Keeping a 600-pound sled packed with gear upright in rough ice is an exhausting, full-time job. How dogs manage to walk, let alone pull, through such ice conditions where a man can scarcely stand upright is to me a mystery.

Jim's advice was to drive inshore just before reaching Sulphur Point and to run along the beach for several miles until the ice offshore became smooth. He said this would be obvious somewhere to the west of the point. Now, normally dog mushers avoid beaches. The snow there is frequently deep and drifted. To advise us to choose the beach for our trail was rare advice indeed.

We stored Jim's advice in the backs of our minds and brought it out to discuss as we neared Sulphur Point. Maybe the rough ice did not go out too far. After all, Jim only said he had done the trip once. Perhaps he did not go far enough offshore. The snow on the beach looked soft and wearying. Perhaps we could just go around the rough ice. Anyway, 1925 was a long time ago. Things might have changed. We decided to attempt to drive around the rough ice. We headed out toward the northwest. Within three miles the rough ice was all around us. Our speed has slowed to less than two miles an hour. The dogs rose and fell among the jumbled ice. We were almost exhausted and soaked in our own sweat from floundering around and righting overturned sleds. We decided to turn back to try the beach. Once there, we found travel quite satisfactory.

Jim Balsillie had been right. Our failure to follow Jim's advice had cost us half a day. However, we had learned something of value. It had to do with respecting and listening to the advice of those who have been there before you.

On a canoe trip down the Snake and Peel rivers in 1981, I learned something about the kind of society a northern river supports. The Snake River has its beginnings in the Yukon high in the Western Cordillera at about the same latitude as Fort Norman in the Northwest Territories. We put our three canoes in where the river was barely deep enough to float a loaded boat and walked our loads a mile or so downstream. The river is one glorious rapid more or less uninterrupted for a hundred miles. The mountains are breathtaking. The country through which the river travels is a garden of Eden full of big game that pay scant attention to humans.

We were six men in a glorious place having the time of our lives. We had little need for company save our own. Indeed, in the first 170 miles, we did not see a soul. There were signs that people had been using the country. The majority of these were winter signs and, for the most part, were confined to the lower sixty miles of the river. From the confluence of the Snake and Peel rivers, however, things changed.

First, there was the bare footprint on the beach. We were close to the Arctic Circle and it was the second week of August. In those latitudes at any season a bare footprint was a thing to be noticed. But this was not merely a footprint but a delicate, slender footprint of the sort one expects to find in a glass slipper or soft Italian leather. Or so we thought at the time!

Poor Robinson Crusoe. He had not seen anybody for ages and had nobody with whom to speculate about the owner of Man Friday's foot. By contrast, we had six healthy imaginations and built speculations onto one another's fantasies.

A day later, we caught up with the owner of the foot. He turned out to be an unshaven young man with a male companion. We smothered our disappointment in laughter as we approached their campfire from the beach. They were Germans travelling in two kayaks and they had just completed paddling the Ogilvie River.

The one with the lovely feet was deep-frying donuts over the open fire. The other was sprinkling them with icing sugar and making coffee. We accepted their invitation and joined their continental breakfast, swapping tales of rapids, Dall's sheep, and grizzly bears. It seems there were plenty of all three in the two river valleys we had separately travelled.

We left them to their baking and pushed on downriver. I knew there were Dene summer fish camps closer to Fort McPherson where the Gwich'in people smoked and dried fish for the fall and winter. Would the Gwich'in be interested in our travels?

We stopped first at Trail Creek. There, Elizabeth Colin had dry fish, bannock, and sweet tea for us. We recounted our adventures for her and the others at the camp. They were hungry for news of the upper Snake River, which none of them had visited for years. A boatload of hunters heading upriver passed us as we resumed our trip downriver. Another went downriver late at night after we had made camp. Although neither stopped to talk to us, it seemed that, within twelve hours, everyone along the river from Trail Creek to Fort McPherson knew we were on our way. Much of the news we had given to Elizabeth Colin had preceded us. We stopped at every fish camp but one. And it mattered little that our tales had already been passed along. Most people wanted to hear them again anyway.

Windbound on the Peel River one afternoon we camped early and rolled into our sleeping bags by 7:00 p.m. We were up at 3:00 a.m. and away one hour later to make some headway before the winds blew up a chop that would beach us. At 4:30 in the morning we arrived at Road River and the camp of John (Tetlichi) Charlie, a respected elder who had previously been chief for many years. I had known him prior to our trip, and I wanted very much to stop and visit. At 4:30 a.m. the Charlie camp was quiet and everyone was asleep.

Instead of waking John and his family, I wrote a note and anchored it to a fuel drum using a large stone. We pushed on. By mid-afternoon a motorized skiff had overtaken us.

It was Elizabeth Colin's husband, Neil, who modestly introduced himself as the "Mouth of the Peel." Neil brought the news from Road River. "John Charlie is sure disappointed you never woke them up," he said. "You shoulda gone in and make fire. People woulda got up for tea. Too bad." I wish that I had known then what I do now. The rhythm of life in the bush is set by events. Seasons are important but the time of day is not. The habits of animals and birds influence the daily habits of those whose lives revolve around the river. Nobody minds being wakened when visitors come to camp. I shoulda gone in and make fire.

What to do? What not to do? It seems those questions continually present themselves to the wilderness traveller. Sometimes one can call on personal or borrowed experience. At other times one may have little but common sense as a guide.

There is an urge to push on inside us all. In some it is stronger than others. Its strength may vary in direct relation to how close our intended destination is or how tempting. Cold, wet travellers sometimes take incredible risks to reach a warm, dry place. I have pushed an exhausted dog team on through the night to be home instead of making a comfortable camp and coming in well rested and safely in the morning.

There are two lessons to be learned. The first is always to have enough equipment and food to be comfortable and well fed even when delayed a few days on the trail. The second is that being stormbound is not a curse and can be something to look forward to.

While I was taught from an early age that you should always take plenty of rations, I was caught short once on a family trip by canoe near Yellowknife. We travelled with my brother, Richard, and his friend, Jim Clark. They were teenagers. Richard loved to fish even when there was nothing taking a hook. Jim enjoyed lifting huge boulders, staggering to the river's edge, and dropping them into the water to see how big a splash they would make. They were both energetic paddlers. All of this added up to huge adolescent appetites. By the second day into the trip, we were rationing the peanut butter and honey. By the third day, we were into the emergency flour supply to make bannock for the fourth day. We began fishing in earnest so we would not go hungry before the end of the trip, which was to take approximately five days. In the end we had enough, but only because we had packed eight days' rations for a five-day trip.

Caribou hunting by dog team is a very sporting way to go after big game. If you only have a few days, the odds are very much in the caribou's favour. You generally go on well-travelled trails to get into the country to make better time. Otherwise, you have to break trail for your dogs on skis or snowshoes.

In February, 1982, my friend Greg McDonald and I were

on such a hunt. We headed northeast from Yellowknife through Prosperous, Shortpoint, Neck, and Duncan lakes. We travelled twenty-five miles in an easy day. There was plenty of daylight left when we decided to camp and we did a good job, pitching our tent in a sheltered place, laying down a deep bed of spruce boughs, and cutting plenty of firewood. The dogs were tethered in the willows off the trail and out of the wind, which by sunset had swept the sky of clouds. We banked snow around the tent walls in the moonlight while the lantern hung golden from the ridgepole and smoke blew down from the chimney of our airtight stove. We planned to leave the camp standing and go off the next day with empty sleds looking for caribou.

During the night the wind blew. If the temperature dropped, we did not know it. Our stovepipe glowed cherry red and our sleeping bags were good. In the morning, however, it was definitely warmer. We went out to find our dogs all but buried in the snow, which was falling heavily and drifting into the trail.

I did not like the look of the weather, but we had come to hunt and, after breakfast, we hooked up the dogs in two teams and left. The portage trail was invisible. The lead dog found it with his feet. If he stepped off it, he disappeared in deep snow. Stopping before we reached the lake, I cut spruce boughs along the trail to set as markers across Graham Lake. It was just as well that I did. Out on the lake you could not see ten feet in front of your lead dog. Instead of putting the trail markers every hundred yards, I was placing them every hundred feet. Greg's leader followed behind me but he was troubled by the storm and turned in a circle for home. I pressed on till I ran out of trail markers and then turned back, too. I had no idea where on the lake I was. However, the trail markers took us back to the portage and the portage took us back to camp.

After we had tied up the dogs, we went inside. The stove was still warm. We stoked it up and made tea and bannock. I got out my sewing kit and began mending a dog harness. Propped up against our sleeping bags, Greg and I chatted and drank tea. A mouse appeared from under the spruce boughs somewhere and, as bold as you please, climbed into the frying pan to nibble on the bannock crumbs.

I dug into the depths of my pack and pulled out a copy of the *Manchester Guardian Weekly* and a harmonica. Between tunes, Greg read me tidbits from the paper, which was several months old. That did not seem to matter. We were shut away from the of the world anyway. Its problems, old or new, seemed far away.

Morning blended into afternoon and then it was dark. Sometime during the day the dogs were fed and harnesses were laid out for the morning. A snowshoe was repaired. Whichever direction we went the next morning (assuming we travelled at all) we would need them. Because of the drifting snow, there would be no trails at all. We would have

to snowshoe ahead of our teams all day. Somehow none of that bothered us. We were at home and comfortable. Except for crossing Graham Lake, which we should not have attempted, we had enjoyed a successful day.

The adventure traveller learns these things one by one, if he learns them at all. He learns them when, beaten by a gale, he is kept in his tent for days at a time. He learns to break camp at 10:00 p.m. and to travel into the dawn of the next morning. In the spring he learns to run dogs at night and rest them by day when the trails are quickly disappearing in the hot sun. He learns to relax and enjoy being where he is when there is nowhere else he can go.

Until 1981 I had never been a paying guest on a guided expedition. That year, partly because the guide was a close friend and partly because I was contemplating a part-time guiding career, I took that canoe trip down the Snake and Peel rivers. My guide was Hector Mackenzie of Yukon Mountain and River Expeditions. He knew the rivers well. He had studied the flora and fauna of the area. He knew its history. He was acquainted with the Dene people at whose camps we visited. Moreover, he made all the arrangements, purchased the food, and found us travelling companions. I enjoyed the trip very much. I wondered why I had never taken a guided trip before.

Certainly it makes adventure travel safer, particularly for the inexperienced. But, it also gives the adventurer immediate contact and conversation with someone who is of the country. And I will wager that fifty years after, when the details of the travel have blurred and the photographs are faded, it will be the people you camped with and whose trails you crossed that you remember best. The people of the North — people constantly on the move in a land where all travel is an adventure.

Western Arctic

Great Bear Lake, at 31,400 square kilometres the eighth largest lake in the world, is located along the Arctic Circle, just south of the treeline. The lake's only settlement is Fort Franklin, but there are several fishing lodges on its long shores. *Wolfgang Weber*

Wilderness travellers on
Keith Arm of Great Bear
Lake. *John Bayly*

July camping at Crossley
Lake, 170 kilometres east of
Inuvik. *Judith Currelly*

Dene and Métis craftspeople of the Mackenzie Valley — as well as Yukon Indian people — for centuries have made and decorated moccasins, ankle-high crow boots, and two-layered *mukluks*, as well as garments, from smoke-tanned moose- or caribou-hides and, in some places, from beaver, with decorative fur trim of beaver and wolf. Long before glass beads came North with the fur traders in the early 1800s, Native women used the quills of birds and porcupine, dyed, woven, and shaped to create symbolic, decorative work. *Fran Hurcomb*

Mackenzie Valley's Muriel Betsine shows the young the art of embroidering and beading. *Fran Hurcomb*

John Truro of Fort Good Hope is one of the many Native artists whose drawings and paintings express deep knowledge of the land and the people. *Fran Hurcomb*

Fort Norman is a traditional community at the confluence of sparkling Great Bear River with the mighty Mackenzie. *Tulit'a* — meaning, where two rivers meet — has long been of importance to the Dene. It wasn't until 1810 that a fur trading post was established here. *Hälle Flygare*

Over the course of many long winters, the church of Fort Good Hope has been decorated with splendid frescos painted with natural dyes from plants and berries, probably one of the most impressive works by Christianized Dene artists. *Fran Hurcomb*

Further down the river lies Fort Good Hope, firmly established in 1805. The energy and enthusiasm of Mackenzie Valley missionaries is evident in Our Lady of Good Hope church, built by Catholic priest Emile Petitot in the 1860s. *B. Wilson*

Most Mackenzie Valley communities still rely on river barges for their bulk freight in summer, as seen here south of Fort Good

Hope with the barge train just having left the Ramparts. *Hälle Flygare*

The ferryboat at Arctic Red River crosses the Mackenzie to service the Dempster Highway traffic, which travels over an ice bridge in winter. *Wolfgang Weber*

Arctic Red River is a tiny Dene settlement at the confluence of Arctic Red and Mackenzie rivers. The site has probably been a major fishing camp of the Gwich'in Loucheaux Indians for centuries. *Wolfgang Weber*

Modern oil town Norman Wells: man-made islands in the Mackenzie bear most of the oil production wells, installed in a technique known as directional drilling. Oil was discovered here in 1920–21; the field was expanded in the early 1940s to supply oil through the Canol Pipeline to Whitehorse, and further west, during World War Two. Increasing demand for oil led to a further major expansion in the 1980s. *Wolfgang Weber*

The latest refining technology has been used at Norman Wells since 1985.
Wolfgang Weber

Gus Kraus has been a prospector and trapper in the Nahanni country for more than sixty years.
Matt Bradley

227

During the fall and winter of 1943–44, Dodo Canyon was one of the key obstacles in the construction of the Canol Pipeline and its service road of 929 kilometres from Norman Wells through the Mackenzie Mountains to Whitehorse, to transport oil to the expected war theatre in Alaska. Today, the Canol Heritage Trail — the 372-kilometre NWT portion to the Continental Divide at Macmillan Pass — is a wilderness area of incredible beauty and rich natural resources, which continues on the Yukon side through no less scenic country. *Wolfgang Weber*

Wrecks of trucks and
bulldozers can be found all
along Canol Road.
Wolfgang Weber

A waterfall near the Canol
Heritage Trail.
Wolfgang Weber

Our Lady of Victory, the "Igloo" church in Inuvik. *Elke Emshoff*

Inuvik, with close to 4,000 inhabitants, is North America's largest town north of the Arctic Circle and can be reached by jet plane or via the Dempster Highway. *Wolfgang Weber*

Most first-time visitors to Inuvik, located just north of latitude 68° N, are surprised to discover that it lies within the northern edge of the forest border. Inuvik was founded in 1954 to replace nearby Aklavik, which was reportedly sinking into the Delta waters — though it hasn't yet. *Wolfgang Weber*

Drilling rig at the edge of the Mackenzie Delta. Oil and gas below the Beaufort Sea were the driving force for industrial development of the northwestern coastal areas of the NWT. The estimated resource potential here is 1.5 billion cubic metres of oil and 2.1 trillion cubic metres of natural gas. The impact of these activities on the fragile environment is still not known, however.
Wolfgang Weber

Aklavik, in the heart of the Delta, was established in 1918 and rapidly became the chief trapping, trading, and transportation centre. The "Mad Trapper" of Rat River,

Albert Johnson, object of the first aerial RCMP manhunt in Canada in 1932, is buried here.
Wolfgang Weber

Cable-layer on the East Arm of the Mackenzie at Inuvik.
Wolfgang Weber

The Mackenzie Delta is one of the greatest wildlife habitats in the world. Besides being the home for numerous small and large land mammals, millions of birds nest here in summer, including large species such as swans, cranes, geese, eagles, hawks, and falcons.
Wolfgang Weber

In early September, snow geese gather along the western Arctic coast to migrate to southern quarters. Here, another example of patterned tundra ground can be seen. *Wolfgang Weber*

Anglers enjoy peaceful nature and good catches on one of the many arms of the Mackenzie River and its delta. *Wolfgang Weber*

Many trappers in the Mackenzie Delta primarily trap muskrat, which find an ideal habitat here. The Delta people are a mixture of cultures of the Dene and Inuvialuit. *Wolfgang Weber*

Mackenzie Delta trapper.
Wolfgang Weber

The predominant
"furniture" in this trapper's
cabin is the stove, made of an
old oil barrel.
Wolfgang Weber

The float plane base at Shell
Lake near Inuvik offers
aircraft on skis a solid
landing strip on ice in winter.
Wolfgang Weber

When metre-thick ice covers the Mackenzie and the Beaufort Sea, a good ice road is prepared on the East Channel from Inuvik to Tuktoyaktuk.
Wolfgang Weber

Drill and supply ships overwinter by riding at anchor near Tuktoyaktuk. Besides man-made islands in the Beaufort Sea closer to the shore, reinforced drill ships are needed for deepwater drilling. Due to the severe physical and environmental problems, the drilling season is only 150 days per year.
Wolfgang Weber

Located near the mouth of Hornaday River on the southern coast of Darnley Bay, Paulatuk is a small Inuvialuit settlement whose people still live a traditional lifestyle based on hunting and fishing. Carving is a common occupation here.
Wolfgang Weber

Paulatuk: airplanes and snowmobiles are today's common means of transportation along the Arctic coast. *Wolfgang Weber*

Paulatuk is a friendly little community, as this girl proves beyond doubt. *Wolfgang Weber*

Small winter camp at Brock
River not far from Paulatuk.
When an intensely cold wind
blows, laden with fine snow
crystals picked up from the
ground that conceal the
landscape behind a white
wall, even the Inuvialuit stay
in camp. *Wolfgang Weber*

The soft sedimentary rock of
the Melville Hills river
canyons is eroding to bizarre
columns and towers.
Wolfgang Weber

Continuously blowing winds are responsible for the erosion of rock into thin needles and rough walls, typical for Brock River Canyon. *Wolfgang Weber*

Ice fishing is easy, once the hole has been cut: a wooden stick, a strong line, and the right hook, plus warm clothing and a little patience, as this Inuvialuit woman demonstrates.
Wolfgang Weber

A proud white hunter, having achieved his goal, a good-sized caribou bull, on the Arctic coast.
Jerome Knap

When spring arrives in the North and temperatures rise to a comfortable −10° or −15°C, Frank Pokiak and his family and friends go hunting and fishing to set up a picnic-camp on the frozen Eskimo Lakes near Tuktoyaktuk on the weekends. *Wolfgang Weber*

The Roman Catholic church
Our Lady of Grace is located
on the spit at Tuk. Next to it
is the restored mission ship
Our Lady of Lourdes,
which, from 1931 to 1957,
carried supplies to the
missions along the Arctic
coast. *Wolfgang Weber*
Modern materials are being
used today for fishing and
hunting boats at Tuk's inner
spit. *Wolfgang Weber*

Tuktoyaktuk today is the supply centre for oil and gas exploration in the Beaufort Sea. The small spit of land in Kugmallit Bay was one of the traditional homelands of the whale-hunting Karngmalit Eskimos, who now call themselves Inuvialuit. A few of the many pingos in the area can be seen in the background, on top of some of which people have built their homes. *Wolfgang Weber*

Yellow and red are the predominant colours of nature in fall, as seen here at the treeline along Anderson River, which reaches the Arctic Ocean at Wood Bay. *Wolfgang Weber*

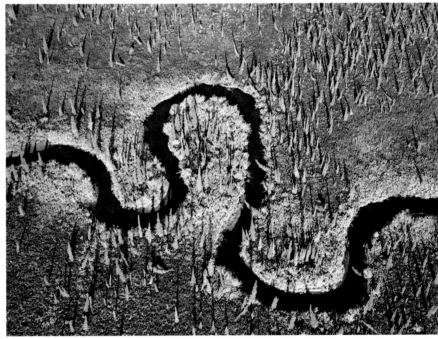

One of the many solid-ice pingos near Tuktoyaktuk, which "grow" as high as 150 metres and are covered with a thin layer of soil with vegetation. *Wolfgang Weber*

A stream in fall in the typical forest-tundra transition zone near Sitidgi Lake. *Wolfgang Weber*

The last survivors of the ice ages: muskox family group in defensive formation on Banks Island. The abundant wildlife on this large island in the western Arctic has always been an attraction for both the ancient and the modern peoples of the North. *Wolfgang Weber*

Sandhill cranes with chick in the warming summer sun of Banks Island. *Albert Kuhnigk / First Light*

Young Arctic fox on the summer tundra near Sachs Harbour, the only community on Banks. *Roddy MacInnes*

One of the Horton River's
big bends, before it cuts
through the coastal hills and
flows into Franklin Bay.
Wolfgang Weber

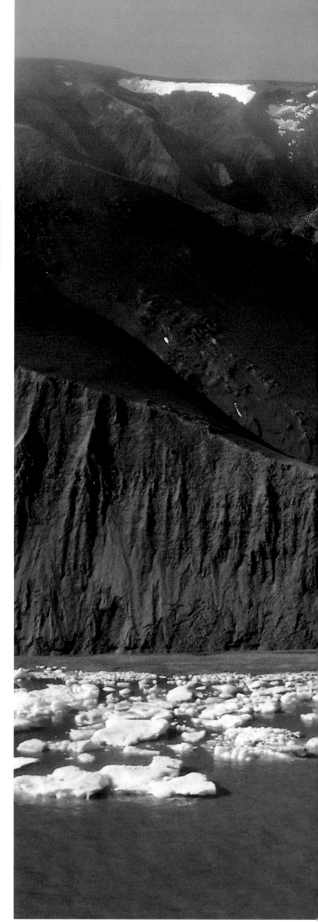

Not far from Paulatuk lie the Smoking Hills at Franklin Bay, a coal and sulphur deposit that burns endlessly, giving Paulatuk its name, meaning "soot of coal." *Wolfgang Weber*

Polar bear on the sea ice along the Arctic coast. *Wolfgang Weber*

The ice pans of last winter
populate the shores of
Franklin Bay south of Cape
Bathurst. *Wolfgang Weber*

Randal Pokiak
Inuvialuit History

The Inuvialuit chose to settle and concentrate along the coastline of the Arctic Ocean. They limited their travels in the geographical area, as we know it now, from Herschel Island to Cape Bathurst, and bartered and traded with the Inupiat of Alaska and the central Arctic Inuit. The Inuvialuit developed this society in this area for several reasons.

1. There was a land base to build permanent community centres, the major centres being Herschel Island, Tununuk, Kittigazuit, Tuktoyaktuk, Warren Point, Atkinson Point, Dalhousie, Anderson River, and Baillie Island. From the migrating Blue Nose and Porcupine caribou herds as well as from moose harvested from North Yukon, the Mackenzie Delta, and Anderson River, they got what was needed for their society — food, clothing, accommodations, and other items. Grizzlies were also harvested.

2. The Mackenzie River is one of the largest in the world. The delta area is used by migratory birds not only for nesting, breeding, and moulting but as a staging area both when they arrive in the spring and when they get ready to leave in the fall. The land around the river is rich and produces plants, berries, and roots that were edible by humans as well as by wildlife.

3. The Arctic Ocean had migratory mammals as well as fish and polar bears. The mammals harvested were bowhead and beluga whales, seals, and *ugyuks* (bearded seals). The richness in wildlife, fish, and migratory birds was the attraction for the Inuvialuit to settle in the area.

The next reality they had to face was the environment. They had to adapt to climatic conditions, learn by trial and error, which at times was costly, even to the point of some people perishing. They had to rely on one another and share their experiences. Under these conditions the Inuvialuit developed a pattern for their society, which I will try to piece together based on the stories of Inuvialuit elders.

"Inuvialuit" means the real people or a people that identify themselves to an area. In our dialect "Inuit" means any human being or people. Inuvialuit understood that there were other people outside their concentration areas and they respected them.

The Inuvialuit followed a yearly cycle or pattern. Things were discussed by a recognized leader and subleader and their trainees, but the overall decision was made by the leader. These discussions were pursued when the Inuvialuit gathered together as a collective group at the Kittigazuit area during the winter months. Discussions focused on what the terrain was like; the animals, fish, and birds, how early or late the migration of various species started, when they left or would arrive again. Each subleader reported on his

area while the leader listened. These kinds of discussions were heard by all present so that everyone had the same information — nothing was held back because if that happened it would jeopardize the social order or lives of the people. The leader, by end of March, dispersed the parties with the subleaders in charge to go to their harvesting locations and use their expertise for the health and welfare of the people as a whole. Each party or community varied in size. The total population of the Inuvialuit numbered in the thousands (5,000–6,000) during this pre-contact time.

Inuvialuit Leaders

Inuvialuit at that time knew the responsibility that came with leadership. Any decision made by a leader would affect the welfare of everyone. A leader is recognized by his wisdom or understanding of the environment and wildlife and by his being able to use this knowledge to make life easier for himself and his family. Those around him see this and usually consult him for his opinion in decisions they plan to make. Thus is started the process of consultation, and the one so recognized by others has no choice but to take the leadership role. The other members of the party then reward him from the fruits of their labour because of the guidance he provides. Because of his initial unselfishness he not only benefits from his own labour but also from the labour of others. He also takes stock of those he has become responsible for and picks out those others who are fulfilling similar responsibilities and works closely with them.

The leader and his subleaders had to administer or distribute responsibility to the parties for which each subleader was responsible. If there were seven parties or small communities, there were seven subleaders. They had to decide what, where, and when small hunting and fishing parties should be sent out to the surrounding areas so there could be more variety in their diet. In times of scarce food supply along the coastal areas and in case of a consequential raiding Inupiat party, the enemy had to be carefully located and repelled, and subleaders had to be able to respond to a cry of help from other Inuvialuit camps when necessary. Each subleader had to make sure that in his community those with patience and communication skills were used to teach and train the young. Community leaders had the ability and skills to do the things each subleader was responsible for so there was no time wasted in understanding a problem or a process. He was there to make sure that there were enough people in each party to meet the overall requirement of the Inuvialuit.

When it was time to gather at Kittigazuit area, the leader was responsible for what could be taken for showing or barter/trading purposes with the other community leaders and their members. He was responsible to report to the ultimate leader of the Inuvialuit on their activities and the concerns of his community.

Ultimate leaders were responsible for the Inuvialuit in the concentration area. They made sure that sufficient numbers of people with distinct abilities and skills were committed to each community. This leader circulated himself between each community to better understand the local concerns, and he also had the opportunity to do some things out of the ordinary that he wanted to try out for himself. He was able to do this because his needs were met by the various communities.

Travel

During the spring and fall travel was done by walking, by sleighs pulled either by the people themselves or by dogs (one dog per sleigh). During the summer and early fall, kayaks and *umiaks* were used. Men had two types of kayaks — one for speed for hunting; another for hauling freight so that, for example, they wouldn't have to drag their catches over long stretches. During some travels they backpacked themselves or used dogs to backpack. When it came to travelling with *umiaks*, the woman paddled with a man responsible for the rudder. *Umiaks* hauled family members and camping gear. Men followed or led in their kayaks. For passing messages they had runners on land, and these used kayaks during water seasons.

Community Activities

Each community had a specific species it concentrated on harvesting. They did not have to worry about any other major species because they knew that another community was harvesting it, just as they had the responsibility for looking after the need of the Inuvialuit people through the wildlife harvesting they were entrusted with. And each species of wildlife harvested was prepared differently for food and other uses.

Each community was close to the migration route or habitat area for the migratory species of wildlife, fish, or birds it was responsible for, although a community never was set up on the exact route or in the heart of a habitat area. During the hunts the leader was followed with no questions asked. At his sign the hunt was started. Anyone who disobeyed was disciplined by not being allowed to take part in other hunts. Usually disciplinary action of this kind lasted for one year, after which time the disobedient individual was allowed to try again. The disobedience was thus not only an embarrassment to himself but he jeopardized the welfare of his community and the Inuvialuit as a collective group. This action reflected negatively not only on himself but also on his community.

After the hunt the workload was shared by all, since what was harvested was gotten in large quantities. Food was stored in the permafrost, was dried, or a fermenting process was begun. All usable by-products were cleaned and prepared for tools, clothing, or shelter. Bones were broken and the marrow stored. For permanent shelter sod houses were built, usually for three to five families, depending on the size of the house built. There were compartments built and each compartment was used by one family. Sod houses were built using the driftwood that came down the Mackenzie, Kugaluk, and Anderson rivers as framing material (along the coast of the Arctic Ocean, over 300 miles of shoreline has driftwood). A wood frame was built, clay was used as chinking between the cracks, then sod was laid over the wood and clay.

Tents were made and used also. Poles were of driftwood and caribou or seal skins sewn together with the fur on the outside were wrapped around the wooden poles. When travelling in early spring and fall the people built snow houses when necessary. Caribou skins sewn together were used for blankets and mats. Polar/grizzly hides were often used as mats under the caribou mats.

The centre of the sod house was a common area where cooking and dining took place, and where storytelling and socializing transpired. Stories told about the results of both the good and bad that happened to an individual. Children were taught by these stories how to live, keeping in mind those around them, especially how to listen to and respect the leaders' words and what they had said. A person's words at that time were considered to be a contract, only it was not written. Words were not taken lightly — "I will," "I'm going to," "I'm ready to," "I'll do" were words that drove the Inuvialuit. That's why, before a decision was made, there had to be a lot of thought and discussion about the matter being contemplated.

For fishing and hunting small game every member of the community knew how to take part. The children and young people developed their skills through such fishing and hunting, under the eyes of adults. Small game varied around each community and fish of all species were plentiful. Fish traps were used and nets were made with sinew tied together for catching both fish and ptarmigan.

When a young member of the community for the first time brought home game for food, the family and close relatives celebrated with him. When the food was eaten it was shared by all except the youth who got the game. They would share the game even though it may be just a nibble for each member. To top it all off the whole community would hear of the success and show their respect to him, because one of their members had just started his maturity process.

Every member of the community knew how to sew and build a snow house because it was required for warmth and shelter. After all, there could be times when one would be alone for long periods of time. Woman and young girls specialized in sewing, house and lantern keeping, caring for young infants and children, berry picking, and gathering roots and other edible vegetation. As well, the womenfolk often waited expectantly for the return of their loved ones.

Some got so they could see and recognize objects from a long distance. This closeness of love brings with it an uncanny invisible tie, to the point where if there is something happening out of the ordinary or an endangerment to a loved one it is felt in some way by those at home. This may be because there is more time to think about (and pray for) them.

Men, when not hunting for harvest, were exploring or searching out new areas that would make life easier for the community. Any new discovery would be recognized by the community and thereby the individual's knowledge would be seen to be worth seeking out. A lot of this "research" or "studying" was done during the months when wildlife was plentiful in the area. Anything noticed in the behaviour of the wildlife would be shared back home and the meaning of that behaviour had to be evaluated until understood (at times answers could take years). Men's lives were dedicated to trying to understand the wildlife and environment.

Food was eaten raw, cooked, fermented, or dried. A lot of oil — whether fat, blubber, or rendered blubber — was eaten. Not only were the meat, blubber, and marrow eaten but also the intestines. After game was cleaned, it was cooked or dried for food. Berries were collected when ripe and were eaten or stored in sealskin bags. (Sealskin bags were used to store berries, fermented meat, and rendered blubber and were also used as water bags.) Roots and other plants were washed and eaten.

Clothing was made of caribou, seal, whale, *ugyuk*, muskox, polar/grizzly bears, and bird skins. Fish skins were used, as well as other skins of small game, for added decoration on clothing. There were winter clothes as well as spring/summer/fall clothing. Sinew, usually from the back spinal cord of caribou, was used as thread. Besides the ordinary clothing, there was also ceremonial dress made for special events.

Tools and equipment for harvesting and preparing by-products included *ulu* knives, lamps, needles, bone drills, stones/bones for scraping, snow goggles, snow knives, shovel, bone/stone picks, fish hooks, seal/whale/bowhead harpoons and lances, bows and arrows, slings, three-stringed slings, sticks for fish traps, nets, and kayaks.

Permafrost and Its Uses

From Herschel Island to Cape Bathurst there are recorded depths of permafrost of anywhere from 60 to 1,000 feet in places. Permafrost is a permanently frozen substrate of rock and soil, which is overlain by an *active* layer of soil that may thaw and refreeze. Here, along the Arctic coast, there are several locations where this is kept from melting by a layer of over-burden, usually peat moss and lichen and in some places clay, sand, or gravel pockets that make a hill or mound. Because of the permafrost pingos form or grow out of the ground. What happens is there is an underground lake just below the permafrost. These lakes vary in size. The water that has contact with the permafrost (ice) begins to freeze slowly, the freezing causes expansion, and thus the permafrost and over-burden begin to heave and lift up, creating a pingo. This process takes place until the underground lake is completely frozen over, at which point the pingo quits growing. These pingos were used as landmarks by those out on the ice floe or travelling by boat across large, open stretches of water. Pingos are a solid cone or core of ice.

The Inuvialuit used this permafrost to their advantage in other ways. They dug into it and made space to store and freeze food. To make coolers they dug to the level of the permafrost and built a shelter with wood frame, clay, and sand. These coolers kept the fermentation of food-processing controlled during the summer months, when at times it gets rather hot and meat/fish can rot quickly. In the summer an ice house dug into the permafrost is very cold and in the winter it's just a few degrees below freezing. This is because, during the summer, the surface of the land or tundra isn't frozen in many places so the coldness of the permafrost escapes and replaces the warmer air in the ice houses. During the fall and winter, the ground surface is frozen and acts like a blanket, so there is no air of any kind escaping. The storage space in the ice house thus warms up and the air becomes stationary and stale. Hence, the food stored during the summer stays in excellent condition but if kept in the ice house in the fall and winter the surface of the food becomes mouldy. To keep the food from getting too mouldy they hauled it to the surface and put it on stages when the ground had been frozen over for a few days and they were certain it was going to stay cold.

Other Aspects of Inuvialuit Life

Games within a community were encouraged when there was time. Various games were played by different age groups. Non-competitive games were played by groups. Competitive games were played by individuals with others watching. The purpose was to develop themselves by practising against each other to be ready for competitions with the other communities. For children, games were developed to teach them to work and think together. Skill, concentration, and strength were to be developed through their games.

Elders were revered within the community, for they had lived the longest and therefore knew more about life. In their own time they kept the community together by listening to *their* elders. Now it was their turn to give council and advice about personal and family matters. The physical strength of old men, for example, was lacking, but they had learned to put to use for the community the strength of young men. At one time, after all, they were the young ones, so they knew the limitations of these young people.

Elderly women, likewise, worked on the character and personality of young women and girls as well as showed them the duties of a wife.

Finally, adoption was important in the community, both to the ones adopting a child or a person and to the one being adopted. Adoption occurred when the natural parents died. Priority was given to childless couples and to the elderly who were living alone and needed help. Adopted persons usually produced more for their parents because they were not only treated like real family but they were grateful and wanted to please them. As they were growing up the adopted people in some ways could better understand how to help others that were in need because they were filling a need and were getting the first-hand experience of being helped themselves. Because of that attitude of going one step further in their duties and by their work pleasing others, they gained respect from those around them.

Louise Profeit-LeBlanc
Sister Greyling

Caches emptied, only leg bones left.
Where the caribou once roamed
There was nothing now!
Even the rabbits vanished.
The time of starvation was here . . .

The man looked at his wife, so weathered and thin.
Breasts emptied of their milk
A babe's crying ceasing to a faint whimper,
Weak in his mother's arms.
Sunken eyes and fontanelles.

He sharpened the knife
The job would have to be done quickly
As the cold would take you down.
Making you like itself.
Where was the fatty flesh?

Out onto the stark white lake,
Glowing in the dark,
All was quiet in the morning
Except for the interaction
Of the snowshoe against the snow
And his breathing.

He had kept the hole open for water
And pulling the tarp off,
Looked into the murky, black waters
Steaming below in the moon-lit morn.
Murmered softly to his Maker.

Swift as the movement of his knife
On an animal's body, he braced himself
And face grimacing with pain
Cut off a small piece of his own flesh
Wrapped it quickly with moss and skin.

Letting his breath off again
Placed the life-giving flesh
On the hook and lowering it into the water,
He waited.

The greyling came . . .
And starvation left.

Jerome Knap
Fishing and Hunting in the Far North

Yukon and the Northwest Territories occupy a land mass that is two and a half times greater than Alaska and yet the population is less than 85,000 people. Both Yukon and the Northwest Territories represent the greatest wilderness left in North America and perhaps the world.

The Northwest Territories is better known for its fishing than the Yukon; the Yukon is better known among international hunters. The main reason for this is that hunting in the Yukon has been open to non-resident hunters since the early 1950s, but even during the gold rush days in the early part of this century, southern newspapers were writing about the abundance of gold and game in Yukon. The Northwest Territories did not open big game hunting to non-resident sportsmen until the early 1960s.

Nonetheless, the Yukon's fishing can almost rival that of the Northwest Territories — certainly it has a greater variety of game fish. Just as certainly, the Northwest Territories can rival the Yukon when it comes to hunting. The Northwest Territories has a greater variety of game.

Fishing in the Yukon

The mountain lakes and streams of this territory have super fishing. Lake trout, Arctic grayling, rainbow trout, Dolly Varden, chinook, coho, and sockeye salmon, along with northern pike and the savage inconnu, can be caught in Yukon waters.

The Arctic grayling are probably Yukon's most widely distributed and most abundant game fish. They are found in just about every stream. Most of the streams crossing the Klondike, Dempster, and Alaska highways offer grayling just by walking to the nearest pool. The opening of the Dempster Highway from Dawson City in the Yukon to Inuvik in the Northwest Territories has opened several rivers to superb fishing. The Ogilvie and Blackstone rivers cross the highway and all of them have excellent grayling fishing, as do Kathleen River and Fox Creek. There are no fishing camps on any of these rivers. To fish these waters anglers have to camp. Arctic grayling are not confined solely to rivers. Most of the lakes also have grayling, with the best lakes probably being Fox, Little Fox, Wye, Snafu, Tarfu, Dog Pack, and the Moose Lakes chain.

Yukon's other stream fish is the Dolly Varden. The best water for these trout is the Teslin River system. Both the Teslin River and Teslin Lake have Dolly Varden. The lake, however, produces the larger fish, up to five and six kilograms. That's big for Dolly Varden! Teslin River also has some big grayling, up to six and a half kilograms. The upper Liard, Rancheria, and Frances rivers have Dolly Vardens while Blanchard, Takhini, Tatshenshini have both Dolly Varden and rainbow trout. For those who prefer to fish rainbow trout in lakes, Watson Lake is perhaps the best bet.

Lake trout are another widely distributed fish in the Yukon. Lake trout don't generally run as large as in the big lakes of the Northwest Territories, but they are abundant. Just about every deep lake in the Yukon lowlands has lake trout. Many of the lakes off the Alaska Highway from Haines Junction to the Alaska border offer good fishing. Other waters are right on the Klondike Highway.

All the major lakes — Teslin, Aishihik, Kluane, Marsh, Kathleen, Fox, Laberge, Little Salmon, Von Wilczek, Ethel, Bennett, Dezadeash, Snafu, Tarfu, and Watson — are loaded with lake trout. The trout in these bigger lakes commonly run up to nine or ten kilograms. All these lakes also have good Arctic grayling fishing.

Probably the best lake trout fishing in the Yukon is at Wellesley Lake, where the Lafevre family operates a fine wilderness fishing lodge. Wellesley is a designated trophy lake were only barbless hooks can be used and anglers may keep only two trout, one under ten kilograms and a trophy fish above ten kilograms. Besides fine lake trout fishing, Wellesley also offers good opportunity to view wildlife. Moose are frequently seen along the shores, as are grizzlies and the occasional wolf. Osprey and bald eagles nest around the lake.

The sun was just peeking over the horizon when we shoved our boat off the dock in Wellesley Lake. It was cool. The water was warmer than the air and here and there mist rose off the lake in patches although it was only early September. The poplar trees and birches were already beginning to turn from green to yellow. Autumn comes early in the Yukon.

Spring and late summer are the best time to fish the lowland Yukon lakes for lake trout. A cow moose with a gangly calf in tow was wading close to the shore across the bay. The water was shallow there with thick stands of aquatic vegetation, favourite summer food for the moose.

As we slowly moved off over the deeper water I started to release metres and metres of line from my fishing reel. The lure on the end was a big and heavy Dardevle and I let it flutter down into the deep water below. Steve Cooke and I had already been on Wellesley Lake for two days, and both days each of us had caught twenty to thirty lake trout ranging in weight from six to twelve kilograms. But Wellesley Lake could produce bigger than this. Lake trout in the fifteen-kilogram class are not that rare and the odd fish of eighteen kilograms has been landed. That's what Steve and I were after.

Steve got the first strike of the day, and after a seven- or eight-minute battle we got a first glimpse of the trout. I estimated its weight at about ten kilograms. The action con-

tinued off and on for an hour. We had caught about six trout each in quick succession. Two of the smaller fish, each about 2−3 kilograms, were hooked rather badly and we kept them for a shore lunch. It was promising to be a good day. The cooler weather may have triggered a feeding impulse among the trout. We trolled our lines about 100 metres from the shore off a deep rocky beach that plunged 50 metres straight down.

Reaching into the picnic basket for the coffee flask my eye caught a movement on the shore. Looking up I saw two wolves emerge from the willows close to the shore and start to gambol on the beach.

"Steve, wolves!" I hissed, pointed shoreward.

That instant two more wolves emerged. They joined the other two in play along the beach. And then two adults, the parents, joined the pack. One adult, probably the female, was a third taller than the adolescent wolves in play, and fuller in the body. The other was almost twice the size of the youngsters.

The female wolf saw us instantly. She froze and stared at us for two or three minutes. We thought afterward that it was rather strange that noise from the boat's outboard motor did not frighten or even alert the wolves about our presence. It is probable that they did not associate the mechanical noise of our outboard engine with humans.

We stopped fishing and slowly turned the boat around to get a better look at the wolves. Our movements in the boats were done very slowly and carefully. We did not utter a single word.

The young wolves were not concerned about us at all. They gamboled along the pebbly beach and played in the shallow water. Even the adults lost much of their concern. Steve moved the boat within twenty metres of the shore. Reaching slowly into the ice chest, I pulled out one of the trout and then heaved it toward the shore, some distance from the wolves. The trout fell into the water with a loud splash some three to four metres from shore.

The splash alerted the young wolves. Almost instantly one of the young pups ran to where the fish landed. The trout was by then floating on the surface, belly up. The pup seized it in its teeth and brought it ashore, much like a retriever would bring a dead duck ashore.

The three other wolf pups tried to grab the fish, and a free-for-all erupted on the shore. I quickly threw them the other trout. When it splashed into the water the same wolf that got the first trout ran for the second. But this time it was smarter. As soon as he grabbed the trout the pup bounded ashore through the shallow water and disappeared with the trout into the willow thickets on the bank. No doubt he intended to have a meal in peace and quiet.

From the body language of the adult wolves, it was obvious they did not like their offspring to be out of sight. The female took off after the pup almost immediately while the male

waited for the other three pups to finish their meal. And then, slowly, all four wandered into the willows.

"Even if I don't catch another trout I have had one of the best mornings fishing," Steve Cooke said in low, hushed tones after the wolves disappeared. "I shot off a whole roll of film."

Silently I agreed with him. Seeing a pack of wolves at such close distance can only happen in true wilderness. But the fishing got even better early in the afternoon. I landed a lake trout that tipped the scales at a shade over seventeen kilograms and Steve caught one that was only a little smaller.

Northern pike are also abundant in many Yukon lakes. They have a wide distribution in all the lowland waters. The northern pike in the small lakes are always hungry, and it is not unusual to have several fish follow a lure on every cast. The pike generally don't run as large as in the waters further south, but the bigger lakes do yield fish up to seven and a half kilograms.

The Yukon's Arctic char and salmon fishing has not even been exploited. Salmon run into all the major rivers, such as the Yukon, Alsek, and Teslin. Excellent coho salmon fishing is also found in Little Salmon, Fisheye, Marcella, and Wye lakes. The Klondike River is best for chinooks. Arctic char are found in the northern streams. One of the top char streams is the Firth River, which empties into the Mackenzie Bay. This is just a short flight from Inuvik in the Northwest Territories. But again, there is no camp or lodge on this river. The anglers have to camp out on the tundra. Other good char waters are Chapman Lake and Blackstone River.

Inconnu, that big and very predatory member of the whitefish family, can be caught in Teslin, Laberge, Little Salmon, and Quiet lakes and in McQuesten River.

Fish of one species or another are abundant in lakes, rivers, and streams in all the major wilderness areas, such as the Stewart and Pelly River area southeast of Dawson and the Ogilvie Mountain range, including the Blackstone and Ogilvie rivers north of Dawson. The fishing pressure in the Yukon is incredibly light, even on waters by the much-travelled Alaska Highway. Anyone contemplating a Yukon fishing trip, however, should bring plenty of bug dope and headnet. Insects can be devastating in the early summer.

Fishing in the Northwest Territories

The countless lakes and rivers, some of which are among the largest in the world, offer fantastic fishing for lake trout, Arctic char, and Arctic grayling, while walleye (or pickerel) and northern pike round out the complement. The inconnu or sheafish, a giant and savage member of the whitefish family, inhabits the Mackenzie River and Great Slave Lake. And giant Greenland sharks, some weighing over 1,000 kilograms, lurk along the Baffin Island coast, and no one even fishes for them.

Walleye are found in the more southerly watersheds of the Northwest Territories, while northern pike are much more widely spread. None of these species, however, are as abundant as the lake trout, the Arctic char, or the Arctic grayling.

The giant lakes, Great Slave and Great Bear, have become world famous for lake trout. The top five world record lake trout came from these waters — trout weighing over thirty kilograms. Both lakes have a number of fly-in fishing lodges on their shores. Several of these lodges offer complete packages, including round-trip transportation by chartered jet from such cities as Edmonton and Minneapolis.

The best fishing news in the last years was that Bern Will Brown, the artist, has reopened his Colville Lake Lodge to tourists. Brown closed the lodge because his paintings of the North and its people were in such demand that he was too busy with his brushes to operate his lodge. But Brown missed the bustle of the tourist season and the talk of fishing, so he has put away his easel for the summer months.

Colville is the gem of the Northwest Territories. It offers outstanding lake trout angling plus grayling in the tributary streams and, of course, pike in the shallow bays. But hardly anyone bothers with the pike except for the local Dene, who net them mainly for dog food. The Colville Lake Lodge, the only camp on the lake, stands right on the edge of the Hareskin Indian village cloistered around the mission station. These Dene still live traditional lives by trapping and hunting. They act as guides during the July-August fishing season. All this gives the lodge a unique atmosphere. The angler has the opportunity to see an aboriginal lifestyle that might vanish one day.

The Keewatin area (in the more eastern portion of the Northwest Territories) has up to now been overshadowed by lakes of the western portion. But such lakes as Dubawnt, South Henik, Smalltree, Snowbird, Kashba, and Nueltin, which straddles the Manitoba border, all have excellent lake trout fishing. Nueltin also has outstanding northern pike, with northerns in the ten- to twelve-kilogram class, and an amazing abundance of walleyes, and whitefish that can be caught on dry flies during the evenings. Many of the fishing camp operators on the Keewatin lakes offer fly-in packages from Winnipeg, Lynn Lake, or Thompson, Manitoba. This makes them easier to reach for anglers from Europe or the eastern and midwestern United States.

Some fishery biologists in the Northwest Territories believe the future of lake trout fishing will lie with the smaller lakes, such as Prelude, Rutledge, Harding, Blatchford, Wrigley, Hearne, Trout, Drum, Willow, and Lac La Martre, which recently produced several lake trout in the twenty-five-kilogram class. The lake to watch is Yamba, one of the last major lakes in the Northwest Territories without a fishing camp.

It represents virgin trout fishing at its best. The only time it ever gets fished is when Bill Tait's High Arctic Hunts operates its caribou hunting camp on its shore.

However, the fish that fires anglers' imaginations in the Northwest Territories is not the huge trout but the Arctic char. The creme de la creme of international anglers come to the Arctic in quest of this hard-fighting salmonoid. The Arctic char makes the other members of his family, the other chars, trouts, and salmons, seem placid and tame in comparison. Arctic char are found only in rivers that empty into the Arctic Ocean. The fish came by their name, Arctic char, honestly. And its delicate dark pink flesh is a gourmet's delight.

Such rivers as Hornaday near Paulatuk in the western Arctic and the Coppermine and the Tree all continue to yield good catches of Arctic char. But these rivers have been subject to more fishing pressure over the years than those found further east. Today the more remote rivers such as Tongait in Kingnait Fiord out of Pangnirtung, and Robertson River out of Koluktoo Bay, both on the huge Baffin Island, and Char Lake on Victoria Island probably have the best fishing in the Arctic. The difficulty with fishing the best Arctic char waters is that they are remote, requiring long air charter or boat travel to get there. But when you do get there you are in a fisherman's Shangri-la.

"What's that white thing down the fiord, a piece of ice"? Steve Cooke, my fishing partner, asked, pointing to the opposite side of the river down the beach. "Put your binoculars on it."

"It's a polar bear," I answered the instant the binoculars were at my eyes. "And he's moving this way. Here, have a look."

Within minutes the ten other fishermen were looking at the bear as we passed the binoculars around. All thoughts of fishing had stopped for the moment. The white bear was now identifiable with the naked eye. It was trotting along the beach right toward us at the mouth of the Tongait River. Joavie Alivuktuk was already cradling his rifle in the crook of his arm. And a couple of the Inuit guides were getting the boat and the motor ready.

We understood the plan. Joavie was going to let the bear come right across the river mouth so that we could get a good look and photos of the polar bear. But if the bear decided to swim across for a closer look at us it would be intercepted by the boat and scared off with a shotgun loaded with rubber pellets.

The bear came directly across to us. Only a forty-metre channel of swift-moving water separated us from the bear. The bear was tempted to cross on several occasions but always decided against it when the engine on the boat was turned up to near full throttle.

After about fifteen or twenty minutes Ipeelie, the senior

guide, aimed the shotgun just in front of the bear and fired. The bear jumped backward as the charge of eighty-odd rubber pellets bounced from the rocks and stung its forelegs and chest. With the second shot, fired in the air, the bear ran back from where he had come and did not appear again.

"What a trip!" Joe Sliva from Chicago said as we all went back to fishing. "First the belugas and now the polar bear, plus all these fantastic fighting fish."

The fishing indeed was fantastic. Everyone of us, even the novice fishermen, was catching Arctic char of four to seven kilograms, every third or fourth cast.

Hunting in the Yukon

The Yukon, like Alaska, is synonymous with big-game hunting. This does not mean that small game are not abundant. Grouse of four species — blue, sharp-tailed, spruce, and ruffed — are all found in the Yukon, as are willow and rock ptarmigan. Waterfowl are also abundant along the waterways. In fact, one of the great nesting areas for ducks and geese in North America is the Old Crow Flats, the huge inland delta of the Crow River in northern Yukon.

Sheep and grizzlies are the glamour big-game species in the Yukon. Caribou, moose, and black bear are too abundant to hold that position, while mountain goats are found only in the southeastern Yukon. Dall's sheep are found in all of the mountain ranges in the Yukon except the southern Cassiars, where stone sheep occur. Some of the stone sheep in the Yukon are quite light in colour and are frequently called fannin sheep by local hunters.

As far as our eyes could see one mountain peak after another crested in front of our Cessna aircraft. Yukon's Ogilvie Mountains could vie with any mountain range in the world for their ruggedness and beauty. We were flying from Dawson to a remote hunting camp on a small mountain lake almost in the heart of the mountains.

As we flew over the peaks and valleys I almost hoped that the flight would not end. But all good things must end. After an hour of flying time the pilot pointed to a lake about fifteen miles away and soon after he started to descend. As he circled the lake to prepare for landing I could see four neat log cabins and a horse corral among a grove of spruce trees. A dozen horses were loose along the lush meadow of the lake. In a few minutes the plane was taxiing to a dock made of spruce logs.

"Tomorrow at sunup we will be heading up that mountain," George Gemmel said as we unloaded the gear and boxes of provisions from the plane. "If you look through your binoculars you'll soon see why."

High on the grass-covered mountain side was a band of Dall's sheep. They appeared to be bedded down for the midday. In the distance they looked like a string of pearls on a piece of green velvet.

"They'll be hard to approach," George said. "They have a clear view in every direction. But there are several really fine full-curl rams among them. A couple must be well over forty inches."

It took a week of hard riding and even harder walking and climbing before we finally found a band of rams that could be stalked within rifle range. We had seen dozens of sheep in the seven days but they were always in such a place that they saw us regardless of what route we tried to use to get close to them. Wild sheep have incredible eyesight. Experienced hunting guides say that a sheep's eyesight is as good as a human's aided with a seven- or eight-power pair of binoculars.

On the eighth day we managed to outmanoeuvre a group of four rams and get above them — the one place sheep never think of looking for danger. The shot was largely anticlimactic, as it always is on a big-game hunt.

Grizzly bears range over much of the Yukon but hunters have a better success on grizzlies in areas north of Dawson and Mayo because the terrain is more open and the bears are easier to spot with binoculars. However, the biggest grizzlies are found in southern Yukon where there are more forests. This makes them harder to hunt. Black bears are common everywhere. Wolves and wolverines are widely distributed and both are regarded as predators and can be hunted under proper licence. Polar bears in the Yukon are found only along the Yukon's short Arctic coast and may only be hunted by Inuit.

Moose are found almost everywhere. The foothills of the Ogilvie, Selwyn, and Richardson ranges provide excellent moose hunting. But there is good moose hunting even within a short drive of Whitehorse, Dawson, and Mayo. The moose in the Yukon are of the Alaska-Yukon type and are the largest on the continent. Most Yukon outfitters, unlike those in the Northwest Territories, use horses for transporting hunters into the forests and mountains and to bring the game out. Without horses, hunting moose can be difficult because the hunter and his guide could spend a week packing out a moose in pieces. The only practical way to hunt moose without horses is by boat or canoe.

Caribou are also numerous, with barren-ground caribou being found on all tundra habitats, while Grant's caribou are found in the alpine tundra of all the major mountain ranges. Yukon shares with Alaska the huge Porcupine herd, which numbers some 150,000 animals.

The Yukon has a number of top outfitters who also hunt with saddle and packhorses. This type of hunt must rate as one of the finest hunting experiences in the world. All non-resident hunters must book through a registered outfitter and be accompanied by a guide. All big-game seasons in the Yukon open on August 1 and close in early to mid-November, depending on the species. There is a spring bear season from April 15 to June 15. The small-game season, including waterfowl, begins September 1.

Hunting in the Northwest Territories

The Northwest Territories is Canada's last frontier, the closest thing to virgin country on the North American continent. This is good news for any hunter or for anyone who seeks true wilderness. Small game can be very abundant — ruffed, spruce, and sharp-tailed grouse are found in the Northwest Territories, but ptarmigans are probably the most abundant of all small game.

Both ducks and geese nest on the many wetlands of this vast land; indeed the Mackenzie Delta is one of the most important nesting grounds for ducks on the North American continent. The waterfowl migrate down the Mackenzie Valley in great profusion. The snowshoe hares and the big Arctic hares are the two principal small-game mammal species. The snowshoes are forest dwellers while the Arctic hares live on the open tundra.

However, it is the big game that draws hunters the world over to the Northwest Territories. The polar bear is the most coveted trophy animal, and the Northwest Territories is the only place in the world where the polar bear may be legally hunted by non-resident hunters. Hunting the *nanook*, as the Inuit call the polar bear, is a supreme adventure. The bears may be hunted only by the traditional method with dog teams and sleds. Each non-resident is accompanied by two Inuit guides on the hunt. The hunt currently costs up to $ 15,000 U.S. with the hunter getting the skin and skull as trophies while the guides (and their community) get the meat plus the cash income. Only the polar bear and the tiger (which is endangered and virtually fully protected) will turn the tables and hunt the hunter.

Between 13,000 to 15,000 polar bears, as estimated by the team of biologists whose job it is to look after the general welfare of the white bears, live in the Canadian Arctic. The polar bear population has increased in the last ten years to this number. Some of the biologists believe that the present polar bear population in the Northwest Territories is about what it was 100 or more years ago. There are two reasons for this. The Inuit today live in villages of anywhere from 300 to 1,000 people, so there are vast tracts of the Arctic coast line where no people live. One hundred years ago, when the Inuit were entirely a nomadic, hunting people, they lived in small camps of three or four families all along the Arctic coast and they hunted incessantly during the winters. Also, the polar bear population has increased because of the very strict quota on how many bears may be taken by each Inuit village. The village elders are allowed to allocate a small part of this quota to outfitters for non-resident hunters. The best polar bear hunting is around Baffin Island and Lancaster Sound, which has the highest polar bear population in the Canadian Arctic. Another good area is Hadley Bay on Victoria Island.

Other big-game species in the Northwest Territories include Dall's sheep, moose, caribou, and muskoxen. Dall's sheep are found over the entire range of the Mackenzie Mountains. Mountain goats, on the other hand, are found only in the southwest corner of the Mackenzie Mountains.

Moose are found throughout the forest lands but only those in the foothills are open to hunting by non-resident hunters. The moose hunting in the forested Mackenzie Valley foothills rivals that of the Yukon. In fact, a large number of moose in the Boone and Crockett Club record books of North America big game come from the Mackenzie Valley.

However, hunting for moose in the Northwest Territories is generally harder than in the Yukon because only two or three outfitters use horses. The winters in the Northwest Territories are simply too harsh to allow overwintering of horses on open range. By contrast, in Yukon horses can overwinter quite well with some supplementary feeding of hay. The Yukon valleys get enough warm chinook winds to melt the snow off several times a year, thus allowing the horses to graze.

Barren-ground caribou range over all the open tundra areas through the spring, summer, and fall. Many of the herds migrate into the forest cover in the winter. Woodland caribou are found in the western forests. The caribou herds in the Northwest Territories have considerably increased in population during the last ten years. There are now over one and a half million caribou roaming the tundra. This has resulted in liberalized hunting regulations and non-resident hunters are even allowed two licences. The best trophies are coming from areas around Little Marten and Yamba lakes.

"Rise and shine. There's daylight in the sky," Joan Cotton, the camp cook, shouted from the kitchen tent. "Coffee is ready and there are caribou running on the ridge."

The words of caribou and coffee brought us fully awake. But I luxuriated in the warmth of my sleeping bag for a few moments. It was a brisk morning. I could feel a hint of frost through the tent wall. I had already shot a fine double-shovel caribou bull the day before, and although I still had a second licence I did not want my hunt to end too quickly. So my plan was to stay in camp and fish for the Arctic grayling and lake trout that abound in the lake. The thought of freshly caught trout for lunch appealed to me.

In less then ten minutes we were washed and dressed and ready for breakfast. As I stepped outside our tent I could smell the freshly brewed coffee and frying bacon. A din of voices rose from the cook tent as some of my fellow hunters were placing their breakfast orders.

Caribou were already moving, silhouetted against a blue sky on the ridge behind our camp on Marten Lake. Through my binoculars I counted well over a dozen animals.

"Many caribou across lake," Tommy Ashweigan, a veteran

Dene guide, said, pointing across the lake.

It took a few seconds for my eyes to adjust. The hillside was in the shadow of the rising sun, but slowly I could make out movement across the tundra-covered hillside — caribou were on the hillside by the hundreds, all moving parallel to the lake.

"My God, the main migration is on!" I said to myself. "Hey, you in the kitchen. Come and have a look. There are caribou across the lake by the hundreds." Everyone, including the cook, bolted out of the cook tent.

During the rest of the week I saw thousands upon thousands of caribou. The great Bathurst caribou herd was on its annual migration. In camp that evening we all talked eagerly about the day's sights and sounds. A couple of the hunters saw wolves actually kill a caribou calf. The wolves had laid a careful plan, with two wolves waiting in ambush while three others chased the caribou to the waiting wolves. Another hunter saw a wolverine carrying a leg bone of a caribou.

But most of the talk was about the caribou migration, their endless numbers, and about the hunt. Everyone in camp had shot his second caribou, even the two bow-and-arrow hunters.

Even the caribou on some of the Arctic islands, where environmental conditions are generally harsher, have increased, which has led to a small number of licences being available for the small, almost white Peary caribou on Victoria Island. This is the first time in over fifty years that white men have been allowed to hunt these caribou.

The grizzly bear and the black bear also can be hunted in the Northwest Territories. Both bears have a fairly wide distribution, but of the grizzlies only the barren-ground grizzly can be hunted by non-resident hunters. The best area for the barren-ground grizzly is around Bay Chimo (Umingmaktok) at the mouth of Bathurst Inlet. Black bears can be hunted in the foothills of the Mackenzie Mountains and in the spruce and pine forests around Fort Smith near the Alberta border. Wolves and wolverines can be taken by any hunter possessing a valid hunting licence anywhere on the Northwest Territories mainland.

The muskox is another unique big-game animal in the Northwest Territories. The muskox herds have increased at such a rate on some of the Arctic islands that winter die-offs have actually occurred. Muskox quotas have been liberalized but the harvest is strictly controlled. Since the only other place where muskox can be currently hunted is on Nunivak Island off Alaska, the Northwest Territories has attracted most of the international hunters who seek this unique remnant of old ages.

The Northwest Territories' other big shaggy bovine, the wood bison, is presently not legal game. Whether or not limited hunting by non-residents will be allowed in the years to come remains to be seen.

Walrus is the only other big-game animal that presently cannot be hunted by non-native hunters, but even that may change one day under the same sort of legislation that allows polar bear hunts to take place. Seals can be hunted. A non-resident hunter is allowed one seal licence per year, which is valid for two seals.

The hunting season for most game begins on August 15 and generally ends on November 15, but for Dall's sheep it opens July 15, while the polar bear season opens October 15 and closes May 31. Non-resident hunters must be accompanied by licensed guides and book their hunts through licensed outfitters.

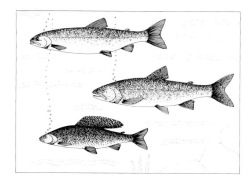

Daniel Lhingit Tlen
The Hunter

I want to look again down on the river flats,
    where donjek berries grow in clusters on their tiny
    bush
    where Arrow Grass Waters rush gold and shallow,
    deadly in its muddy melody,
To see where the moose had eaten, lain, and gone.

Tomorrow, early when the sun still lies in its warm pine bed
in the
    western hills,
Dreaming of the same horizons somehow somewhat
changed,

I will prepare my packsack with meat and tea
And my gun and shells for the moose and me.

Could it be that moose know of me and my necessary inten-
    tion?
The Elders, hunters from the beginning of time,
Have said that game will know upon
    awakening from their coolish sleep,
    that it is time for the ending of another round:
    Ending life for other life is life's big confrontation.

The night is cold.
The stars are active behind the dance of the Northern Lights.
    With violent grace and pastel technicolour the play of the
    Fire-in-the-sky must forcedly unfold.
The cosmic actors of another time and place have come to tell
    Their story upon the screen
    And skein of night.

And I lay in the bed-roll with the pillow piled high,
    Dreaming of unrelated events.

Somehow it seems when my brain sorely teems with that
disconcerting
    thought,
    That I should dare be more aware,
    That my anguish is nothing but a scare,
    And that life flows like the flying sun returning
All but once.

Our business must needs go on.

And I lay in the bed-roll with the pillow piled high,
    Dreaming of unrelated events.

The morning is crisp, and the snow crunches under my brisk
steps.

The frosty air stings my nostrils.
I exhale a cloud of steam.
The charge renews my feelings of the chase,
Refreshing my reeling, rolling breath.

The flats are shrouded in an icy fog,
    The hillside hot in the steely greyness of the sun.
Trees creak in their frozen roots, while the Whiskey-jacks
and
    Magpies
    Flip and glide about their morning chores.

The quietness suddenly starts ringing in my ears.
    I enjoy the company of the stepped-on snow
    And the scratch of branches on my coat and pack.

The morning passed quickly
    As I watched from the look-out on the river bank.
    With my elevated view
    I could peer at any goings-on in sight, and listen.
I gathered frosted, frozen sticks.
    They snapped like popping rabbit bones,
Light a fire,
    Boil some tea,
    Roast fat moose meat.

Ritually,
    Just as my Ancestors had wished with hope,
    Over countless generations,
In prayer for a good outcome to the hunt,
    I threw some moose fat in the fire,
Good luck in the chase.

My sacrifice? My superstition?
    I couldn't have eaten all that fat meat anyway.

I undid my moccasins and removed them to wade the Arrow
Grass Waters
    I felt I was crossing my life.
The freezing water scraped my shins and speared my brain
with
    searing icy points. The glacial ooze-covered stones
    slipped under my step as the river pushed and tugged
    my knees.

Suddenly, there, a moose,
    Meeting me
    At his crossroads.

There I was.
    The reason for his disconcerting dream.

I didn't feel the rifle kick. Boof!
 I only heard bullet hit the body. Thup!
Those clear eyes,
 The great proud head, held high
 So slowly fell.
Great fierce legs,
 To gelatin turned,
The struggle for his breath.

I wish I would have been a Healer,
 Sucking out the hurt,
 Spitting it through the fullness of space,
 Splashing it amongst the stars,
Absorbing the life with ease and painlessness.

I wish I could have been a dead and frozen branch,
 Blown by a steady cold, metallic wind
 Across the bleak and drifted reaches of the Arctic.

"Thank you, *Takenakau*, for bringing us this food this after-
 noon!
Thank you, Our Creator!" I prayed.
 I numbly skinned and cleaned the gift of life and death.
Why must I kill to live each day?
 Who chose this way to grow?
How will I ever know?

My grandfather says, "You cannot think like that!
 Leave it alone! Let it be? *Ukandhän!*"

Daniel Lhingit Tlen was born in Burwash Landing in the
Yukon and is of Southern Tutchone descent. He currently
resides in Whitehorse, is the father of four children, and
teaches Native language at Yukon College. As well as being
a musician and song-writer who has put the traditional songs
of his people into contemporary music, he has written a
book, *Speaking Out*, documenting the state of aboriginal
languages in the Yukon. He was the first chairman of the
Council for Yukon Indians, a group endeavouring to unify
Yukon Indians for the purpose of settling land claims.

Florence Whyard
Welcome to Beringia!

"The Yukon!" Say that to almost anyone and the automatic reply is "The Klondike gold rush." That comes first. Then, "Ice and snow. Eskimo people." And frequently, as a question, "It's in Alaska, isn't it?"

If, as someone has said, it is not deeds or acts that last but the written record of those deeds, the events of the Klondike gold rush must last forever, as they have these past 100 years. Thousands of books, brochures, articles, and newspaper stories poured forth all over the world before, during, and many years after that most exciting of all great stampedes to riches.

In the Soviet Union, school children for generations have read socialist Jack London's stories of the North's cruel hardships. In Czechoslovakia the fabulous adventures of Jan Welzl caught the imagination of his countrymen; in Ireland, the Klondike success of Michael MacGowan, who came home a wealthy man, inspired his Gaelic readers. In French, even in Japanese, the first-hand adventures are told, and in their telling attract more and more visitors to see this country for themselves.

The ballads of Robert W. Service convinced thousands (including some real Klondikers in the Yukon) that he had personally struggled over the Chilkoot Pass and survived the hardships of the Trail of '98. In fact, he wrote his first two books of verse working in the Whitehorse branch of the Canadian Bank of Commerce, where today a bronze sculpture on Main Street pays tribute to the poet. Transferred to Dawson City, the bank clerk arrived there some years after the gold rush had peaked, but he was soon making more from his verses than the bank manager. When he left to be a Red Cross ambulance man in World War One, he said good-bye forever to his little log cabin, but years later his two granddaughters came from Monte Carlo for a visit and fell in love with the Klondike, just as he had done.

The Yukoner who has made the greatest literary contribution to the Klondike record is, of course, Pierre Berton, whose encyclopedic research, combined with memories of living in Dawson City as a small boy, has produced very readable Yukon history. He and his family continue to make regular visits back to the Klondike. Klondike creeks are still producing millions in placer gold, but only under protest. Gone are the days of the lonely prospector panning at the edge of a stream. Huge, expensive machines roil through the gravel beds today and their operators are connected by phone and fax to world markets and daily prices in the gold rooms in London and Tokyo.

But, as Yukon author Allen Wright pointed out in his *Prelude to Bonanza*, "it was not an empty land" when the Klondikers came. First, there had been the waves of people who, through centuries, had walked across the land bridge from Asia. The continental shelf of the Bering Strait, exposed during times of glaciation elsewhere in the Arctic regions, is thought to have formed that ancient land bridge between vast areas of northern Siberia and similar parts of Alaska/Yukon.

Together, these land areas formed a geographical refuge from the ice, known to scientists as Beringia. The Yukon portion of that "Beringian Refugium" is Canada's largest archeological treasure storehouse, located on what Dr. R.E. Morlan of the National Museum of Civilization calls "the presumed pathway for human immigrants to the New World." Years of careful digging in the Old Crow area have produced the oldest dated evidence of human occupation yet found in the Western Hemisphere.

Eventually, archeologists such as Dr. Morlan and Dr. Richard Harrington hope to put together an integrated picture of environmental change spanning more than 100,000 years of eastern Beringian history. The sophisticated bone technology displayed in some of the tools used by the ice-age inhabitants of the Old Crow Flats has been carbon-dated at 35,000 years and is visible proof that those people were not clumsy, crude, ignorant, or unskilled.

Hundreds of miles farther south, the oldest known remains of Yukon's first inhabitants indicate that a small group of hunters once camped on a bluff north of Canyon Creek, near the Aishihik River, not far from today's Alaska Highway. That was between 7,000 and 8,000 years ago. They left some spear points behind, and it is known that some of their hunters used a throwing board to cast spears or darts with greater force when hunting bison, caribou, and moose during the 4,000 years they inhabited the extensive grasslands of their time . . . today a spruce forest.

In the Kluane Lake area, where today's visitors to Kluane National Park can see fascinating exhibits at the park headquarters at Haines Junction, the glaciers halted about 13,000 years ago; and 1,250 years ago clouds of ash from an erupting volcano in the White River area covered the land for hundreds of miles. Visitors today can spot the tell-tale white layer as they drive along the Klondike Highway or paddle down the Yukon River. (One especially large deposit of the white material is known locally as Sam McGee's Ashes!)

The mountains in the Kluane Lake area are part of the magnificent St. Elias range . . . and that is a direct connection with the earliest stories from Yukon's "modern" history. A Danish sailor in the Russian navy, searching for that ancient land bridge to the New World, first sighted the mountain peaks from near the coast of what is now Alaska. It was on St. Elias Day, July 16, 1741, so Vitus Jonassen Bering named them for the saint; his own name has been given to the narrow stretch of water separating the two continents, a strait so narrow that on a clear day northern neighbours in North America and Asia can see each other's coastlines.

Vitus Bering died after his little ship ran aground on a sandy island and his men buried him there, but they took back with them enough velvety sea otter pelts to the Empress Catherine II that she provided funds for other naval expeditions, which resulted in exploration of the Aleutian Islands and opened up a new chapter of fur trading for the Russians. It grew into the story of modern Alaska.

Unlike the Russians from the west, British traders and explorers came through eastern Canada and filtered into the Yukon from the posts they had established along the Mackenzie River system in what is now the Northwest Territories. Robert Campbell of the Hudson's Bay Company was one of the earliest, travelling in 1838 to establish new trading areas with the Indians at Dease Lake and Frances Lake. The primitive shelter he and his men established that winter makes Fort Frances the oldest "white" settlement in Yukon. Campbell also opened the post of Fort Selkirk, near the forks of the Yukon and Pelly rivers, abandoned later after being sacked by hostile Indians who resented losing their monopoly on trade in the interior.

The Tlingit people had controlled the mountain passes from the sea, trading as middlemen between European "wholesalers" and the source of furs in the inaccessible Yukon; the Europeans brought metal tools, rifles, and beads.

"Guns and beads! Beads and guns! is the cry through all the country!" So wrote Hudson's Bay Company trader Alexander Hunter Murray in 1848, after working his way from the Mackenzie through the mountains and marshes to build the post at Fort Yukon. "The rise and fall of our enterprise on the Yukon River depends on these supplies." He had met and married seventeen-year-old Anne Campbell the year before, en route to the new wilderness post, and their daughter, born that year, was the first white child in that northern region.

Other traders followed. So did scientists, explorers, missionaries. Roman Catholic and Anglican priests made their way from Fort Good Hope and Fort Simpson, NWT, into the Yukon in 1861. The Rev. Robert McDonald, a part Cree from Red River, Manitoba, in 1862 established an Anglican mission and also a family dynasty, which continues today in northern Yukon.

The Russian era ended in 1867 when Alaska was sold to the United States for $7.2 million. By then some 1,000 miners and prospectors had made their way up the rivers and streams to camp in the interior — at Circle City, Eagle, Fortymile. Small riverboats steamed upstream from St. Michael on the Bering Sea coast, bringing traders, missionaries, prospectors, camp followers, and the ever-vigilant North West Mounted Police.

In 1882, twelve miners who had survived a winter together, sharing their meagre rations, formed the first chapter of the Yukon Order of Pioneers, whose motto, like the Alaskan Brotherhood's, was "No Boundary Here." Today, their legal right to exclude female members is being challenged in Canadian courts by some pretty authentic pioneers who also put up with the hardships of early days in the Yukon — without recognition by their menfolk.

That same year, two German geographers, Arthur (mapping) and Aurel (culture and language) Krause, came from Bremen to study the Tlingit Indians. They climbed the Chilkoot Pass and with Indian guides travelled on foot through the Yukon interior, actually sighting Kusawa Lake in June before they had to turn back. The book they published in 1885 included excellent maps and much new and accurate information, which was used by many who followed in their footsteps.

Young Frederick Schwatka, a lieutenant in the U.S. Army, actually made the first complete trip down the entire Yukon River system in 1883. He named every prominent feature along the way for equally prominent Americans despite the fact that most of them already had been named — a process repeated a number of times, as local usages are succeeded by officially determined and sometimes less appropriate names, for a variety of reasons. (One of the distinct advantages of being a Yukoner is that after your death, if your contribution to the territory has been found worthy, you might very well have a mountain named for you by the national board entrusted with such responsibilities.)

Canadian surveyors followed the trail to the Yukon. Dr. George Dawson led the Yukon Expedition in 1887, accompanied by Richard McConnell and William Ogilvie. Their maps and detailed reports were published just in time for the Klondike gold rush, and their names are to be found in many places; Dawson City was named for the brilliant young man who headed the Geological Service of Canada and died in mid-career.

By 1894, the little settlement at Fortymile on a tributary of the Yukon River boasted quite a cosmopolitan population. According to records kept by Captain Constantine of the NWMP that winter, 260 men, women, and children resided there — predominantly Americans, then Canadians, some English, and some Scandinavians. There were three Armenians, one Arab, one Greek, and one Chilean. All these men were working the creeks nearby, looking for gold and finding just enough to keep them looking for more.

Meanwhile, off the Yukon's north coast, whalers from many parts of the world were getting rich in the Beaufort Sea. First came the Russians, then the American whalers, mainly from the eastern states. A captain from Bedford, Massachusetts, provided names for Pauline Cove and Simpson Point on Herschel Island in 1889. John Meyers, a black seaman from Baltimore, was the first of his people to be buried in the Yukon; he died at Herschel in the winter of 1892 from "inflammatory rheumatism."

Polynesian, Danish, French, and English were among the languages spoken by the whaling crews. Some of the captains brought their wives and families along to share the long, cold winters, frozen in the ice. On May 8, 1895, a daughter, christened Helen Herschel, was born there to Captain and Mrs. Albert Sherman. Anglican missionary Isaac Stringer and his wife Sadie, both from Ontario, named a boy Herschel. Their presence on the island served to temper somewhat the alcoholic orgies of the crew members and protected the Native women from them. Mrs. Stringer created a welcoming, homelike atmosphere in their tiny quarters in a warehouse, made the seamen work at self-improvement in their idle hours, and even taught some of them shorthand and typing!

The NWMP established a post on Herschel in 1903, the result of Rev. Stringer's concern for the Eskimo people in the area, and the police presence improved the situation. The detachment was used in later years as a breeding station for the beautiful white sled dogs used on long police patrols through the Arctic winters. The last of these handsome animals raced in the Yukon Sourdough Rendezvous dogteam races at Whitehorse and were then given to mushers at Old Crow. Today, the RCMP travel by plane or motorized vehicles and their only dogs are specially trained for tracking.

The Yukon's only offshore island has now been declared a territorial historic park. Efforts are being made to preserve its history and fragile environment, a task made difficult because there are no permanent residents to stand guard against unwanted visitors. One Inuvialuit family comes from Aklavik in the Mackenzie Delta each year to hunt seals, camping in the weathered old abandoned buildings. Announcements from time to time that oil rigs wish to winter in Pauline Cove or that runways are to be built for military use spark immediate and vocal opposition from Yukoners and their government.

So, for some 150 years after Vitus Bering named the St. Elias Mountains, there had been outsiders coming into the country, though little was ever heard about it in other parts of the world. By 1898, with telegraph wires humming and headlines blazing, the magic word "GOLD!" brought overnight knowledge of the Klondike and few stopped to wonder who had been in the country before that. The presence of the NWMP in Dawson and along the trail ensured that the Klondike stampede, if not the dullest in history, must certainly have been the most law-abiding. Six weeks on the woodpile or a "blue ticket" to leave the county seemed to be effective deterrents to crime.

The arrival of wives and families led to the establishment of schools and hospitals — the churches were already there — and social mores. The organization of some kind of local government became necessary. The police and a few govern-ment officials had been charged with all the recording of mining claims and land transactions in the hectic first few months, and Ottawa seemed very far away indeed when mobs of angry American miners tried to introduce their own methods of administering frontier justice!

By 1898, with passage of the Yukon Act, the first government of the Yukon Territory was established. It consisted of a commissioner and a council of six members (including the judges of the territorial court) all appointed to aid him in the administration of the Territory. The commissioner was himself a federal appointee. Now, more than ninety years later, the Yukon Act is still the basis for establishing the powers or the limitations of the government of Yukon. The commissioner is still appointed federally, but through the intervening years many important changes have occurred. The size of the council grew and elected members were included, five of them by 1902. A fully elected council took charge at Dawson in 1908 and excluded the commissioner from their legislative sessions.

But with the waning of the gold rush population, and the slowdown as miners left for overseas during the Great War, minimal activity in the Klondike prompted the federal government to abolish the council entirely and revert to government by bureaucrats. By 1919, three elected councillors again represented the entire territory and it was not until 1951 that the population had increased sufficiently to warrant five members.

Meanwhile, another mass invasion changed the face of the country. In 1942, thousands of American soldiers arrived by train on the White Pass & Yukon route (there were no roads into Yukon). Their assignment was to construct an all-weather road to carry military supplies from the lower forty-eight states to Alaska. After decades of proposals for such a highway, ignored by both federal governments, a Japanese pilot's bombs on Dutch Harbor, Alaska, provided the incentive!

Almost overnight, Whitehorse supplanted the traditional seat of government at Dawson City, now isolated except by river or air. Trucks supplanted riverboats; woodcutters no longer lined the banks with cordwood, fuel for sternwheelers' boilers. A major shift occured as people moved into new settlements along the highway and the territorial roads that soon followed. Bridges supplanted ferries. Government offices moved south to Whitehorse. After the departure of the thousands of construction workers a short eighteen months after their arrival, it was years before Yukoners settled down again, and they never really recaptured the same peaceful way of life enjoyed before the Alaska Highway cut its way for more than 1,300 miles from Dawson Creek in British Columbia to its junction with the Richardson Highway in Alaska. The engineers made history, breaking every record in the book, and a formal ceremony was held at Soldiers Summit, above Kluane Lake, on November 20, 1942, just eight months from start of construction. Civilian contractors took over the assignment then, to improve the military road, and that process is still continuing as "The Alcan" gradually receives paving and blacktopping along its entire length.

One of the last great motoring adventures, the Alaska Highway and Klondike Highway funnel visitors north to the newest artery, the Dempster, named for a famous sergeant in the NWMP, which crosses from northern Yukon into the Northwest Territories, ending at Inuvik. Thus, today's traveller can sail up the Inside Passage along the west coast to the port of Skagway, drive up to Whitehorse, just 110 miles from the sea, continue through magnificent scenery to Dawson, then head up the Dempster to another ocean. Nowhere else can one get such a clear impression of the vastness and the stillness of the Yukon. Crossing the Arctic Circle on the Dempster and still heading north is a rare and wonderful experience.

Today, annual invasions of friendly visitors, numbering ten times the total population of the Yukon, sweep through the territory, leaving money and taking with them photographs, memories, and northern souvenirs. No longer a dangerous challenge (unless one seeks white-water river rafting or attempts a mountain climb in avalanche season), the Yukon now provides an oasis where magnificent scenery, comfortable accommodation, and modern transportation systems combine with a peaceful political climate to welcome visitors.

For nearly a century, the Klondike has provided material for hundreds of books, authors, and filmmakers as Yukoners watch visiting writers come, make a quick tour, and depart. But in the last ten years there has been a tremendous flowering of the arts in the North, resulting today in one of the most supportive environments in Canada for artists, writers, musicians, playwrights, actors, and photographers. Yukon scenery has inspired European-trained artists to set aside their traditional methods and produce lively new interpretations of northern surroundings. Native carvers are sculpting in bone and antler; some of the finest galleries in Canada, flourishing in Yukon, display their works, sponsor their shows, and sell their creations to an ever-increasing flow of collectors from the South.

Not long ago, in a Whitehorse gallery, a visitor from New York City asked for the latest work by a Yukon artist. How did she know of him? Before leaving home she had asked Vincent Price, the actor and art expert, what to look for in Canada. He told her, "Buy anything you can find by a man named Ted Harrison; he paints in the Yukon." Harrison has had one-man shows in Tokyo, London, Philadelphia, New York, Montreal, Ottawa, Toronto, Edmonton, and, of course, Whitehorse.

In a magnificent setting on a hilltop above Whitehorse, the modern buildings of the new Yukon College complex include not only the ever-changing displays of art works in gallery and hallways, but the handsome new home of the Yukon Archives and the almost-completed Yukon Art Centre, which will provide theatre- and concert-goers with spacious, comfortable seating and state-of-the-art technical equipment for drama and musical productions. Surely there can be no other small community in Canada with so many facilities encouraging cultural activities — as well as the many other recreational opportunities — as the 20,000 residents of Whitehorse enjoy.

From being a place along the river where Klondike stampeders stopped just long enough to dry out their socks, Whitehorse has grown into a cosmopolitan capital city — the most westerly in Canada. In addition to being the hub of transportation systems and the seat of government, the community supplies services and goods to major mining centres linked by territorial roads. Mining is still the number-one industry in Yukon, and has been since the gold rush, but as mineral prices fluctuate on world markets tourism has occasionally slipped ahead.

Today's miners are likely to be operators of heavy equipment in massive open pit developments, such as at Faro, where concentrates are milled from lead and zinc ore and trucked down the Klondike highway past Whitehorse to seagoing freighters at the port of Skagway. The oldest operating mine, underground at Elsa, has at times been the richest silver producer in Canada, growing and retrenching through its more than fifty years as the world market prices dictated.

Near Whitehorse, ever since Klondike-bound prospectors spotted copper-bearing rocks on their way to richer gold, there have been sporadic copper-mining operations. Elsewhere in the Yukon, development of a fascinating variety of minerals has kept prospecting an active industry, now made considerably easier with helicopter and road support. The discoverer of the huge Anvil Mine lead-zinc deposit, Al Kulan, was on a budget of fifty cents per day when he walked with packsack on his back through swamps and over mountains, but he ended up as Yukon's first "modern" millionaire, driving a white Rolls-Royce around the tiny settlement of Ross River.

Through exploration and mining (both hard rock and placer) the mineral industries of Yukon and northern British Columbia now generate some $400 million in exploration and production annually. Statistics for 1988 show placer output reached over $64 million and exploration spending topped $50 million, much of it spent on local services, supplies, and leased equipment. Currently high gold prices, compared with between $11 and $16 at the time of the gold rush and $32 when dredges were operating, have resulted in vigorous exploration and the development of several hard-rock gold-mining operations in southern Yukon. Asbestos, antimony, nickel/copper, and multi-metal properties mark the mineral map of Yukon, from Clinton Creek north of Dawson to Tungsten at the southeast corner on the NWT border. Further deposits of lead, zinc, and tungsten await improved world markets, and at Windy Craggy, near the Haines Highway and the B.C./Yukon border, a huge mineral find of copper/gold/cobalt could have a tremendous impact on Yukon's economy in years to come.

In Yukon's modern schools, children from an increasing variety of racial backgrounds are becoming not just bilingual but some of them will be trilingual, choosing to be taught in English, French, and also one of the Native dialects. They are learning about cultural traditions, Native storytelling and legends, as well as their A-B-Cs. At the new $50 million Yukon College on its hilltop site overlooking Whitehorse, an incredible variety of courses attracts Native and non-Native students of all ages.

A new generation of students is growing up in the North, preparing for leadership not just in Yukon or the Northwest Territories but for all of Canada. Living at "the top of the world" they acquire a broader, more objective viewpoint on national problems. They have not been crowded into a narrow, over-populated, over-priced, polluted strip of real estate along the southern Canada/U.S. border, oblivious to their world to the north.

A former judge in Yukon, Mr. Justice John Parker, who had also been a resident of the NWT, once told a northern conference that in his opinion the most important export from the territories in future years would not be the minerals, the oil or natural gas, the lumber, fish, or furs, but leaders for the Canadian nation — young men and women from the vast third of the Canadian map above the 60th parallel that forms the core of the Canadian spirit. Today, those young leaders are already becoming familiar names on the national news.

Unlike the Northwest Territories, where the population is 75 per cent of Native origin, Yukoners are just the opposite, with non-aboriginals in the majority. (Many third- and fourth-generation "whites" consider themselves to be natives of the Yukon, their children and grandchildren having been born here.) The Yukon Native land claims now in final stages of negotiations with the territorial and federal governments, after some eighteen years of progress and delays, will directly provide money, land, and self-governing benefits to about 30 per cent of the Yukon population. Indirectly, however, they will affect everyone in the North for years to come with the removal of a land freeze that has constricted development for many years and the infusion of millions of settlement-fund dollars.

Another difference between the two territories, now gradually diminishing, has been their growth into self-government. Yukoners have experienced some eighty years of a totally elected legislative assembly; only recently has the NWT reached that stage.

The Yukon is still more industrial, having had an economic infrastructure since the Klondike gold rush, and like Alaska, it has more miles of modern highways providing access to mineral/gas/oil development. Ever since Americans outnumbered Canadians in the Klondike, Alaskans have been close friends and business associates. The Alaska and Yukon governments mesh a number of programs, such as tourism and road construction, and a feeling remains of "Us against them" when northerners are frustrated by federal governments in the south, whether in Washington or Ottawa.

Accustomed to international railroads, highways, and airlines, Yukoners needed no special arguments to approve free trade with Americans; long accustomed to using an Alaskan port as their access to the sea, they are looking forward to gradual eliminination of tariffs and duty on goods and services crossing their borders. Tourists should benefit as well.

In fact, the first waves of people who, through centuries, walked across the Bering land bridge from Asia travelled east into what is now the Northwest Territories, then gradually made their way south, as far as the Navajo country in the United States. There were no political boundaries, only those of survival. Some of those people stayed in the North, survived the glacier age, the volcanoes, the invasions by others. Their numbers were not great because tribal sizes were limited by the food supplies available. As Dr. Julie Cruikshank explains in *Their Own Yukon*, the Indian people in the subarctic regions of North America came to terms with their harsh and unpredictable physical environment; that was better than trying to fight or alter conditions more powerful than men. So they adapted to and worked with nature rather than fighting against the natural environment. Today's Yukoners bear little resemblance to the first families of Beringia, who came looking for a better place to live. They were followed by explorers and exploiters. Some stayed and put down roots, adding their strengths and skills to those of the people who had come before them.

Again, a new wave of immigrants from many parts of the world is weaving bright new colours into the Yukon fabric. Some thirty languages are spoken by Yukon government employees listed as staff interpreters, from Afrikaans to Vietnamese. A quick glance at the new restaurants specializing in national dishes, the shelves of specialty foods in the supermarkets, strange new ingredients for Oriental and continental cooking — all are indications of recent changes in the Yukon lifestyle. European smoked meats vie for shelf space with Mexican tamales; wine shelves in government liquor stores are burgeoning with hitherto unknown brands.

Northerners watch the same television as any other North Americans; they see the same movies, read the same books, hear the same newcasts. Travelling outside is a routine matter now; no longer are Yukoners embarrassed by the wrong hemline when they step off the plane! Whitehorse is small enough to be friendly but large enough to support art galleries, bookstores, concerts, theatre groups. Yukoners enjoy what must be the world's highest percentage per capita of tax-supported recreational programs of all kinds.

And the world is finding its way to Yukon sites for top-grade competitions, in cross-country skiing, dogteam racing, triathlons, and all kinds of outdoor sports. Hundreds of hockey players vie for ice time with figure skaters each winter; basketball, badminton, volleyball, squash, and racquet courts are filled. The growing population seems to provide more than enough people to use all the new facilities mushrooming up in many communities, from swimming pools to art centres.

In the village of Old Crow, north of the Arctic Circle, a little man with a weathered face and lots of smile wrinkles, a former chief of his Loucheux people, now teaches twenty grandchildren the ancient arts of trapping muskrat, hunting caribou and moose, catching salmon. He proudly wears a tiny white pin on his blue denim jacket. Its centre motif is a silver maple leaf, surrounded by a stylized snowflake. Charlie Peter Charlie is one of the newest Yukon members of the Order of Canada. Its motto is: "Desiderantes Meliorem Patriam" — They desire a better country.

Since the Order was established during Canada's Centennial Year in 1967, more than a dozen Yukon men and women have been nominated by their peers to go to Government House in Ottawa and be inducted into the Order by its commander, the Governor General. They have included a Klondike placer miner who served his constituency long and well in Territorial Council; an Anglican deaconess, known as "mother" to many Native prisoners, who had worked among the Chinese in Vancouver for thirty years; an Indian Chief who headed the first movement toward settlement of Yukon Native land claims; a businessman who gave years of public service at municipal and territorial levels, working toward autonomy for northerners; an English-born mountain climber, member of international expeditions, author, and photographer, who opened the eyes of Yukoners to the magnificence of the peaks around them; a Royal Canadian Mounted Police veteran who patrolled his huge area by boat in summer, by dogteam in winter, often as the sole representative of government in lonely places; a woman journalist, community worker, and historian; a river traveller and expert in Arctic survival, who had been with Richard E. Byrd at the South Pole; a young entrepreneur who rose to nationally known levels of commerce; a native woman who spent her lifetime keeping her Tlingit language, tradition, and stories alive among her people; a Yukon artist whose delightful, brightly coloured paintings and books about the North have given thousands a new image of the Yukon; and the Old Crow chief whose service to his people bridged years of dramatic changes in their lifestyle.

Would a composite portrait of these men and women present a true picture of a "Yukoner"?

About twenty-five years ago, reporter Rusty Erlam wrote a piece for the annual program of events for the Yukon Sourdough Rendezvous, published by the *Whitehorse Star*. It is still being quoted, though rarely with a credit line. She talked about the space — 20,000 people (then) sharing almost 200,000 square miles — and the freedom to move about at will, one clue to what makes a real Yukoner tick.

Her analysis continued: "His love for this country is inarticulate — he can seldom explain it and would be embarrassed to try. He puts up with atrocious weather during the winter. He often does without the amenities of modern civilization. He grumbles about the lack of green grass, the slowness of development and the indifference of the rest of Canada, but deep down, he hugs a secret — a certainty that when all things are tallied, he comes out 'way ahead.'

"He knows his country is more beautiful, more unspoiled than any other, and his history is more exciting. His sense of humour is mischievous and goodnaturedly directed against those from Outside. His clannishness with other Yukoners in the outside world is phenomenal. His excitement over new Yukon mining discoveries is intense.

"His energy in undertaking anything he likes is tremendous. His impatience with senseless regulations can get him into trouble. His attitude is optimistic and his inverted snobbishness is comical. Un-awed by visiting celebrities, skeptical of experts, contemptuous of phonies, he is helpful to newcomers, fond of eccentrics and he leaves his door unlocked. It never occurs to him to worry about his 'identity', because he's a Yukoner.

"He is also one of the best hosts anywhere in the world, for where people are so few, each individual is worth more. He really means it when he says WELCOME TO THE YUKON!"

Yukon

The coast of the Arctic Ocean in northern Yukon with Nunaluk Spit around the deltas of Malcolm and Firth rivers. This area around Herschel Island was a traditional whale-hunting ground for the Karngmalit Eskimos. *Wolfgang Weber*

Herschel Island, located just off the Yukon northern coast, was the place where, from about 1890, the many Beaufort Sea whalers from all around the world overwintered. Today, the island is protected as a territorial historic park. *Wolfgang Weber*

The Firth River winds through the British Mountains in the Northern Yukon National Park, a mountainous wilderness paradise with abundant wildlife. *Wolfgang Weber*

About thirty species of ducks, geese, loons, and swans nest in the Canadian North, including the rare trumpeter swan, now making a comeback in the western part of the Northwest Territories and in the Yukon. *Richard Hartmier*

Arctic terns leave their nesting grounds in August to migrate as far south as the pack ice of the Antarctic. *Wolfgang Weber*

278

The Peel River in late summer: Fort McPherson, just north of here, and Arctic Red River are settlements on the eastern edge of the wide lands of the Gwich'in (Kutchin Indians) that extend deep into Alaska, and its people have inherited a colourful and complex culture. For centuries, the Gwich'in, especially the Loucheaux tribe, have traded with both the coastal Tlingit and the coastal Indians of British Columbia, as well as with the Inuvialuit and other Eskimos of the Arctic coast. The Gwich'in already had iron spears and other Russian trade goods from Alaska when Alexander Mackenzie encountered them in 1789.
Wolfgang Weber

Stephen Frost from Old Crow, speeding down the Porcupine River, is returning from his caribou hunt. His mother Clara has long been known as "the knitter" to the people of Old Crow. *Richard Hartmier*

Old Crow hunter with blue geese harvest on the Old Crow Flats. *Jerome Knap*

Caribou on the summer
tundra of the central Yukon
Plateau west of the
Richardson Mountains.
Wolfgang Weber

European soccer — as well as other sports, such as skiing — has made its entrance with the youth of remote Old Crow, although this small settlement is not serviced by road or by scheduled flights. Reverend Robert McDonald went north from the Red River Colony in Manitoba and established the first Anglican mission in the Yukon in 1862, married a Loucheaux woman, and one of their several children, Neil McDonald, settled in Old Crow. The Loucheaux people here, who call themselves Van Tat Gwich'in, largely still subsist on hunting, fishing, and gathering.

Pat Morrow / First Light

Housing development in
Old Crow — with
traditional skills and modern
tools. Logs are floated down
the Porcupine River for
about 110 kilometres.
Pat Morrow / First Light

One of the two log churches
— Anglican and Catholic —
in Old Crow.
Wolfgang Weber

The Dempster Highway, the only Canadian all-weather road that crosses the Arctic Circle, in the loneliness of the Richardson Mountains with the first September snow. *Wolfgang Weber*

John Bayly's camp on the Snake River, with the Mackenzie Mountains to the east. *John Bayly*

This modern motel at kilometre 372 is, apart from various campgrounds, the only accommodation in the Yukon portion of the Dempster. *Richard Hartmier*

Fall-coloured tundra along the treeline on the Eagle Plain along the Dempster Highway west of the Richardson Mountains. *Wolfgang Weber*

Grizzly bears are found almost everywhere in the Yukon up to the Arctic coast. Their number is estimated to be 6,000–7,000 and their diet consists primarily of roots, grubs, berries, and small rodents. *Wayne Towriss*

Moose bull in the fall tundra brush north of the Ogilvie Mountains.
Brian Milne / First Light

Wilderness adventure on
horseback at the Hart River,
which flows into the Peel at
around latitude 66° N.
Richard Hartmier

Log cabin in the wild Hart River country, with food cache and black bear trap. *Richard Hartmier*

Portaging a canoe around the rapids of a crystal-clear stream. *Wendy Stephenson*

The all-vehicle, solid gravel Dempster Highway, opened in 1979, leads through 721 kilometres of untouched landscape from Dawson City to Inuvik. It follows the route of the winter patrol of the North West Mounted Police, which was established between Fort McPherson and Dawson City to deliver mail to the gold miners at the turn of the century. *Wolfgang Weber*

From North Fork Pass of the
Dempster Highway, the
view reaches all the way up
to Tombstone Mountain in
the distance, a crucial
landmark for the NWMP
winter patrols by dogsled.
In 1910, Constable
Fitzgerald and his three
companions starved to death
on the Peel River, just a day's
travel from Fort
McPherson. The next
spring, Corporal Dempster
found the "Lost Patrol."
Wolfgang Weber

Winter traffic on the
Dempster in the Ogilvies.
Wolfgang Weber

The raven is a bird of
mystical significance to Dene
and Yukon Indians.
Wayne Towriss

The craggy peaks of the
Tombstone Range in the
Ogilvies rise as high as the
2,200 metres of Tombstone
Mountain. *Wolfgang Weber*

Tombstone Mountain and other peaks reflect in the mirror of Talus Lake. *Wolfgang Weber*

David Howe is angling for Arctic grayling in Ogilvie River. *Wolfgang Weber*

Remnants of Venus Mine at Windy Arm of Tagish Lake in the southern Yukon. The mine produced silver from 1966–71 and was abandoned afterwards. *Wolfgang Weber*

Signpost in Keno City on the original Silver Trail of Mayo, Elsa, and Keno. In 1919, Louis Beauvette unearthed a rich silver ore deposit in a mountain named Sheep Hill, which later was renamed Keno Hill. Along with neighbouring hills at Elsa, it became one of the richest silver properties in Canada. *Wolfgang Weber*

Name: Judith;
profession: bush pilot;
location: Atlin Lake,
Yukon/B.C. border.
Wolfgang Weber

Started to be built in 1898, the narrow-gauge White Pass & Yukon Railway has mainly served to transport metal-bearing ores from Whitehorse and Carcross to the deep-sea docks at Skagway, Alaska. When world market prices dropped and modern mills in the Yukon refined the ore on location, the economic basis for the railroad was gone. In the 1970s and early 1980s, the train brought tourists from and to Whitehorse during the summer. Now that there are two highways available — the Haines Highway and the southern part of the Klondike Highway — trains operate only during the summer travel season between Skagway and Fraser, B.C. *Wolfgang Weber*

The "Trail of '98". Upper left: Today, hundreds of hikers climb the Chilkoot Trail from Dyea at Lynn Canal to Bennett Lake, one of the major headwater lakes of the Yukon River, where the gold seekers built boats to travel up to the Klondike: 7,124 crafts set sail here on May 29, 1898. Lower right: At the northern end of Bennett they reached Windy Arm of Tagish Lake at Carcross (Caribou Crossing). The SS *Tutshi* is one of three remaining sternwheelers out of a fleet of some 250 riverboats of later times. Lower left: Once they had reached Fort Selkirk, established by HBC's Robert Campbell near the confluence of the Pelly River, they were only a few days away from the gold fields. Upper right: A few miles south of here, where the Klondike joins the mighty Yukon, they had finally reached their destination. *Wolfgang Weber*

"Arizona Charlie" Meadows built the Palace Grand Theatre during the town's heyday in a style finer than any one would have expected for a boom town. It was built from the wood of two stranded riverboats. Today, it is the home of the Gaslight Follies, performing daily during the summer season. *Richard Hartmier*

The "old-timers" of the Yukon Order of Pioneers lead the yearly Discovery Day Parade in Dawson, commemorating the gold strike of Rabbit Creek. *Wolfgang Weber*

(Upper):
Dawson miner Pierre Monfette pans gold in Hunker Creek, obviously providing him with the means for a good life. *Wolfgang Weber*

Dawson City, a lovely little town of the gold rush days with legacies of the past found everywhere, is located at the confluence of the Klondike and Yukon rivers. The tailings of its former gold fields and the present gold-mining activities are seen along the Klondike River and especially on Bonanza Creek, to the upper right. Dawson City has been declared a national historic site. *Wolfgang Weber*

North of Carmacks are the Yukon River's treacherous Five Finger Rapids, which posed a navigational hazard to both the boats of the gold seekers and the riverboat skippers of later times. Overpowered by the currents, the boats had to be winched through a narrow channel of the river.
Wolfgang Weber

Boreal owl with its prey.
Wayne Towriss

Snowshoe hare in summer.
Wayne Towriss

(Upper):
Red fox near Little Salmon
Lake. *Jochen Rothmann /
Wolfgang Weber*

Loucheaux camp on the
banks of Porcupine River —
drying and smoking caribou
meat and skin.
Pat Morrow / First Light

I. McKintosh tans moose
hide at Laberge, with her
grandchild watching.
George Adamson

Southern Tutchone summer
camp on the southern Yukon
Plateau lands.
George Adamson

Emerald Lake alongside the Klondike Highway north of Carcross. Its colour is said to be caused by the copper-bearing rockbed underneath. *Wolfgang Weber*

The "Alcan," as the Alaska Highway is called in the Canadian North, traverses the alluvial lands of the Slims River, as this main tributary flows into Kluane Lake. *Wolfgang Weber*

The "delta" of this stream at Kathleen Lake in Kluane National Park becomes visible during snow melt. *Wolfgang Weber*

Summer fireworks over Whitehorse, the Yukon's capital, with more than 20,000 inhabitants the largest city in Canada's North.

In the past, scores of sternwheelers steamed up and down the Yukon River on a length of more than 3,000 kilometres from St.

Michael's at the Bering Sea to Whitehorse, and sometimes further up to Carcross, delivering freight and transporting passengers.

Launched in 1937, the stately SS *Klondike II*, now a national historic site, was the largest of them all plying the river. *Richard Hartmier*

Northern Lights over a
hilltop near Whitehorse:
the aurora borealis is now
known to be an electrical
discharge powered by a
"generator" composed of the
solar wind and the earth's
magnetosphere.
Wayne Towriss

The Alaska Highway not far
from Haines Junction at the
foot of the Kluane ranges.
The "Alcan," which begins at
Dawson Creek, B.C., and
stretches more than 2,400
kilometres to Fairbanks,
Alaska, is by far the most
travelled route in the Yukon.
Built as a wartime gravel
track in 1942, the highway is
now almost totally
asphalt-surfaced.
Wolfgang Weber

Historic log cabin at Silver City. *Richard Hartmier*

Prospector's cabin near Dezadeash Lake next to Kluane National Park, built

almost a century ago. *Wolfgang Weber*

Dall's rams can be frequently seen in the Kluane mountain ranges. *Wayne Towriss*

Mountain goats can be observed high on steep cliffs in Kluane, such as this goat and its young near Kathleen Lake. *Richard Hartmier*

Mountains in the Kluane
ranges: eroding of
mineral-rich rock creates
luminous colours.
Wolfgang Weber

Mount Logan in Kluane National Park, at 6,050 metres the highest peak of the St. Elias Mountains and Canada's highest mountain. The spectacular region of mountains, icefields, and glaciers was named a world heritage site by UNESCO in 1979. *Wolfgang Weber*

Mountain climbers' camp in June, en route to conquer Mount Logan. *Mike Beedell*

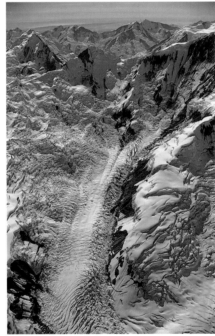

One of the hundreds of "mini" glaciers in the area. *Wolfgang Weber*

The flowing rivers of the Kaskawulsh Glacier are being nourished by the mighty icefields of the St. Elias Mountains.
Wolfgang Weber

White-tailed ptarmigan in
higher reaches of Kluane
National Park. *Jochen
Rothmann / Wolfgang Weber*

Hoary marmots like to sun
themselves on the warm
rocks, seen here in the
St. Elias Mountains.
Wolfgang Weber

The annual Yukon Quest, held in February-March: top mushers from across North America compete for a $ 100,000 purse in this 1,000-mile dogsled race between Whitehorse and Fairbanks, Alaska, via Carmacks and Dawson City.
Richard Hartmier

Yukon Quest musher near
Dawson. *Richard Hartmier*

Dick North
Yukon Gold

Gold is the most exotic mineral on Earth, and as such it is a synonym for riches. Throughout history, because of the ease by which it can be handled, this metal has been used as a medium of exchange. A little gold can represent a maximum of purchasing power. Not only did gold dust or coinage replace the ancient and awkward barter system, but with the rise of nation-states it evolved as a backing for currency, thus facilitating the exchange of goods and services in trade and commerce. Even today, as sophisticated as we have become in our use of complicated financial formulas by international institutions, gold's permanence as a practical increment of value has never been surpassed.

The reasons for this are many. Gold has an attractive lustre that is rarely disguised by the vagaries of nature. Its relative softness enables it to be easily moulded into jewelry and coins. An individual needs little more than a pan and a shovel to retrieve gold because in its placer form the yellow metal has been washed free of its host rock. Gold represents a maximum of worth in that it can be transported at a comparatively low cost. For example, an individual with a one-pound poke of gold dust in his pockets at the present price would be toting approximately $5,000.

Georg Bauer (a.k.a. Agricola) of Germany was the first individual to write a truly comprehensive book on mining. Translated into English from Latin by Herbert Hoover sixteen years before he became the President of the United States, Bauer's observations fit in as well today as the year his work was first published — in 1556.

He wrote: "Many persons hold the opinion that the metal industries are fortuitous and that the occupation is one of sordid toil, and altogether a kind of business requiring not so much skill as labour. But as for myself, when I reflect carefully upon its special points one by one, it appears to be far otherwise. For a miner must have the greatest skill in his work, that he may know first of all what mountain or hill, what valley or plain, can be prospected most profitably, or what he should leave alone; moreover, he must understand the veins, stringers and seams in the rocks. Then he must be thoroughly familiar with the many and varied species of earths, juices, gems, stones, marbles, rocks, metals and compounds."

Prospecting is probably one of the oldest human activities. Almost half a million years ago, early human types foraged for likely looking rocks and branches, which they put together to create weapons. In a sense, therefore, they were prospectors sizing up rocks for their needs. As time passed nuggets of gold, turquoise, and other precious stones attracted attention and were worn for their ornamental qualities.

In North America, as whites moved westward they began to find mineral deposits, and with each newly located metal came inevitable "rushes" to get in on the good ground. Promising discoveries were made throughout the Rocky Mountain states, but the greatest of the mid-nineteenth century took place when gold was found in northern California, instigating the stampede of 1849. This discovery electrified the peoples of the eastern part of the continent and they headed west to seek their fortunes.

Other discoveries were made: silver in Nevada, copper in Montana, gold in the Black Hills of South Dakota. Each find created a fraternity of men who dedicated their lives to pursuing ever-illusive metals. Eventually they turned their eyes northward, and almost immediately a major gold field in British Columbia was found. The prospectors and miners descended like locusts on the new field and almost as quickly cast their eyes beyond the new strike.

Rumours of gold in the Far North were substantiated as early as 1850 when Hudson's Bay Company explorer Robert Campbell found flakes of gold in the gravels of a sand bar in front of his newly erected trading post at Fort Selkirk on the Yukon River in the Yukon District of the old Northwest Territories. Campbell, like most traders at that time, was busy searching out profitable areas for purchasing furs, and other than briefly mentioning his find in a report he was generally uninterested in exotic minerals.

Gradually, the gold seekers worked their way north, edging toward the Yukon District. Gold was found near the headwaters of the Stikine River in 1861. Several years later, Archdeacon Robert McDonald of the Anglican Church Mission at Fort Yukon found gold at Birch Creek, near the confluence of the Porcupine and Yukon rivers 300 miles downriver from the scene of the ultimate big strike near the Klondike River. This, like Campbell's report, though not followed up, contributed to the legend that there was gold in the Yukon. The Yukon District, which was to become the Yukon Territory in 1898, was bounded on the north by the Arctic Ocean, on the east by Canada's Northwest Territories, on the west by Alaska, and on the south by British Columbia.

Oddly, both the Stikine and Porcupine areas spawned lost gold mine stories that have lured gold seekers to search for them. Rumours of the "Lost McHenry" mine enticed prospectors from the Cassiar area of northern British Columbia to the southern Yukon in the early 1870s. The legend was that a man named McHenry showed up at Dease Lake with forty pounds of gold, contending he had obtained it from a placer deposit marked by a huge snow cross that formed above it on a mountain when the spring thaws came. McHenry puportedly said the small creek he had worked was in the vicinity of the Gravel River, but his directions were too general for anyone to follow. If, per chance, a prospector was to find this deposit and mine gold to the extent of McHenry, he would earn at today's prices roughly $250,000. One man, subsequently known as "Old Man" Wilson, searched for this mine for forty years without success. Geologist Joseph Keele, for whom Wilson worked as a guide, named a peak for him. This mountain and a lake of the same name are situated at the head of Ross River near the Yukon-Northwest Territories border. One theory of some geologists is that the "cross" may be under an area of perpetual snow, and that only an unseasonal early hot spell will reveal it.

The Porcupine River also has its legendary lost gold mine, supposedly in a stream marked by the presence of a cabin that was not of the customary four sides, but rather of three. This triangular structure was thought to have been built along the upper reaches of one of a number of tributaries of the Porcupine. These included the Driftwood and the Bell and their tributaries. The man who reportedly found this bonanza made his way into the community of Fort McPherson, Northwest Territories, with gold that weighed in the dozens of pounds and stated that his three-sided cabin was the beacon marking the location of valuable gravels. Financier Washington Dodge of San Francisco launched an expedition to find the diggings but was unsuccessful.

The principal springboard for the Yukon gold rush was the rediscovery of a "mine" in southeast Alaska that probably had once been "lost." This was the Alaska-Juneau mine, where prospectors were later to earn grubstakes that financed their trips into the interior of the Yukon drainage searching for gold.

The possible predecessor of this Alaska mine was known as "The Lost Rocker," documented in the log of the Hudson's Bay Company steamer Otter captained by Herbert G. Lewis. The ship was on one of its seasonal fur-trading jaunts when Lewis and his crew plucked a half-dead prospector out of a canoe floating aimlessly off Stockade Point near the mouth of Taku Inlet. The man, Fred Culver, had been wounded and was suffering from starvation. The Hudson's Bay men nursed him back to health while he told them his story. Since he had a poke filled with $1,500 worth of gold to back up his yarn, Lewis and his men were prepared to listen. Culver claimed that he and two companions went ashore looking for gold. They climbed up and over a steep ridge, descending the far side to a stream where the men found colours. Following the pay streak, they ascended, eventually making camp in the most likely spot. They built a rocker, and in a short time accumulated an impressive amount of gold. However, in their preoccupation, they had neglected to take into consideration the dreaded Tlingit Indians who jealously guarded their lands against all intruders. The Indians learned the presence of the miners, possibly by observing the disturbed waters of the creek, and attacked and killed two of the miners. The survivor, though wounded, grabbed a gold poke and fled. He explained his success in getting away as probably due to the Natives thinking he and his companions had ascended from the Indians' side of the mountains rather than from the other side. When the Natives discovered their error, it was too late to catch the gold miner, and when they finally did track him to the beach he was successfully away in his boat. His account seemed accurate, for in any other circumstance the Tlingits would have had canoes available to pursue the wounded man.

Thirteen years later, in 1880, Joe Juneau and Richard Harris, with the Indian's approval, ascended what is now called Gold Creek to find gold in substantial quantities. This was probably the same creek found by the earlier party. As a consequence of this discovery the Alaska-Juneau mine came into existence and the city of Juneau was built. Eventually men from Juneau spread out like so many ripples in a pond, ever pushing in the direction of the northern interior. One of these men was George Carmack, the eventual discover of a bonanza on Rabbit Creek.

A sub-tribe of the Tlingit Indians, the Chilkats, guarded a route to the interior called the Chilkoot Pass. This was the shortest trail to the interior, being only about thirty-three miles from salt water at the mouth of Taiya Creek at Lynn Canal to the headwater lakes of the Yukon River.

The first white man to evade the Indians successfully and cross the pass was George Holt in the late 1870s. It is hard to believe he could have made this without at least tacit permission from the Indians of the region. He followed the headwater lakes to what is now called McClintock Creek, missing the Yukon River by only a few miles, then ascended the incredible snake-like bends of the creek to traverse the headlands and reach the Teslin River. Here, he found enough coarse gold to impress his associates in Alaska that the trip was worthwhile. Holt was not so fortunate, however. Several years later the Indians killed him along the Copper River in Alaska.

The importance of Holt's feat was underscored by its results. Like a scout bee returning to a hive, his incantations stirred miners in Alaska to a fever pitch. One group demanded that the United States Navy provide for their safety and at the same time negotiate a treaty with the Indians guaranteeing safe access to the interior by way of Chilkoot Pass. Commander Lester A. Beardslee, skipper of the navy ship *Jamestown*, was the right man to ask about opening a new area. (He had been with Commodore Matthew C. Perry when he opened up Japan in 1853.) Beardslee showed up in front of an Indian delegation with the heavy guns of the ship at the ready. The Tlingits grudgingly accepted mediation, knowing full well the power of those guns if they did not. Thus, in the summer of 1880, the first full-blown prospecting expedition, comprising nineteen men, traversed the pass, employing Chilkat packers in the process. However, it would be another decade and a half before the gold rush.

During the intervening years, gold seekers persisted in their search for the yellow metal. However, less than 200 men at any one time could be found along the upper reaches of the Yukon River.

Gradually, they returned to outposts of civilization with respectable showings of gold. For example, just south of the Yukon District, on the northern borders of British Columbia, 1,500 miners poured into Dease and Thibert creeks in a "mini" gold rush. These creeks are still being worked today.

Farther north, circa 1878, Jack McQuesten and Al Mayo built a trading post at Fort Reliance, which was located only six miles from where the town of Dawson City was to be established two decades later. Thanks to the foresight of these two men in their efforts to keep miners supplied, the latter were able to spend the winter in the country. This extended the time they could work their ground and also afforded them more time to search for new ground.

Gold is a very general term. What were the prospectors really after? In a practical sense a miner considered himself a success if he could pan out an ounce of gold a day. The customary measurement of gold was twenty pennyweight to the ounce. A pennyweight in those early days was worth about eighty cents, meaning $16 an ounce. To put this into proper perspective, $16 a day or approximately $500 per month was a hefty sum in times when a man could purchase a nickel beer in a Seattle pub and be given a free lunch. However, when balanced out with the expenses of an outfit and the cost of packing it into so remote a country, and then eventually having to tote it out again, the daily wage was slim.

The "curse" of gold beckoned the peripatetic prospectors back again year after year. Gold was found on Cassiar bar on the Yukon River. Six men averaged about an ounce a day each for the short summer season. Farther down the Yukon River, miners uncovered a small bonanza on the bars of the Steward River, one of the largest tributaries of the Yukon. They averaged 400 ounces in the summer of 1884. Jack McQuesten made a special trip to the new field and in five days he took out fifteen ounces, which was enough to inspire his setting up a trading post on Stewart Island at the confluence of the Stewart and the Yukon.

Almost as quickly, Stewart was abandoned in favour of yet another strike downriver at the mouth of Fortymile Creek. The name arose from the fact it was that distance from Fort Reliance.

Frederik Schwatka's expedition of 1883 had served to publicize the Yukon area, but not until the Canadian government had dispatched its own scientists to the region did it begin to take on a more viable veneer for those looking for precious metals.

Three men were sent to the Yukon District of the Northwest Territories in 1887. Their basic goal was to describe the region and to explain what was going on up there. Dr. George M. Dawson and R.G. McConnell of the Geographical Survey of Canada were ordered to determine the mineral potential while William Ogilvie, a Department of Interior surveyor, was to survey the boundaries and to ascertain the general activity in the region. The latter not only traversed from the Alaska-Canada border at Chilkoot Pass all the way down the Yukon River past the town of Forty Mile but also established an astronomical observation post.

Ogilvie's description and photos of the Yukon were to give the Canadian government its first adequate insight into the distant region. A photo taken by Ogilvie's photographer was to become one of the few ever taken of Jack McQuesten, Arthur Harper, and Ogilvie together. One great contribution of Ogilvie was his suggestion to the miners that they pierce the permafrost that shielded the gold on bedrock by the simple method of burning their way through the frozen muck, thus thawing the ground.

The reports of Dawson and McConnell were more basic in nature. They literally walked the land and dug into the soil to see its value. Dawson predicted that the discovery of a major placer deposit of gold was imminent.

By 1889, the Yukon was explored from yet another quarter. Seafarers searching for bowhead whales found them in the Beaufort Sea, a bight of the Arctic Ocean off the Yukon's north coast. In order to exploit the season to its maximum, the whalers began to winter in the safety of Pauline Cove at Herschel Island, located only a few miles off the coast near the delta of the Firth River, and not far distant from the Babbage and Malcolm rivers. Even here, gold was found in scattered pockets before 1900.

The Yukon as an entity was at least casually explored from north to south by the close of the ninteenth century. However, the area was similar to an iceberg with only the tip showing. The larger under-portion was like a ripe tomato ready to be plucked.

More discoveries were tallied, one being on Sixtymile River late in the century. Fred Harper demonstrated his faith in the strike by erecting a trading post he named Ogilvie on an island located at the mouth of the river where it met the Yukon River. He selected Joe Ladue to manage the post. Ladue, an itinerant gold seeker (yet clear-headed thinker) from Plattsburgh, New York, was appropriate for the job. This appointment was to prove an important one in the ultimate fate and history of the North.

The mines of Juneau were still spewing out prospectors who headed to the Yukon like so many ants to a bowl of sugar. One of these was George Carmack, a self-educated chap with some culture. His forte was his geniality and his ability to get along with people, particularly Indians. He teamed up with an Indian woman, Kate (or Kitty as she was sometimes called), who took his last name. He lived with Kate and was accepted by her family, which included her brothers Jim and Charlie. The former was to adopt the surname Mason, and Charlie took Dawson as his given name and Charlie as his last name.

Carmack drifted with the Indians from season to season, harvesting fish, moose, and caribou and taking furs. His interest in prospecting was casual compared to some of his peers, who turned over every twig and rock looking for gold. George Carmack took life as it came and was proud of his status with the Indian people, who were of the Tagish band, living around the lake of the same name where they spent most of the year. Carmack was known as a man of his word and was respected by those who knew him — Indian and white alike. He discovered a coal vein at Tantalous Butte and erected a cabin there, and even packed-in an organ, which he played for his delighted though somewhat astonished Indian guests.

Farther downriver, Robert Henderson, a man of strong likes and dislikes, one of the latter being Indians, prospected the creeks near the mouth of Sixtymile River. Henderson originally from Nova Scotia, had fled the silver mines at Aspen, Colorado, to better himself in the Yukon. In 1895 he was grubstaked by Joe Ladue, who saw in him a certain vitality that made for a good prospector. Ladue suggested that he try the area north of his post, which Henderson agreed to do. He headed up Indian River sampling gravels as he went. Presumably he met Billy Redfort and worked for him on Quartz Creek, a tributary. Not satisfied with this, he climbed over a divide were he found another creek more to his liking, and there he staked a claim. He called this stream Gold Bottom.

The stage was now set for the ultimate discovery — the almost literal pot at the end of the rainbow. This was to evoke a controversy that even today stirs arguments as to who should have been given the credit.

Carmack was joined by his Indian friends at the mouth of Thron-diuck River. Here, they set up a fishing camp that Carmack called their Klondike camp, Klondike being the anglicized version of the Indian name. The name derived from the custom of hammering posts into the river bottom in order to trap fish. This tributary was known to have been one of the finest in the country for catching salmon.

Carmack's entourage at this time was composed of Skookum Jim (Jim Mason), Tagish Charlie (Dawson Charlie), Kate, and Patsy Henderson (so named by Carmack), who was Kate's nephew and about seventeen years old at that time. Fishing was poor, and Carmack and his friends were pondering what to do about it when Bob Henderson showed up. He and Carmack were acquainted, and after the usual salutations Henderson waxed exuberantly over the new creek he had staked. He described its location and invited Carmack to stake there, pointedly ignoring Carmack's companions while granting the invitation. Carmack noticed the slight but said nothing. He told Henderson if he ventured into the vicinity he would take a look at Henderson's diggings.

Several weeks later, Carmack, Jim, and Charlie, leaving Kate and her nephew to watch the salmon camp, struck out up nearby Rabbit Creek and almost immediately found gold that washed out ten cents to the pan. Then they ventured over a series of ridges in a ten-mile trek through tortuous grass hummocks and deep moss to visit Henderson. When they finally did arrive at Henderson's camp, the latter refused to allow the Indians to stake on "his" creek or even to sell Carmack's Indian companions any tobacco. Carmack took exception to this and decided not to stake on the creek. However, he did extend Henderson an invitation to join him and said his ground was better. Carmack and his companions returned the way they had come, back to Rabbit Creek, again traversing the ten miles of swamp, buckbrush, and moss to poke around the area where they had found gold worth only ten cents to the pan. While so doing, one of them, probably Jim, found gold in almost unmeasurable amounts. Right then and there the three men realized they had found a bonanza, and that is what Carmack named the creek.

Carmack staked the discovery claims, being allowed two under the mining laws, and Jim and Charlie staked one above and one below. Indicating that Jim actually made the discovery was the fact that he insisted that the discovery claims go to him. Carmack, however, suggested that it might be better to file it in his name as Native rights might be questioned by government in such a case. It was a moot point, as they all made fortunes on the deal. Jim was to sell all of the claims for $65,000 in 1904 after they had been worked for eight years. At today's prices this would have brought Jim roughly $1.3 million.

Robert Henderson later insisted that he should have been made aware of the strike by Carmack. Close examination, however, reveals no other conclusion than that it would have been almost impossible for Carmack to have done this. Henderson's insult of Carmack's companions was bad enough, but even if he had not been offensive toward the two Indians, one cannot see either of them or Carmack making a twenty-mile trip over exceedingly tough country to advise Henderson of their discovery. It was just too dangerous and too far.

To comprehend fully what Henderson's demand would have entailed, an individual would have to retrace the twenty-mile hike. Only by doing this could one understand how difficult the conditions were. The logical option for Carmack under the circumstances would have been to split his claim with Henderson, which he did do with Jim. This would have reduced his portion to a third. If the circumstances were reversed, would Henderson have done the same? Though

Henderson did lose out, the Canadian government later officially recognized Henderson as the co-discoverer of the bonanza and bestowed a monthly honorarium of $200 on him. This sum, though seemingly paltry in this day and age, was a hefty income at the time it was awarded.

Carmack's discovery set in motion a gold rush the likes of which had never been seen. The strike was made during the world-wide depression that had commenced with a stock market crash in the United States in 1893. This meant a residue of jobless people were ripe for any beacon indicating wealth that flashed on the horizon.

The stampede did not really become apparent until almost a year after Carmack's discovery because winter closed in on the Yukon, freezing the rivers by which easy access was possible. Thus, except for those who were in close proximity, the rest of the world waited until the summer of 1897 to bolt for the diggings.

Those nearby rushed upstream from Circle City and Fortymile, while others vaulted across the coast range from Juneau and Sitka to stake claims before winter set in. These men, and those with sufficient funds to buy in with the original stakers, were virtually the only ones (along with suppliers) to sustain a profit as the result of the gold strike.

The discovery was made on August 17, 1896. By November 17, 500 claims were staked on the Klondike creeks (tributaries of the Klondike). Bonanza and Eldorado creeks proved to be two of the richest ever found. One claim 425 feet in length yielded 125,000 ounces of gold. This would amount to roughly $50 million at today's prices.

The gold rush saw 100,000 men heading out for the Klondike over a three-year period but only 40,000 people arrived there. The first wave comprised mostly locals who reached the ground in 1896. The second wave of "argonauts" was inspired when those from the first went ashore in Seattle and San Francisco in the summer of 1897. The gold they lugged along was tabulated in tons rather than ounces or pounds! No sooner had these ships docked in Seattle and San Francisco than thousands of gold seekers began to line up to go north.

Most chose the closest and obvious routes — over Chilkoot Pass or White Pass at the head of Alaska's Lynn Canal. Others followed trails blazed by earlier pioneers. Each of these routes, however, had a certain element of difficulty that tested to the utmost the patience and/or the stamina of those determined to get to the gold diggings.

The rush itself brought out the best in people — and the worst. Father Judge was an example of the good. An unselfish, giving man, he was one of the first clergy on the scene. Not only did he deal with the psychological and religious side of man's nature, he also set up St. Mary's hospital to look after the physical ills of the stampeders and forfeited his own life in the process, dying only a few years later of disease in the same hospital. However, the institution continued his good works under the Sisters of St. Anne, administering to the people of Dawson City for half a century until it was destroyed by a fire.

A graphic example of the bad was the racketeer Soapy Smith. A man with a likable personality, Soapy preyed on the stampeders with a variety of ruses, and one has to wonder how his dupes could have been so naive. As one example, he ran a telegraph service, charging outlandish rates to his "marks," yet there was no such technology available in Skagway at that time. Legend has it that he even charged the dupes for "collect" telegrams answering those originally dispatched. When queried about his shenanigans, Soapy had a standard answer. Any man *that* ignorant deserved to be skimmed of his funds.

Soapy, however, was evil before he joined the gold rush, having previously plied his "trade" in the Colorado mining districts. Others demonstrated their lack of character under the pressure of the conditions. One unforgettable scene is an actual photo of a man being flogged on Chilkoot Pass for stealing supplies — an unforgivable sin where men depended entirely on the honour of their associates.

There were also the beautiful aspects of the gold rush — the unspoiled, raw, rugged grandeur of the land itself with its towering mountains, its absolute wilderness, and its wildlife. Few stampeders who ever saw a migrating herd of 50,000 caribou ever forgot it, or the land in which it was seen. The Klondike gold rush story has been told and retold, of men who were poor one day and who became millionaires the next. In fact, these stories lured the masses to the gold fields. It was a lottery, a ticket to a possible fortune.

The luck of the draw took strange turns. Dick Lowe, a chainman on a government survey crew, was tipped off by the government engineer in charge of a wedge-shaped fraction eighty-six feet in width that existed above Carmack's claim. After searching around for larger fractions to no avail, the chainman finally staked it. The fraction proved up gold worth half a million dollars, which turned Lowe into a bar-hopping spendthrift until death overtook him, virtually penniless, in San Francisco only eleven years later.

Clarence Berry was cut from another cloth. He was hardworking and frugal. He'd drifted north from California in 1894, mortgaging his property to make the trip. He was tending bar in the community of Fortymile when Carmack showed up to reveal his gold discovery. Berry scurried upriver and staked number 40 above Carmack's discovery shortly afterward. He returned and traded half of that and secure funds for half of number five. Luckily, the owner of five sorely needed cash. Berry was to take $1.3 million in gold out of both claims. He moved to claims in Alaska and earned several million more at Esther Creek. His luck even followed him back to California, where he completed a triple parlay by acquiring rights to land near Bakersfield that was later found to be located over a sea of oil. He died in 1930 with his millions intact.

Lust for gold, and what it meant in wealth, led men to kill for it. One of the more celebrated of such events involved a seemingly "good guy" who was really bad, and a "bad man" who was basically honourable. A dispute over gold was the catalyst that brought forth this strange reversal of personalities.

Nelson Soggs was a prominent jeweller in Dawson City in the year 1900. He, with a group of four partners, invested funds in mining several claims, including number 34 on Gold Run. Soggs was made the nominal superintendent of the operation. After several months his partners voted him out as supervisor because he was basically unsuited for the task. His replacement, James Rogers, was the manager of a gambling hall and saloon in Dawson City. He represented one of the partners. Soggs was bitter over the fact that he had been removed as the titular chief of the operation. Under normal circumstances, and in his own element, namely the jewellery store, the merchant would have shrugged off such a minor reversal, but at times greed can bring out idiosyncratic devils that take over a man's normal psychological make-up.

This apparently happened to Soggs at the claim on May 8, 1900. Rogers was observing several of the men "cleaning up" (i.e., separating gold from the gravels) sluice boxes on the claim when Soggs emerged from a nearby cabin and strolled down to stand opposite Rogers. The latter was a big man, six-feet-two and well over 200 pounds. He exuded good health, and would need it. Rankled by the other's presence, Rogers commented: "Did you think we were going to take some of your money?"

The jeweller evidently had presupposed such a remark and, without further ado, drew out a revolver. Rogers, figuring Soggs to be relatively stable, ignored the gesture and turned to walk away. The jeweller nurturing pique over his dismissal, aimed the gun with one hand and fired. He missed. Soggs corrected this by holding the gun in two hands, then pulled the trigger three times, every one of which was a hit. Incredibly, Soggs had to shoot over the head of a miner sitting on the edge of the sluice box immediately below him. For a man like Nelson Soggs, who had never shot a revolver before, it must have been a tremendous step to take. He was in for an even worse shock when he realized the man he had shot did not go down! Rugged giant that Rogers was, he walked to his own cabin while others summoned help. Soggs, in turn, strode back to his shack satisfied that he had done the world a favour.

Witnesses had never seen such an unprovoked attack and were not hesitant in saying so. Examining Rogers's wounds, they found that the first effective shot had pierced his left shoulder to lodge right behind the collar bone. The second shot was decidedly less noble, being in the back. The slug penetrated his torso and came out over the heart. The third slug entered on the left side of his spine and ripped into the stomach. This proved to be the wound most onlookers figured would finish off Rogers.

Rogers's magnificent physique saved his life. He was able to appear at the trial of Soggs, who received two years in prison for his deed. Oddly information that rose to surface after the shooting indicated that Soggs was not as bad a fellow as he was pictured to be, and Rogers was not as honourable as he was portrayed.

The gold rush of 1896–98 was only a part of the history of gold in the Yukon. The initial discoveries saw miners work their claims via the old windlass and bucket arrangement, the viability of which quickly dwindled and was replaced by more efficient methods of recovery. However, even using relatively primitive methods, miners took out an estimated $10 million in gold in 1898.

The first dredge was put into production on one of the river bars in 1899 but was not a success. Later, it was moved to the discovery claim on Bonanza Creek to work claims bought from Skookum Jim Mason. This proved to be more viable than on the river bar and set the tone for the huge dredges that were to follow.

Great ideas seem to evolve simultaneously. More than one man had visions of amalgamating hundreds of claims to mine areas that were quickly becoming unprofitable due to antiquated mining procedures. Probably the most famous of these was an Englishman by the name of A.N.C. "Arthur" Treadgold, an ironic moniker for a man with a fixation on the yellow metal.

An Oxford graduate, he had taught in a private school in Bath, England, but quit the job to return to the university. While there he met an attractive Canadian girl who happened to be the sister-in-law of Inspector Constantine, among whose duties at that time was that of mining recorder in the territories. Through letters the girl received from the inspector's wife, Treadgold heard intricate details of the great strike of 1896. This spurred the intrepid thirty-three-year-old to journey to Dawson City. He was not unprepared for the adventure, having previously taken a course in geology and read everything he could get hold of that was written about the Klondike. He also managed to have himself appointed a special correspondent of *Mining Journal* and *The Manchester Guardian*. With the clout of those two august journals as a door opener, and potential financing available if he needed it, Treadgold was granted an interview with Canada's Minister of Interior, Clifford Sifton, in Ottawa in May of 1898. He then proceeded to the gold diggings. The stories he filed were interesting and his descriptions of the conditions, including notes on how overtaxed the federal employees were, unintentionally served to ease a barrage of criticism directed at Sifton by miners who charged that some of his staff workers in the recording offices at Dawson City were incompetent. The upshot of the whole thing was that a certain camaraderie was established between the two men. This resulted in Treadgold, after proper and prolonged research, being granted a mining concession on Hunker, Bonanza, Bear, and Eldorado creeks in 1901. The key to the order-in-council was Treadgold's promise to deliver water to the gold fields, an important ingredient for placer mining. Since gold is a heavy metal, when washed it is easily separated from muck and gravel.

Treadgold's concession was fiercely fought by local miners and eventually rejected. However, he patiently continued staking and purchasing ground as the years of bureaucratic haggling continued. Finally, a break came his way. The mighty Guggenheim family backed his proposals and a company was formed under the name Yukon Gold, with Treadgold on the board. This resulted in the building of the Twelvemile Ditch. Commencing at Twelvemile River, and seventy miles long, the ditch and flume brought water into the mining area with a sufficient head to employ in hydraulic operations washing down White Channel gravels on Lovett Hill, situated between Bonanza Creek and the Klondike River. Power from plants on Twelvemile River went to run seven dredges put into operation in 1908.

Even dredges, however, were not unassailable. In late February, 1913, Dredge #1 sank in its pond when it was dynamited by unknown saboteurs. One of the world's first "bugs" was employed in breaking the case when Yukon Gold's electrical superintendent planted a listening device in a cabin where a number of Scandinavians often gathered. His reason for picking that particular shack was that ski tracks had been found near the dredge, which of course was not operating in the winter. The amateur sleuth took notes while listening to the occupants as they made fun of the police and the Guggenheim family. He heard a suspect say he had chosen Dredge #1 to destroy because it was closer to town and his ski tracks would be easier to explain. The man was later convicted.

The Yukon Gold Company gradually phased out its holdings in the Yukon, transferring its attention to gold mining and dredging in Alaska, Nevada, and California. By 1927, Yukon Gold dispersed its last Klondike holding to Treadgold. It was reorganized as the Pacific Tin Consolidated Corporation in 1939. The name was derived from its activities in Malaya. Yukon Gold's Klondike operation had yielded about $25 million from dredging 49 million yards of gravel and $6 million from hydraulicking 34 million cubic yards for a total of $31 million. The totals were far short of Treadgold's estimates that the gravel would yield $58 million in gold.

Yet another Yukon giant was Joe Boyle, who set up the Boyle Concession covering about forty square miles of the Klondike River valley. After half a decade of wrangling, Boyle finally made progress by interesting yet another wealthy family, the Rothschilds, in his property. As a result, the

Canadian Klondyke Mining Company was formed with a capitalization of 30,000 shares at $24 par value. The Rothschilds group would hold 20,000 shares and Boyle 10,000. Boyle received $250,000 in the form of a 25 per cent royalty on gross gold production. To mine the gold, the new corporation introduced the first electrically operated dredge into the Klondike in 1905. The dredge was placed on rich ground on Bear Creek and earned its cost back in the first six months of operation. Within a few years, Boyle and the Rothschilds went their separate ways after a lengthy court battle. Boyle eventually won full control of the company through legal action.

Dredging continued in the Yukon under the guise of the Yukon Consolidated Gold Company until 1966, when the last dredge finally shut down. In the boom of the 1980s a dredge operated for a brief period on Clear Creek.

The price of metal determines its worth and at the same time imposes limitations on taking it out of the ground. In a sense, mining has come full circle from the men who first panned gold in the nineteenth century to the present. When in 1971 the pegged price of gold was abolished in favour of a floating price determined by the market, it set in motion modern mining methods by which "Mom and Pop" operations became viable. For example, if a man could afford a bulldozer, with which he could move huge volumes of gravel, he could work a claim himself and live from it. Thus, when gold rose from its pegged price of $35 an ounce to prices consistent with its market value, a new influx of miners descended on the gold fields abandoned by dredge operators. These men perfected earlier procedures developed with the coming of the bulldozer in the 1920s, and as such have kept the production of gold in the Yukon at a respectable level.

Fairly typical of a smaller operators one finds in the Yukon today, is that of Berthold Liske, who came to Canada at the age of sixteen in 1946 from East Prussia. In a short time he became a "cat" operator and worked on such projects as the Lynn Lake railroad. From there he travelled farther west, doing the odd mining job, until he wound up in the Yukon Territory employed by the United Keno Hill Mine. While there he prospected the surrounding country and ultimately purchased mining claims on Ledge Creek, first staked by Australians in 1903. Like many of the smaller operators, Bert would work another job in the winter, such as underground at the mine, in order to finance his summer operations digging gold. He started off working his claims by hand, than as he accumulated more equipment he graduated to more sophisticated methods and quit the mine altogether.

Bert explains it this way: "I had a limited education that I realized would doom me to shift work. Since I knew equipment pretty well, I figured that owning my own gold operation would suffice for the type of life I was looking for. My property is far out in the bush (the wilderness end of Yukon's Mayo Lake) and even if I did not make a bundle of money, I could always survive on moose meat and potatoes."

Bert Liske's comments present the essence of the appeal of gold mining in the northern wilderness. Men from around the world can be found scratching out a living in the Yukon with various degrees of success. Most of them agree that, as much as anything, the simple outdoor life they lead makes the effort worth the risk.

Today the story of gold is reflected in the many exhibits that may be visited in the Yukon. In the immediate area of Dawson City, gold can be panned at specific locations along Bonanza Creek. The famous gold room of the Bank of Commerce displays the implements by which gold is weighed. The complex of machine shops at Bear Creek has equipment used to operate and maintain bulldozers and the like. Here, too, is the lab where gold was melted down and ingots made for shipment. Dredge #4 has been restored at its last resting place on Bonanza Creek, and its operation is patiently explained by enthusiastic Canadian Parks Service tour guides. "Loop" tours through the Klondike gold fields enable the visitor to see actual gold mining progress. One can glimpse just about every technique known for extracting gold from the ground, from hydraulic methods that employ giant hoses to the more common bulldozer and sluice-box method.

Mining techniques

☐ Panning — Gold pans vary in sizes and shapes, but the most common is the sixteen-inch pan. The pan is used predominantly for testing a creek for its gold-bearing potential. Gravels are swirled in a pan with water. This causes the heavier gold to settle on the bottom of the pan, making it relatively easy for the placer miner to estimate the value of the ground he is examining. A rule-of-thumb guide published in a Canadian government publication (*Yukon Placer Mining*) is as follows: coarse gold — pieces over 1/10 inch in diameter; medium gold — 2,200 colours (flakes) per ounce; fine gold — 12,000 colours per ounce; flour gold — 40,000 colours per ounce.

Prospectors usually discuss the value of new ground in *cents per pan*. In other words, ten cents a pan would convert into $18 per cubic yard. Since one man — if he desired to do so — can run roughly 100 pans a day, he would make $10, which is not much in this day and age. However, he can increase his production tenfold by using a sluice box or rocker.

☐ Sluice box or rocker — A U-shaped box with riffles and mats to trap the gold is a simple mechanism by which water is run through the box either by pump or by force of the stream being mined. The miner shovels in the creek gravels, which are washed away by the water, leaving the heavier gold to collect behind the riffles. In this manner our miner could increase his income to $100 a day. A *rocker* is more efficient if operated by two men. In essence, it is a box mounted over the sluice. Gravels are shovelled in by one man, who deposits the gravel onto a screen. His companion "rocks" the box, which separates the smaller-size gravel from the larger. This finer material passes through the grizzly (screen) into a flow of water and a sluice box where the gold is deposited.

☐ Windlass and bucket — A shaft is dug to bedrock and then material is shovelled into a bucket and hauled up the shaft with a windlass. This primitive method was often used in the early days, and on occasion is still employed today by miners testing ground.

☐ Bulldozer and sluice box — This is the most common method used in placer mining today. "Mom and Pop" operations have great success because a maximum of gravel can be moved with a minimum number of personnel. A "cat" or loader dumps gravel into the sluice box and a pump supplies a head of water to wash the gravels.

☐ Monitor — Huge monitors wash down the pay dirt from the side of a hill, flushing the water and dirt through a sluice box. This is fairly commonly employed today.

☐ Dredges — Ground is thawed by the use of points and then mined by a dredge, which lifts the gravels via giant buckets that dump into a sluice for washing. Dredges entail extensive crews, principally in making ready the ground to be mined. There are no dredges operating presently in the Klondike.

☐ Drifting — Drifts are driven along bedrock and mined much like in quartz mining. The drifts are in permafrost in much of the Klondike area. Rails are laid in the tunnel and the pay dirt brought out in small rail cars. There are a few such operations still employed in the Yukon today.

☐ Hard-rock-mining — Regular mining techniques are followed. There are two or three gold mines in operation in the Yukon today. Rock is mined, then processed through a mill where the gold is separated from its host rock.

Beth Mulloy / Louise Profeit-LeBlanc
The Yukon Indians

The world view of Yukon Indian people is complex and ever-changing. It is a combination of old traditions and values, legends, and spiritual practices as well as an ever-adapting lifestyle in a hurried, troubled, and changing world. The struggle of adaption is by no menas only a Yukon Indian struggle but one by which the Yukon Native people can be an example to all of us, by the courage and steadfastness of their struggle to integrate their lives. The following is a look through many voices at the past, the present, and wishes for the future. This story is told using quotations from Indian people interwoven with an ancient legend shared by elder Kitty Smith.

First you listen — this is the beginning. (Annie Ned, elder, Hootchi)

There are four areas necessary for proper education — mental, emotional, spiritual, and physical. . . . Once they have gained this knowledge and have firmly established a strong sense of identity they are then ready for new material from any source. (Elsie Netro, educator)

> In the time before time there was a chief who lived on an island with his two wives. One was quite old and the other was young and beautiful. They lived peacefully together but the younger wife was lonely and longed to have a child to keep her company. One day she realized that she was pregnant. She was so happy. Time passed quickly and she gave birth to a beautiful baby boy. Now her life was complete — she had become a mother.

In the traditional Native community the family was very important. The family included husband, wife, their parents, children, their aunts and uncles, and all the children of these people. It could also include several unrelated people who have been adopted into the clan system. Indeed, the whole community could be looked at as one's family.

You have to teach your children well so that when they grow up they will be good people and will be able to take care of their families too. (Dora Wedge, elder, Carcross)

> But this was not to be. For some reason her husband killed her son. She didn't understand why this was.

> She cried and grieved the loss of her little son, but tried to understand it that perhaps her husband knew something that she didn't know and that he knew what was best. She quietly acquiesced.

With religion our lives make sense. We become healthy and spiritually in balance. Everything begins to make sense and fall into place. (Mary Battaja, language specialist)

> Time went on and she found herself pregnant again. This time she prayed for a little girl child, for she thought maybe her husband was jealous of having another male in the camp.
> Again she gave birth to a boy child. And again the father killed his own son.

To reach out for that higher power and to always rely on this, to remain strong and try to be spiritual in all matters no matter what happens to us in our life is our challenge and part of our purpose on this planet. (Mary Jane Smith, addictions counselor)

> Her heart was so heavy that she lost her appetite and could not sleep. She cried for days. Finally she realized what she had to do. She could no longer live with this grief.
> She decided to take her life.

Children were taken away from their parents and put into schools and the people lost their roles as parents and teachers. Grandparents were no longer listened to and we were no longer responsible to ourselves and to each other — least of all the community. The Native lifestyle contributed to a healthy well-being. We were very well balanced. We were in harmony with the land, we were in harmony with each other. We've lost that but there is a chance for it to come back, maybe not as traditional, but taking the best of both worlds. (Betsy Jackson, health liaison officer)

To understand the Yukon Indian people today it is important to understand their history and the land they live on. Yukon Indian people comprise Athapaskan language speaking Gwich'in (Loucheaux in the older terminology), Han, Northern Tutchone, Southern Tutchone, Kaska, and Tagish (who are nearly extinct), as well as the Tlingit with a different language. The Yukon is about 480,000 square kilometres. The land is covered by huge mountain ranges, some mountains over 5,000 metres in height, with Mount Logan, Canada's highest peak, at 6,050 metres. Many of them are snow-capped even in the hottest summer months. The mountains and their valleys are full of large game and other smaller fur-bearing animals and birds. There are also minerals in these mountains — silver, gold, copper, lead and asbestos, red and yellow ochras, flint, and obsidian. Copper, ochras, flints, and obsidian were useful to the Yukon Indian for paints and tools.

The climate is cold and harsh, with very few frost-free days. The winters can be bitterly cold for weeks on end and the summers warm with very little darkness. The seasons are extreme, winter seeming to last forever. One day spring will appear, then summer seems hardly to have begun and there will be fresh snow on the mountains and winter will soon return.

With its abundant game and varied vegetation, the Yukon is very changeable, depending on the weather and the time of year. The terrain, besides the mountains, varies from tundra to forested valleys and marshy ponds, and each animal has its own cycle, at times being very abundant and at other times very scarce. Mammals generally have a population cycle of five to ten years. These cycles were of importance to Yukon Indians. Most Indians had their regular hunting and migratory areas, but when the animals were at a low population ebb, Yukon Indians were forced to travel to new and sometimes unknown areas.

And that winter, people had tough luck — no caribou. They pretty nearly lost their lives. Anyway, they kept on going. They had nothing to eat. And they went down to Alaska, away, and just about all (the food) was gone. They ran into a bunch of people that actually saved their lives. (Joe Netro, Old Crow elder, from Catherine McClellan, *Part of the Land, Part of the Water*)

Caribou and moose are very important to the Yukon Indians. They are used for meat and the skins are important for making clothing, such as boots and mitts. Other animals available for hunting are rabbits and hares, gophers, squirrels, muskrats, otters, beavers, bears, mountain goats, Dall's sheep, porcupines, mink, lynx, foxes, wolves, coyotes, and wolverines. Some of these animals were hunted and some were not. Even today many Indians do not hunt bears. Some Indians only hunt wolves and coyotes for their pelts; mink, otters, and wolverines, except in the cases of extreme hunger, are used only for their pelts.

Birds and fish are also very important. The fish have their spawning grounds and their cycles. There were times of feasting when the fish were running, and then some extra would be put away for when the run was over. Salmon, whitefish, trout, and grayling are just a few of the fish that were, and are still, snagged, netted, and hooked for food. Birds were used for a variety of purposes — meat, eggs, and feathers for ritual ceremony.

Animals and vegetation were the essentials of traditional Native life, without which there would be no food, medicines, and culture. The Indian had tremendous respect for the natural laws of the land, and individual animals and birds were known to have special powers. This is evident in the legends from the beginning of time, when Crow made the earth.

The traditional Indian believed that the elders were very important members of the community. Through their age and life experience they were thought to have gained great wisdom and a special link with the next world. Information, knowledge, and ritual ceremony were passed on through the elders. The elders would tell much through stories about animals. The animals were said to hold special qualities. So when an animal was mentioned, it was not the real animal, but rather the qualities it was believed the animal held.

You could take and put it (the umbilicus) in the beaver dam. Take the cord and wrap it in something and you go to the beaver dam thinking to yourself, "I wish for my baby to work as good as the beaver." (Jane Smarch, elder, Teslin)

The traditional family groups were divided into two clans, with lineage through the mother. Each clan had crest animals such as the beaver. Clans were divided in half, one side would be a wolf and the other a crow, or perhaps an eagle. A crow could only marry a wolf and vice versa. This would also ensure protection against intermarrying. In death your clan will pay the expenses. The other clan would handle the body and all arrangements. (Paddy Jim, elder, Whitehorse)

Each clan had its own songs, Wolf and Crow. They did not sing each other's songs. (Johnny Johns, elder, Tagish)

What we had were varied cultures of people living in different parts of the Yukon, living nomadically, following the fish and game, taking from the earth, and through ceremony and good sense returning an equal portion back to the earth. Living with strong social law tied up extensively to the harsh climate and fluctuating game cycles.
There was plenty of room for the expression of Indian talent and character, not only through the making of clothing, tools and weapons, but through singing and dancing, story-telling and oratory, and managing the social ceremonies that were a part of the Indian world in earlier days. (from *Part of the Land, Part of the Water*)

Just a little more than 100 years ago white people moved into the North. They came for the land and for what the land had to offer, and more recently they have come as tourists visiting remote and beautiful landscapes. Many Native people see the lifestyles of the whites as being very contradictory to the traditional way of living in the North.

Two races have occupied the Yukon — the white and the In-

dian. A comparison of their methods of operation brings no shame to our ancestors, who for thousands of years lived on, by, and with our land; shelter and food and clothing were taken from the rivers, the lakes, and the plants and animals of the forest. Those who have lived in the Yukon realize that only an industrious and intelligent people could have stayed generation after generation, surviving bitter weather and combatting disease with the assistance of only Nature's gifts. In all of this we did not deplete the forests, or the rivers, or the animals, nor did we pollute or despoil.
The white man's role over a short one hundred years has been somewhat different. Minerals have been taken and the river valleys choked with gravel. Lands have been flooded and fishing eliminated to provide power. Fur-bearing animals are being destroyed through the poisoning of wolves to protect white guide-outfitters' horses turned out to forage during severe winters; food animals are now being shot for sport by hunters using guides, helicopters, airplanes, and pack horses; garbage is dumped in waterways while raw sewage pumped into rivers will bring pollution and fish kill. In short, the white man's role has been one of single exploitation, taking and wasting, but adding nothing. Indians find it very difficult to change to the white man's way, even after over one hundred years. (from *Together Today For Our Children Tomorrow*)

A struggle for the Yukon Indians today is preservation of what was important in the past, while embracing what is important today — and becoming a whole person, through the process of integration.

Total well-being is the well-being of the person including the mental, spiritual, physical, and emotional . . . if we don't express our anger and grief we become ill at ease (disease). (Betsy Jackson)

> She packed up all of her things and moved away from her husband and his other wife. She moved way down the other end of the island and it was there that she decided to let the ocean come and take her away. She no longer had any desire to live.

The white people brought with them many things, a lot of which caused great anguish to the traditional Indian — disease, alcohol, missionaries, miners.

The missionaries brought a way of thinking that led us to believe our way was no good. So the elders buried the knowledge that they had about medicine, about caring for ourselves. We came into contact with a lot of diseases for which we had no immunity and those diseases literally wiped out whole villages. Throught the beliefs of the people we thought that we got sick because of inappropriate behaviour or a

curse, because we were not in harmony with our way of life. (Betsy Jackson)

The missionaries did not understand that, like Christianity, the Indians' own religion was deeply spiritual, nor did they understand that the Indians were guided by their traditional beliefs to live good lives. (from *Part of the Land, Part of the Water*)

Let us see the reflection of the Creator's face in all things. (Anonymous)

In the old days you treated all people as if they were your children. (Annie Ned)

The Missionaries felt it was their job to bring European education, standards, and social community to the Indian people. They began this by taking away the school-age children and putting them into newly opened residential schools.

The main object of this school is to send the boys and girls back to their own people not Europeanized and contemptuous of their surroundings, but able to stand alone, living sober, well-instructed, high-principled Christian lives, and there gather others around them by the daily exhibition of a standard of truth and goodness never known before. (Pamphlet, Missionary Society of the Church of England, Canada)

They starved us up there! We got one egg a year — at Easter. The rest of the time we got corn meal and skim milk. Them in the staff dining room, though, they got bacon and eggs every day. We never saw fruit from Christmas to the next, but they sure had it. Why, some of those kids just starved to death. One year there was six of 'em died right there in school . . . starved to death. (Anonymous)

They sure didn't live their lives the way they preached. There was so much prejudice it made me sick about religion. I never been much for church since then. (Anonymous)

. . . while many Yukon Indians came to accept the white man's God and the gospel of Christ, they did not necessarily give up all their earlier religious beliefs about spiritual power, the need for good relationships with animals, and how best to deal with sickness. (from *Part of the Land, Part of the Water*)

Alcohol speaks many voices, the voices of fear, anger, violence, sexual promiscuity, and self-loathing. Alcohol is thought by some to be a disease, a disease that results from the loss of selfhood and the loss of culture. The Yukon Native people have been struck heavily with the disease of alcoholism. Some have thought that perhaps Native people have a genetic disposition to alcohol, one that causes very low tolerance and creates an alcoholic after only a few exposures to the substance; others believe that the reason so many Native people are alcoholic is because of the loss of culture.

It really hurts me to think of all the bad I've done to my loved ones. I've lost their trust. I said I would never hurt them again, but they just ignored me because I have said this before, repeatedly. They still care, sure, but not much after that. Now it's up to me to win their feelings back, give them happiness once again. I've been drinking so long now I don't remember any happy feelings, so the best thing to do is to start over, start a better life. (Ron Macintosh, Whitehorse)

God is the most great counsellor. When you have a hard time, speak to God. He'll give you the strength and allow you to grow. In my own life God has shown me miracles. Most of the time you usually think it's things outside of yourself which makes you sick but it's usually something inside. Fear is overcome when you put your faith and trust in God. Why does the Lord wants us to go through these problems and tests? So that we can be a good servant to him. Always give thanks to God that he gives us guidance. He created everything good and it's us as people that turn it into something bad. We can't waste our time dwelling on the past but move through our struggles and be happy and joyful despite our many problems. This way we are in a better position to deal wholeheartedly with our problems. (Mary Battaja)

Between 1898 and 1900 rumours of gold brought some forty thousand prospectors and speculators from all over the world to the Yukon. The Indians were overwhelmed by the white strangers and their lives were drastically affected. (Yukon Indian News, 1985 summer edition)

The miners from the gold rush profoundly influenced the traditional Native way of life. The rush came suddenly and left suddenly but the impact was long-lasting. It changed the subsistence level of living off the land. Many young people began to work part-time; people moved in closer to white settlements and built more permanent homes near the mines. This drastically changed the traditional cycle of nomadic living.

The Alaska Highway was built during World War Two. Again the Indians moved in from the bush and took jobs in the highway construction. More permanent settlements were built and the traditional lifestyle was slowly disappearing as more and more integration between Natives and whites took place.

She covered herself with her gopher blanket and lay on the beach waiting for the tide to come in and take her away. She could hear the waves drawing closer. All of a sudden she felt something tug on the blanket. Throwing the blanket off she glanced around to see if there was anyone around. There wasn't. She thought she must be becoming delirious from her suffering. She lay back down and covered herself once again. Again she felt a tug on her blanket. She thought to herself she must be going crazy as three times she looked and there was nothing there. The last time she decided to look out of a little hole in the blanket to see if someone was indeed there. Peeking out she saw this old man come out of the sea. Just as he was about to tug the blanket, she threw it off.
"I see you there!"
"I see you too! What are you trying to do? Drown yourself? What's the matter with you?"
The young woman burst into tears as she began to tell the old man about her tragic life and the death of her two sons. The old man sat down beside her and comforted her.
"Gee, that's sure a sad story you told me. That's too bad that happened to you. Maybe if you perform this small ceremony things will get better for you."

In the olden days they always had to have respect for the elders. No matter who it was as long as they were older they'd have to listen to them. They never talked back. That's how they learned. They didn't open their mouth. If somebody told you, "This is how it's supposed to be done," they'd have to do it that way. (Dorothy Smith, Ross River, from Part of the Land, Part of the Water)

We had these things, these sweatbaths — we called them hot-tents. (Roddy Blackjack, elder, Carmack)

When a girl become a woman she was put in a tent for one month to learn the ways of a woman. (Mary James, elder, Carcross)

There are many reasons for the potlatch, always it was for sharing. (Edward Jackson, elder, Teslin)

At the time of death everyone came to the potlatch. All people were served a meal in a circle. The opposite clan was served first. All the man's possessions were placed in a pile in the centre of the circle. People from his clan could go and take what they wanted. (Paddy Jim)

Potlatch in the days of old was the root of communication. . . . There was some older people, my grandparents for instance, were telling me there were a hundred and ten differ-

ent potlatches for every different project, any kind of project, anything worthy of community development you could call a potlatch. Or even family affairs: the ceremony of giving names, marriages, engagement parties, and stuff like this . . . some of them lasted for months. (Pete Sidney, elder, Tagish)

The Canadian government prohibited the practice of the potlatch in 1884, saying it interfered with "civilizing Yukon Indians." Anyone caught practising a potlatch was subject to six months in jail. Potlatches continued for the Yukon Indians, however, mainly because of their isolation and because, compared to west coast potlatches, the Yukon ones were much smaller. The government lifted the ban in the 1951 Indian Act.

Long time ago Indians, they go around to make potlatch. Big pile of blankets, everything. After that they cook a big pot of food. They cook big dinner. They eat. After that they dance, they do that, they hit drum. They all dance. Oh, lots of fun. (Charlie Johnson, elder, Carcross)

"I'll tell you what, you go back to your camp. When you get back there you're going to find a dish there. On the dish you gonna find a rock about the size of your little finger. It's the kind of rock you see through. Make a big fire and heat that rock up, red hot. Get some water ready. Get two sticks to pick up that rock. Throw it into your mouth and swallow that water down behind it. Try this and maybe it will help you." With that the old man went back into the sea.

The young girl thanked him and went back to her camp. Sure enough, the plate and the rock were where the old man said they would be. She did as he instructed her to do. She wanted to take her life anyway so perhaps this was the quickest way to go, she thought to herself.

When the rock was red hot, she took those two sticks and tossed the hot rock into her mouth. She swallowed the water down right after. It didn't burn her lips, her throat, her stomach. Nothing. She didn't feel any pain.

That night she slept for the first time in several days. She even felt hungry and went to rustle up some food. Her spirit had lifted. She felt as if she had had a new breath of life breathed into her once more.

Today the revival of the potlatch, which was almost stamped out by the church as a pagan practice, is gradually becoming the norm in the Native community with the rise of identity being practised among the people.
(Mark Wedge, president, Yukon Indian Development Corp.)

The curriculum (school) must be tied to this land base and focus around that particular relationship. (Mary Easterson, teacher, Burwash)

Sometimes there is much doubt about eternal life. According to the Bible scriptures this is all we have to do is to give our lives to him. Serve his cause. God is the Holy Word. The Word is God. (Mary Battaja)

A lot of things from my own culture have helped. Things I didn't know were there before. I've found spiritual strength, laughter, closeness, people who are not afraid to approach someone on the street for a hug. For the good feelings they can share. I've found I can be a wanted person, just for myself. Our culture has a lot to offer white society, especially respect for the way people live. (Albert James, "Religion and Native culture," *Whitehorse Star,* 1982)

We need not be shy — we are here for good reason. We must speak straight out — as it is. (John Dickson, elder, Liard)

Before long she realized that her body was beginning to change. Her stomach was beginning to swell. She was pregnant. She was so happy. She smiled as she remembered how it felt to feel the baby's little kicking movements in her womb. Now her life would be complete. One day during one of her afternoon naps the young woman didn't even know, but she gave birth to Crow boy. When she awoke he was already running around. And as we all know in the Yukon it was Crow who made the world.

Angela Sidney
The Story of Creation

Long time ago there was a girl whose father is a very high man. Him and his wife kept her in the house all the time. Lots of men try to marry her but that big shot man he thinks she's too good for them.

That time Crow wanted to get born. He's going to make the world. He thinks how he's going to do this. He changed himself into a pine needle. Here, pretty soon that girl she tells her slave to go get water for her. That slave does it. That girl's mother always tell that slave to make sure the water is clean for her daughter: "Rinse out that pot really good!"

That slave brings water back to that girl. Here that pine needle is inside that water. That girl tells that slave, "How come you bring me dirty water? Get me some clean water!"

That slave goes back and the same thing happens again. He rinsed it out good but just the same that pine needle is in there yet. Four times this happen like that. Finally that girl gives up and drinks the water and tries to spit out that pine needle. Just before she spit it out it blew right in her mouth and she swallowed it down. Pretty soon that girl she got pregnant.

Gee! Her daddy sure was mad! Her mother cried and asked her what man she was with. "Who's the father of that baby?"

The daughter was honest when she said, "I never been with any man."

That baby it starts to grow really fast. She have it real quick. When it got born it just started walking around. Talking and everything! That baby's gramma and grampa sure love their grandson. They don't know that's really Crow.

That girl's father he had a big house. All light inside. He's got the sun, the moon, and all the stars in that house. They're all hanging up in his house.

That little boy, he's starting to play around now. He sees those things all hanging up there and he points to them. At that time the world it's all dark. The only one who has daylight is that high man. He owns the daylight.

Pretty soon that little boy he cries for the sun. He wanted to play with it. His gramma tells him, "No. That belongs to your grampa."

That child begs some more. He started to cry for the sun. He cried so much, his face got all swollen up. He can't hardly breathe. His grampa saw him like that and gave into him. "Let him play with it! He's going to get sick if he cries too much for it!"

That kid just got happy. He rolls it around, plays with it. He having lots of fun with that sun. Just then it rolls by the door. It's open I guess because it's too hot in there. It rolled right out!

That boy start to cry lots again. He cries now because he lost that sun. He doesn't have anything to play with. He's looking up at the moon now. He cries for a long time again. This time his gramma says, "No! You already lost the sun, now you want the moon? You not going to take care of it!"

Just the same his grampa feel sorry for him. "Give that moon to him!"

That little boy he starts to play with it next. He gets sleepy after a while and forgets all about it. That moon rolls right out the door, too. When he gets up, next he cries for the stars. He cries to his grampa again, "Give them to me! This time I won't lose them."

He promise but just the same he's not careful and he lost the stars that time, too!

"Wonder where she got that kid from? He loses everything!" That's what his grampa says.

That Crow he takes off then. He has all those things with him in a big box. The sun, the moon, the stars, everything. He's going to make daylight now. He starts walking around. Pretty soon he comes to a river. All kinds of animals there. Wolverine, rabbit, mink, fox. That time everybody was fishing. That's the time animals they talk just like human. The world was pitch dark that time.

That Crow comes up to those guys. He says, "Give me some fish!"

Those animals just ignore him. They don't pay any attention to him.

"Give me some fish or you're going to see me make daylight!" he tells them fellas.

They all laugh at him. They don't know he's got the daylight.

That Crow he started to open that box. He let out a little bit of daylight. Those animals they sure got a surprise. They started to pay attention to him now. Crow opened that box a little bit more. Now they're all scared! Finally he just broke open that daylight box and throw out all the daylight. They don't know what it is that time. That's the time they all turn into animals and don't behave like human anymore. The same time the sun, the moon, the stars all come out in the sky. Crow tell them to stay there forever.

"Now you just don't belong to one man. You going to be for everyone!"

That Crow he knows. He's right when he say that animals not going to talk like humans anymore, too . . .

Now that Crow, he's travelling around and bumps into Sea Lion. That Sea Lion owns a small island. Just him and his baby live on that island. He's the only one that owns land that time. All over everywhere there's water. Ocean.

That Crow he sat down for a rest. He's tired out. Here he sees that Sea Lion with a piece of land all to himself. That island. He wish for it. So he stole that Sea Lion's kid.

"Give me back my kid!" That's what the Sea Lion shout to that Crow. Crow he wants to make a deal though.

"You gotta give me some land first. Give me some of that sand!"

That Sea Lion he's got no choice, he gave Crow some sand. That Crow he threw that sand all around the ocean. He said, "Be the world!" And that's how it became the world.

After this, that Crow he walks around again. Fly around too. He's getting tired and he lonely too. He wish for people, that Crow. He needs company. So he took poplar tree bark and he carved it into human body. He breathed into it, that poplar bark. "Live!" he told that tree bark. He made person that time. That's the time he made Crow and Wolf too. Long time ago they don't talk to one another. They just shy of one another. They can't even look at one another. Crow man and Crow woman and Wolf people same way too.

Crow say, "That's no good! I'm going to change that!"

That's how come Crow made Wolf woman to sit with Crow man and Crow woman to sit with Wolf man. That's how it's supposed to be. They're partners, you know! That's why Crow gotta marry Wolf and Wolf marry Crow. That's how the world all began.

(Transcribed by Louise Profeit-LeBlanc, May, 1989)

———————————

Mrs. Angela Sidney was born in 1902. Her ancestors came from the Tlingit tribe at Angoon on the Pacific coast, but she has spent her life in the Yukon. Mrs. Sidney has travelled over much of the southern Yukon and her stories reflect the history of the Tagish, Carcross, Teslin, Marsh Lake region. She lives in Tagish.

Contributors
Text

Valerie Alia is a journalist and social scientist whose work focuses on the circumpolar North. She is on the faculty of the Graduate School of Journalism at the University of Western Ontario. A New Yorker by birth, she received her Ph.D., in social and political thought, from York University. She has worked for First Nations organizations and programs, including Inuit Tapirisat of Canada, and has written on northern social and political issues, arts, and artists for various publications.

John U. Bayly, QC, is a Yellowknife lawyer whose house sits at the water's edge on Great Slave Lake near the mouth of the Yellowknife River. When he isn't in the courts he can be found in his canoe or dogsled travelling in the wilderness, or at the lodge he built with family and friends seventy-five miles southwest of Yellowknife. Bayly has worked on aboriginal rights issues for the Inuit, Dene, and Métis of the NWT and is the chairman of the Denendeh Conservation Board, a member of the Historic Sites and Monuments Board of Canada, and a member of the executive of the International Commission on Folk Law and Legal Pluralism.

Ethel Blondin was born in the small northern community of Fort Norman, NWT. At three months, she was adopted, in customary fashion, by her aunt and uncle. She spent most of her formative years living in the bush with her extended family. At the age of nine she attended a residential school and later in her teens a school designed for the leadership development of young Native and northern youth. After receiving a B.Ed. degree from the University of Alberta, Ms. Blondin taught for eight years in various remote northern communities. She then worked as a Native language program specialist for the Department of Education in Yellowknife, instructed teaching methodology at the University of Calgary and at Arctic College, and was also the acting director for the Public Service Commission of Canada in Ottawa. Prior to being elected to the House of Commons in 1988, Ms. Blondin worked as national manager of indigenous development programs for two years and was also Assistant Deputy Minister of Culture and Communications in Yellowknife. She is the mother of three children.

Jonquil Graves holds degrees from McMaster and Carleton universities. After teaching English at Louisiana State for two years, she moved to Yellowknife in 1974 and since then has spent many summers on the barren lands, doing everything from working as a camp cook to assisting in geographical surveys. She has worked for the NWT Department of Renewable Resources as a conservation education officer and has written many publications for the department. More recently, she taught English at Arctic College in Yellowknife. In 1990, with her daughter and husband, a geologist, she moved to Australia.

Anne Gunn has worked for the NWT Department of Renewable Resources since 1979. She spent three years as a caribou biologist before becoming regional biologist for the Kitikmeot region in 1984. Previously, Dr. Gunn worked for the Canadian Wildlife Service, studying Peary caribou and muskoxen in the High Arctic. She lives in Coppermine.

Ann Meekitjuk Hanson, whose original Native name was Pilituq Enosiq Pudloo Lutaq, was born in 1946 near Lake Harbour, NWT, and was baptized as Annie E7-121. It was government policy to give disc numbers to all Inuit at birth. When it was time for baptism, easy-to-pronounce names were picked so the government would have an easier time with records. Annie E7-121 became Annee Meekitjuk in 1965 when she began to work for the federal government as a secretary, translator, and interpreter. She picked her father's name as surname because this was how it was done in the Qadlunaaq way. She married Robert L. Hanson in 1966 and they have five daughters. She is a freelance journalist in the Baffin region in Inuktitut and English. In October, 1987, she was appointed Deputy Commissioner of the Northwest Territories. She assisted in translating two books with Canadian author Dorothy Harley Eber, including *Pitseolak: Pictures of My Life*, and had a leading role in the movie *White Dawn*, a saga by James Houston.

Jerome Knap is a wildlife biologist who turned to writing. For ten years he was an outdoors writer for a large Canadian newspaper, Canadian editor for *Field and Stream*, and columnist for several other outdoor magazines. During his writing career he authored thirteen books and won the prestigious Kortright Award for outdoors writing a record four times. In a career change, Knap became a tourist outfitter in northern Ontario and later moved his operations to the Northwest Territories. Knap's company, Canada North Outfitting, which has operated for more than ten years, offers wildlife, cultural, and adventure tours as well as big-game hunting and fishing trips throughout much of the Arctic.

Brian Lewis was a school principal in small Inuit communities from 1963 to 1970. In 1968 he wrote a fifteen-volume reading program for Inuit children that was used throughout the eastern Arctic. He was a regional superintendent of schools in Iqaluit but moved to the western part of the Northwest Territories after the territorial government established its headquarters in Yellowknife. A former director of the Department of Education, he was elected to the Legislative Assembly of the NWT in 1987. Lewis earned his B.A. from the University of Wales and an M.A. from the University of Toronto.

Jeff MacInnis led the first team to sail the Northwest Passage with no motorized power. The journey covered 3,000 miles over 100 days in an eighteen-foot Hobie catamaran. MacInnis chronicled this adventure in *Polar Passage*, a bestseller. A former member of Canada's downhill ski team, MacInnis won the Belgium National Downhill Championships in 1984. He now gives human performance presentations to corporations and is currently developing a television series on adventure and the environment.

Lynn Maslen earned her B.Sc. (zoology) and M.Sc. (biogeography) from the University of Alberta. She has worked extensively in Alberta and the Northwest Territories on such projects as Alberta's Humane Trapping Program and reclamation prescriptions for northern development. While doing research for her Master's degree, Maslen spent two summers in a bush camp near Fort Norman, NWT, where she studied new methods of revegetating terrain disturbances. She currently works in Edmonton as an environmental scientist assessing the impact of industrial projects on the environment.

Beth Mulloy was raised in the Yukon and has spent many years developing northern theatre — as a director, actress, playwright, and teacher. She is also a poet and has recently published her first book of lyrics. Most of her work is cross-cultural and she keeps close ties with the Yukon Indian people.

Dick North has lived in the north country for thirty years and has edited and worked as a reporter for various journals. He has written four books, the most recent being *Arctic Exodus* (1991). Currently, he is curator of the Jack London Interpretation Center in Dawson City, and is working on a book about Jack London's participation in the Yukon gold rush. He and his wife Andree live in Whitehorse.

Randal "Boogie" Pokiak, one of twenty-one children of Bertram and Lena Pokiak, Inuvialuit hunters and trappers, was born in 1949 and grew up on Banks Island and at Tuktoyaktuk. After graduating from Sir John Franklin School in Yellowknife, he returned to Tuk, from where he trapped and hunted under the guidance of elders and later participated in the land claim negotiations (1979–84) for his people. Pokiak has been chairman and president of the Inuvialuit Development Corporation since 1982 and is a tour operator/outfitter in Tuk and surrounding areas. He is a board member of various Native and non-Native corporations, and also serves as a consultant to cross-cultural workshops and on wildlife management and environmental issues.

Louise Profeit-LeBlanc was born and raised in northern Yukon and is a descendant of the Northern Tutchone people of the Athapaskan nation. She has raised a family of three daughters and has devoted much of her life to the cultural revival of her people, both politically and socially. She is Native Heritage Advisor to the Yukon Department of Tourism.

Erik Watt has been associated with the NWT since 1943 when, as a teenager, he deckhanded aboard the HBC paddlewheeler SS *Distributor* on the Mackenzie River. A newspaperman for thirty years, he covered the NWT for the

Edmonton Journal and the *Winnipeg Free Press*, freelanced as a magazine, radio, and television writer, was managing editor of papers in Alberta and Ontario, and was editor-in-chief of the *Sudbury Star*. In 1976 he moved to Yellowknife and has since travelled extensively in the NWT as Director of Public Affairs for the Department of Indian Affairs and Northern Development and, since 1985, as president of his own public relations company, Erik Watt & Associates.

Florence Whyard has a lifelong background in journalism. She has lived north of 60 since 1945, first in Yellowknife and since 1954 in Whitehorse, Yukon, where she continued her writing and broadcasting while raising a family of three with her civil engineer husband. First woman editor of the *Whitehorse Star*, she was Canada editor for *Alaska* magazine and other publications of the Alaska Northwest Publishing Company, from which she resigned when elected member of the Yukon Legislative Assembly in 1974. She also served as mayor of Whitehorse in the early 1980s. Now in her seventies, Mrs. Whyard has begun publishing Yukon history for children and continues to be active in community organizations. A member of the Order of Canada, she was awarded an honorary Doctor of Laws degree by her alma mater, the University of Western Ontario.

Renee Wissink first came north from Ontario in the early 1980s as a teacher for the Northwest Territories Department of Education. He then developed Arctic adventure outfitting businesses in Iqaluit and Igloolik, operating kayaking, rafting, hiking, dogsled, and sightseeing tours throughout the Baffin region from Lake Harbour in the south to the North Pole. In 1987 Wissink led the Qitdlarssuaq Expedition, a dogsled trek of some 3,000 kilometres that retraced the mid-1800s route of the last great Inuit migration, from Baffin Island to Greenland. Wissink currently is senior park warden for the Ellesmere Island National Park Reserve, Canada's most northerly national park.

Photography

Mike Beedell, one of the best-known Canadian wilderness photographers, who lives in Ottawa, teamed up with Jeff MacInnis early in 1986 as photographer for the three-year sailing trip through the Northwest Passage. A graduate in recreation studies from the University of Ottawa, he is an experienced trekker in the North, having taken part in many expeditions, including the Qitdlarssuaq expedition and one to the top of Mount Logan, Canada's highest mountain. The Arctic is also the subject for his first book of photographs, *The Magnetic North*.

Barbara Brundege is a widely published photographer whose work has been featured in such magazines as *National Geographic, Equinox*, and *The Atlantic*, as well as in publications of the Smithsonian Institute and the National Audubon Society. She has presented lectures on her work at the United Nations and for the National Park Service, as well as at various universities. She has lived for extended periods with Baffin Island Inuit and the Navajo, and now owns and operates a photographic workshop in Los Gatos, California.

Eugene Fisher is an award-winning photographer and writer whose work appears worldwide in such publications as *National Geographic, GEO*, and *Equinox*. His many projects, spanning two decades, include profiles of peoples of the High Arctic, Navajo Indians of the U.S. Southwest, and most of the major wilderness areas of North America. He currently resides atop a 2,300-metre ridge in California's Sierra Nevada Mountains.

Richard Hartmier was born in Toronto, brought up in Beaverton, Ontario, and attended the University of Western Ontario. He came to the Yukon in 1974 for the summer "to see what it looked like" — and he stayed. His four-wheel-drive vehicle is as much his office now as is his home in Whitehorse. Most of his work is done in the Yukon and Alaska, the Dempster Highway being one of his favourite areas. His photography has appeared in many national and international magazines, as well as in books.

Douglas C. Heard is a wildlife biologist with the Northwest Territories government. He has been studying the behaviour and ecology of caribou and wolves in the North since 1976. His interests include photography, windsurfing in near-freezing temperatures, and trying to find out why Yellowknife ravens do what they do.

Fran Hurcomb, who studied photography at the University of California, arrived in Yellowknife in 1975 and spent three years out on a trapline. Her life in the bush became the focus of her photography, which portrayed the vanishing way of life of the trappers. Her photographs and articles have appeared in numerous Canadian magazines. She currently lives on a houseboat in Yellowknife with her new baby, and she still keeps a dogteam.

Tessa Macintosh, a graduate of the Nova Scotia College of Art and Design, arrived in Cape Dorset in 1974 to photograph the community's artists for the West Baffin Eskimo Co-operative. She has been photographing the people and the land of the Northwest Territories ever since, currently as photographer for the NWT government. Exhibitions of her work have appeared in Vancouver, Edmonton, and Yellowknife galleries.

Kim G. Poole, a wildlife biologist with the NWT government, has worked on many species of wildlife since arriving in the North in 1981. He spent three years conducting research on gyrfalcons in the central Arctic and is now studying the ecology of lynx and marten populations.

Richard A. Popko, earned his B.Sc. with honours in wildlife biology from the University of Guelph. His Arctic experience began as a field researcher under Stuart D. MacDonald in 1974 studying Ivory gull breeding biology and distribution in the High Arctic. From 1977, he was working as a renewable resources officer throughout Baffin Island for the government of the NWT. Recently, he and his Inuk wife Napatchee, and their two children, moved to Norman Wells, breaking new soil for a vegetable garden at the banks of the Mackenzie. Popko works there as a resources development officer to strive helping maintain a meaningful lifestyle for Native people based upon hunting, fishing and trapping.

Wendy Stephenson moved to the Northwest Territories in 1977 and has taught school in the small Dogrib communities of Rae-Edzo, Snare Lakes, and Detah. She has two small children, and is presently developing school programs for the Northern Heritage Centre Museum in Yellowknife, where she lives.

Wayne Towriss, originally from Saskatchewan, is a former newspaper reporter and editor whose photographs have appeared in many national and international publications. He moved to Whitehorse in 1971 and was supervisor of photography with the Yukon government for seventeen years until he left his government position in 1988 to freelance.

Wolfgang R. Weber, the principal photographer represented here, grew up in the German state of Hesse and graduated from the Technical University of Darmstadt with a degree in mechanical engineering. While building up his own industrial company specializing in laser optronics, Weber began to write about and photograph the places he visited. For the past dozen years he has regularly spent many months each year in the Northwest Territories, the Yukon, and Alaska, extensively travelling the land on foot, by canoe, and by plane. He has contributed photographs and articles to travel guides, books, and calendars about eastern and western Canada, Alaska, and the southwestern United States, and his photography and writing have appeared in numerous magazines.